T0366938

Trans Figured

In memory of my parents:
William Gerald David Chappell, 11/4/1935–24/12/2019
Gillian Patricia Chappell, 30/4/1937–13/12/1989

TRANS FIGURED

On Being a Transgender Person in a Cisgender World

Sophie Grace Chappell

polity

First published in 2024 by Polity Press

Polity Press
65 Bridge Street
Cambridge CB2 1UR, UK

Polity Press
111 River Street
Hoboken, NJ 07030, USA

ISBN-13: 978-1-5095-6150-6

A catalogue record for this book is available from the British Library.

Library of Congress Control Number: 2023942966

Typeset in 11.5 on 14 Adobe Garamond
by Fakenham Prepress Solutions, Fakenham, Norfolk NR21 8NL
Printed and bound in Great Britain by CPI Group (UK) Ltd, Croydon

For further information on Polity, visit our website:
politybooks.com

Contents

Acknowledgements

The timeline of this book's writing is complicated. I had various parts of it in print well before spring 2020, when I first reached the reluctant conclusion that I really had to write this book, and began in earnest to try to. Putting those constituents together, and adding the other material that the project seemed to require, was a complex and time-consuming process, and interrupted, during the COVID lockdown, by some real crises of confidence and indeed mental health.

At times I tried to write parts of this book, especially Part II, as a kind of real-time diary. That means that some of the book's 'real times' are no longer real; it also means that some of the most significant developments in the politics of transgender in the UK do not map squarely on to what I say here. The most obvious example is Scotland, December 2022 to May 2023, a period that, as I write, is barely past, and undoubtedly not yet in proper historical perspective. To me, from where I stand today, it looks absolutely outrageous that a lying and bigoted London-based government, backed by a lying and bigoted London-based press, has robbed Scotland of the chance to make a genuinely progressive change in the direction of trans equality – one that is happening everywhere else in Western Europe – that demonstrably poses no conceivable threat to anybody's safety, and that Westminster itself still favoured right up until August 2020. And it looks no less outrageous that slurs and slanders about people like me have become convenient political weapons against the Scottish independence movement. But all of this is very recent; and on the whole I don't regret that it isn't properly discussed in this book. Another time, and another place, will no doubt be available soon.

Various parts of this book (in earlier versions) have already appeared elsewhere, online or in print. Some of Part II has been published as 'Being transgender and transgender being', *Therapy Today* (the British Association for Counselling and Psychotherapy magazine), March 2017. Part III is based on 'Is consciousness gendered?", *European Journal of*

Analytic Philosophy, 19(1) 2022. Part IV, 'The Adoption Analogy', has been published in various forms on the Crooked Timber blog, the American Philosophical Association blog, and in *Think*, 2021, pp. 25–30. A different edit of Part V, 'Gatekeepers, Engineers, and Welcomers', is forthcoming in J. Beale and R. Rowland, eds., *Wittgenstein and Contemporary Moral Philosophy* (Routledge, 2024). Part VI, 'An Open Letter to J.K. Rowling' (June 2020), also appeared on Crooked Timber and on a number of other blogs. 'Lissounes: A Thought Experiment', is forthcoming in Katherine Dormandy and Gertraud Ladner, eds., *Liminal Lives: Female Scholars Challenging Boundaries in Theology and Philosophy of Religion*.

For their invaluable help and encouragement and critical reader eyes, I want to thank Chris Belshaw, Kurt Blankschaen, Imogen Chappell, Miriam Chappell, Philip Chappell, Thalia Chappell, Tristan Chappell, Vanessa Chappell, Zsuzsanna Chappell, Ben Colburn, Rach Cosker-Rowland, Matt Cull, Helen De Cruz, Cora Diamond, Katherine Dormandy, Miranda Fricker, Raimond Gaita, Jim Hankinson, Stanley Hauerwas, Simon Kirchin, Stephen Latham, Alasdair MacIntyre, Ian Malcolm, David MacNaughton, Michael Morris, Sasha Lawson-Frost, Danièle Moyal-Sharrock, Peter Momtchiloff, Claudia Richardson, Miriam Ronzoni, Constantine Sandis, Jennifer Saul, Leonie Smith, Eleonore Stump, Kurt Sylvan, and many others whose names I will be embarrassed to have left out of this list when I realise my mistake. None of these good people, obviously, is in any way responsible for what I have to say here.

Simply by being a majority, cisgender people create the world that trans people live in.

Shon Faye, *The Transgender Issue: An Argument for Justice*

Life is freedom, and ... consciousness [is] the flame of freedom ... What constitutes the freedom, the soul, of an individual life, is its uniqueness. The reflection of the universe in somebody's consciousness is the foundation of his or her power, but life only becomes happiness, is only endowed with freedom and meaning, when someone exists as a whole world that has never been repeated in all eternity. Only then can they experience the joy of freedom and kindness, finding in others what they have already found in themselves.

Vasily Grossman, *Life and Fate*

For when my outward action doth demonstrate
the native act and figure of my heart
in complement extern, 'tis not long after
but I will wear my heart upon my sleeve
for daws to peck at. I am not what I am.

Shakespeare, *Othello* 1.1

When someone shows you who they are, believe them the first time.

Maya Angelou

PART I

That Was Then

1.1: 'I just want to'

I was four and three-quarters when I asked my mother if, from now on, I could please go to school as a girl instead of as a boy.

Four and three-quarter years old; but even that wasn't anything like the beginning of something. I wasn't so much asking to start something new as asking to carry on the way I was, only in the new circumstances of school. By then I'd already been dressing as a girl at home, on and off, for as long as I'd been able to dress myself at all. (So, maybe eighteen months.) On and off: not always but quite often, when I thought I could get away with it. And preferably, but not always, when I was alone: I was getting more self-conscious about it, and opportunities to be alone were getting rarer now I'd started school.

Actually, my question was more like the end of something, because my mother's response was 'Why?'

Why? I was four and three-quarter years old, so most of the things that can happen to us in life had not yet happened to me. Certainly, no one had ever asked me that before. I'd never put the question to myself either. I hadn't the faintest idea why I dressed as a girl, or why I felt so happy when I dressed as a girl. I had no clue why I wanted to be seen as a girl, or why, in fact, I wanted to *be* a girl.

I just did.

'I just want to', I said eventually.

My mother already looked furious – and scared – and now she looked angrier still. 'Why?' she repeated in a louder voice. I wanted to repeat 'I just want to', but I could see what would happen if I did: she'd ask me 'Why?' a third time, in an even louder voice, and I'd say 'I just want to' a third time, maybe also in a louder voice, and at some point she would stop repeating the question, lose her temper, and smack me instead.

I don't remember what happened next. Maybe I did say 'I just want to' again, and maybe she did ask me 'Why?' again, and maybe we did go on like that until she started smacking me. Nor do I remember whether this was my only conversation with my mother on the subject. Maybe, before this conversation, there was a whole series of other conversations like it.

But it was definitely the last conversation like this, because something happened afterwards that was enough to stop me ever asking again, at least in that direct way, if I could go to school as a girl. Something, too, that made me bury the whole experience in my subconscious for a very, very long time. Until quite recently, until getting on for fifteen years after I began moving towards transition in 1998, I didn't remember any of this confrontation at all. And I still don't remember how it ended.

But I'm guessing that, whatever happened next, it wasn't good.

1.2: The opposite of a Tom-boy

My mother died in 1989, so I only have my own recollection to rely on for this first thing. (And if she was alive, would we be able to talk about it? Impossible to say; but the little evidence there is, is not encouraging.) However, there are other little parcels of memory from the same time period that have, as it were, the same postmarks, and for those I have my older brother's confirmation.

At about the same time as that conversation, I was learning to read, and got to *The Famous Five*. And there I read that there was a name for a girl who wants to be a boy, as George does (who was christened Georgina): she's a Tom-boy.

'Right', I said when I first came across that word, all excited. This was decades before the internet. I had no idea that I wasn't the only boy in the entire world, ever, who wanted to be a girl instead. I didn't even learn the word 'transgender' until about thirty years later, in 2000 or thereabouts. But now – 'Right! Perhaps after all I am not the only one, perhaps people do have words for what I'm like. So if "Tom-boy" is the word for a girl who wants to be a boy, what is the word for a boy who wants to be a girl? Because that's what I am.'

My brother remembers me asking this. (He was about seven.) He also remembers me asking the connected question, 'What is the feminine form of "Tom"?' because, whatever it was, I was clearly a *that*-girl – a

Tamsin-girl, if 'Tamsin' is the girl-form of 'Tom'. And he remembers too that my questions were met with a nasty silence from whichever adults were listening. He didn't himself, he tells me, make much of it at all. As he rightly points out, I talk a lot, and a lot of what I say is nonsense that doesn't really add up to much.

Not all of it, though.

1.3: One secret wish

In the movies, there were fairy godmothers and magic wands and secret transforming spells. And that all looked pretty good to me, at six years old. In the movies, you could become anything, anything you wanted – with a bit of luck and a plot twist.

So why not a girl?

And at primary school I joined in with the girls' games sometimes, and one game they quite liked to play was Weddings.

So why could they all get a turn at being The Bride, but not me?

And I used to hear other kids answering the question, 'What would your one wish be?' and think, 'Are you crazy? You get this Magic Wish, this one and only Magic Wish, and you blow it on that?'

I don't think I was much older than six when I twigged what you do with a Magic Wish, anyway: you wish for an unlimited supply of Magic Wishes, of course. But leaving that aside... Suppose they plonk me down in front of some fairy godmother or vat of secret elixir. Do that, and there isn't the slightest doubt what I am going to ask for. No contest. Just one thing. Just the one same thing that I prayed for with my whole heart, secretly, desperately, again and again, as I went to sleep at night: please turn me into a girl.

Nope.

'You can have anything in the world – but you can't have that.'

'Simply by being a majority, cisgender people create the world that trans people live in' – as Shon Faye observes.[1] And that makes the cisgendered world an uncomfortable one for transgender people to live in.

But maybe it doesn't have to be quite *this* uncomfortable?

[1] Shon Faye, *The Transgender Issue: An Argument for Justice* (Allen Lane, 2021), p. xvii.

1.4: Eden, and a snake

It starts in Eden where everything starts, in the unconsciously known of early childhood. It starts out as the snake hidden in the garden; the thing about yourself that you know and don't know, can't avoid but can't admit, can't ever say but can't honestly gainsay either.

Self-knowledge is extremely hard when there is something about yourself that no one around you wants you to know, and that you yourself – once you begin to pick up others' inhibitions – start trying as hard as you can not to know.

'Let kids be kids', people say today. What do they mean by this rather sentimental and (I would say) deeply misleading slogan? Apparently quite often, in Florida and Texas for example, what they mean is: 'Don't let transgender kids be transgender kids.' As a transgender child in a society like ours, you are rapidly taught not to be yourself. Which seems to be what they want; the same people frequently say: 'There is no such thing as a trans kid', which is just a flat refusal to listen to millions of us, including me (see 1.18 below).

But apparently these people don't mind if their ringing pronouncements don't fit the facts. Because saying 'There is no such thing as a trans kid' does fit their gender ideology. It also fits what seems to underlie that ideology: namely, a deep *desire* that there should be no such thing as a trans kid.

The wish is father to the thought; and the wish is this: *they want us not to exist.*

Once that lesson is in – that you mustn't be yourself – the fact of your own nature becomes, even for you, something you yourself don't want to know either. Simply because it's so 'wrong'. It's so strange, so unexpected, so contrary to everything that you've been taught and told ever since you had ears at all. Above all (and the more you pick up others' standards, the more this matters), it's so deeply embarrassing.

But there, inescapably, it is. You have the body of a male; you want to have the body of a female. You want to be female; and you want every-thing that goes with being female. (And presumably it's the other way round if you're a trans boy; though I should let trans boys/men speak for themselves.)

'You want to be a girl, not a boy': is that it, though? Do you want to be a girl, not a boy, or do you just ('just'?) want to dress as a girl, not a

4

boy? Is it about your sex – femaleness, the actual physical body? Or is it about your gender – femininity, the social role? Do you want to dress and present feminine as a means to the end of being female (or getting as close to it as you can)? Or do you want to be female as a means to the end of dressing and presenting as feminine (again, as far as possible)?

This book is, designedly, a personal book. In everything I say in it, I can only speak authoritatively for one transgender person: myself. But for me it was, and is, both: it's about changing gender as a means to changing sex, and it's about changing sex as a means to changing gender. I wanted to be feminine in order to be female, and I wanted to be female in order to be feminine. It ran in both directions. It still does.

(Though one thing that isn't relevant in *either* direction: I was never really confused, I think, about the difference between 'liking girly stuff' and wanting to *be* a girl. True, it was hard to see a way to express my wish to be a girl *except* to go for girly stuff. Still, I always understood that boys could like dolls and ponies, or girls could like tractors and Action Man, without any of this in any way compromising their status as boys or girls. Being feminine, being female, and liking girly stuff are three different things. Some trans-exclusionaries claim that people who diagnose themselves as transgender do so because they don't understand these differences. They are simply mistaken.)

And is it nature or nurture? What trauma or hormone triggered it? Was it the wrong mix in the chemical brew of the womb, or was it too many Saturday mornings spent furtively reading *Ballet Shoes* instead of *Biggles*? Was it in my parents' DNA or in mine?

Well, I know there is embryological science that seems relevant to transgender. Who knows, maybe it's true. And if so, maybe true of me. I also know that my parents wanted one son and one daughter, and when I arrived they were disappointed that I wasn't a daughter, so they tried again (successfully, this time).

We can speculate about all these possible causes, but it's never very convincing. For any supposed triggering condition for transgender that you care to name, it seems like that condition is going to apply to lots and lots of people who aren't transgender – and not apply to lots and lots of people who are. In the end, I find these questions as unanswerable as 'Who started it?' about the Eden narrative.

What made me transgender?

What made *you* cisgender?

'If someone shows you who they are, believe them the first time.'

1.5: Auditioning for the angels

At five or six I had a certain reputation as a funny little joker. With adults, charm was my trump-card. Charm got me on *Braden's Week* once: that old light-entertainment TV programme had a regular slot where they interviewed small children with a view to getting a laugh from 'the things they come out with'. I don't remember at all what I came out with. I enjoyed the recording process, but when I saw the output, I felt betrayed. I already knew that adults were (among other things, of course, many of them good) perfidious, untrustworthy gaslighters. But to trick me into being ridiculed by other adults, on telly? Even for adults, that seemed like a new low.

What charmed adults was partly my unexpected articulacy, and partly my cheeky-monkey looks. At that age I was ash-blond with a lopsided quizzical grin, big round hazel eyes, and long dark eyelashes, like my mother. And though I didn't spend a lot of time in front of mirrors (I have always been a bit of a scruff about my appearance), I did look all right, I thought, in a dark green satin dress.

In a dress at six years old, I was not definitely a girl. But at least I was not definitely *not* a girl. Things would have been more satisfactory if my mother had let me grow my hair long, as (in vain) I begged her to. But even short-haired I was ambiguous in a dress, and that was – that was a start.

I joined the village church choir because of the vestments. Long floaty white surplices with frilled lace collars: they were dresses, really, and boys got to wear them too. And not only to wear them in public, but to wear them on ceremonial display. Mind you, I couldn't read music (I only learned in 2015) and I bored easily, sniggering with the other choristers while we knelt on the hassocks and something long-winded and unintelligible went on from the pulpit. And, in reality, the surplice, when you put it on, was cold and faintly damp from the dusty cupboard, easily ripped fragile old white cotton, faintly hinting at mothball-must and a rusty iron, pre-worn by who knows how many previous choristers. But it was worth it to be dressed like that for an hour and a half a week. And it all fitted with what was going on inside me.

Which was what? Well, two things in particular. One thing was a bedtime routine in my own head. 'If you can't sleep', my parents often had to say, 'then tell yourself a happy story.' The recurring story that I told myself to get to sleep was a story about arriving in heaven, and being fitted for angel's wings and robes; about being transformed from whatever it was that I was, into a kind of impossible, blissful, celestial, and definitely-not-male purity. ('Where like stars his children crowned, all in white shall wait around': a line in a carol that I latched onto the moment I heard it.)

And the other thing was the presence to me of God's love. Quite simply, he was there, like a heat source, a fire or a radiator, in the corner of the room. To be conscious was to be conscious that he was present, in my consciousness, as much as I was present there myself. He was maybe not obvious all the time, but he was in there somewhere. And the less distracted I was by other things, the quieter I and my surroundings were, the more I was aware of him.

It's still like that today. It is perhaps the most important thing of all for me that God is just there, and always has been.

Not that, at first, I was aware that it was God's presence that I was aware of. But in Sunday School one day we had a story from 1 Samuel 3. It's a time when hardly anyone in ancient Israel hears God speak to them (a bit like Britain now); but the worn-out old prophet Eli has a small boy-servant Samuel who keeps coming to him in the middle of the night saying 'You called?' when Eli hasn't called at all, and is just trying to get some sleep. But eventually it dawns on Eli: the voice that Samuel is hearing is Yahweh's voice. So Eli tells Samuel to stop bothering him when he hears the voice. Instead of bothering him, pray: 'Speak, Lord, for your servant is listening.'

And so I discovered that though the people around me apparently didn't have words for boys who wanted to be girls, still they did have words for this warm happy watching Presence that was in me, and of me, and yet was not *me* but someone else present to me, and loving and watching over me: silently mostly, but always there.

A lot of my childhood games were about running off and disappearing. But wherever I disappeared to, He came too.

7

1.6: The vanishing

Hidden in you as the sleeping deer is hidden
warm in the highest cairn of the furthest hill,

I am snow-bound, thin-air-remote, unwatched
by the spies of the woodsmoke glens.

Or I am barred and locked, your secret garden: sealed
with soft flowers' fragrance, quiet rumours of water,

rumours relayed over blank and roughcast walls
that shut in the shining green, the sunburst lawns;

and all that bustles beyond our walls goes by
my paradise and pleasance of your joy.

Or fast in your arms, I sleep the sleep of dreams
in the deepest bed in the house of the perfect eaves.

He who dwells in the shelter of the Most High
She who rests in the shadow of the Almighty
disappears.

1.7: 'Please God, let me be a girl'

If you actually want to get trans figured, if you actually want to understand transgender –

And do you, by the way? Do you actually want to understand transgender? Or is transgender something weird, alien, threatening, ridiculous, contemptible to you, and you've just come here to get a clearer fix on exactly why you find us – me – so contemptible? You've just come here for ammunition? For target practice? You're not here to get trans figured, you're just here to get the dirt on me?

I'm sorry, what a rude, hostile, gatekeeping interrogation that all was. The question does need asking, unfortunately; it'll become obvious why as we go along. But anyway, as I was saying:

– If you actually want to understand transgender, the first things you need to understand are how serious it is and how early it is.

How serious is it? Well, at least from my own experience, and from what I know of the experience of all the trans people I know well, it is no random whim. It is no casual fad. It is no passing fancy. It is absolutely the biggest thing that you want, so big that sometimes you can't even get it in focus or perspective, like a passenger on an ocean liner trying to get a photograph of the ship itself. And it is the thing that you want most urgently and unavoidably and permanently and inexorably. (As the psychiatrists say when diagnosing 'gender dysphoria': consistently, persistently, insistently.) It is crushing. It is suffocating. It colours everything else; it is your burden and your delight; it is your deepest anguish and your highest bliss. It is everything. And it is life or death.

> *How cis people think trans people decide to transition:* Well, that was an interesting essay by Judith Butler. I'm convinced. I think I'll start wearing skirts and put she/her in my email footers as a political gesture.
>
> *How trans people decide to transition:* I CAN'T GO ON LIKE THIS ANY MORE OR I WILL DIE.

On 'gender dysphoria', by the way. I have already accepted that talking about gender dysphoria is *one* way to talk about being transgender. Is it the main way? Is it the only way?

Some current commentators evidently think so. And in our state of society, they're certainly on to something. But maybe we should question our state of society? Ask yourself this (a good question for me, given that, as well as being transgender I am also a keen mountaineer): why is there no such general thing as 'mountain dysphoria'? Why, broadly speaking, does no one in our society succumb to mental health problems because they can't get at mountains?

As a matter of particular fact, I myself *have* sometimes suffered a bit from depression and frustration because I was living too far from the hills. But in general, the answer to my question is obvious. There is (generally speaking) no such thing as mountain dysphoria, simply because people *can* get at mountains. They want to climb mountains, and they get to climb mountains, and the result is a great deal of mountain *eu*phoria. Mountain dysphoria would only be a big social phenomenon if, for some reason, our society took mountaineering to be a dubious, eccentric, perhaps perverted activity that needs to be banned, suppressed, and denied. But since people who want to climb mountains are typically allowed to climb mountains, there just isn't a problem here, just a great deal of human happiness and fulfilment... you can see where I'm going with this analogy.

And on suffocating. Everyone, I suppose, is a something-phobe; I am a claustrophobe. I've always had a deep anxiety about being trapped inside things. I don't get panic attacks underground any more, like I used to as a child, but caving has never appealed, and wide-open spaces like mountain tops always have. Some people, for reasons that escape me (see 1.17 below), are militantly opposed to the idea that anyone can be 'born in the wrong body'. But the predicament that you feel, or at any rate I felt, in looking in the mirror and seeing a male me when I wanted to see a female me: that little phrase expresses how it feels exactly.

And how early is it? As early as can be. From the very beginning. As much as a religious sense is there (in those in whom it is there, like me), your sense of yourself as transgender is in everything, right from the off. Of course, there can be times when you hide it from yourself: as we'll see, mine is the story of someone who hid it from herself for decades and decades, who spent half her life trying with all her might *not* to be trans – and in the end failing. Conversely, of course, there can also be times when you cop on to yourself, when you realise what you want and who you are, and it seems that through some epiphany you 'become more transgender' – as we'll also see. But it's there all along, running right through you, through everything you are, like the lettering through a stick of rock. As long as you have any awareness at all, you're aware of that. It's who you are right from the start.

In this book I write personally, as I say. I don't claim to speak for anyone else, and I'm sure that I'll say some things that other transgender people will disagree with, or not find 'relatable'. I'm not trying to make universal, exceptionless generalisations. But I do know, from talking to other transgender people, that I am in many ways very similar to a lot of other trans women.

The thing about praying every night to be changed into a girl, for instance. I did it; lots and lots of trans girls do it. There have presumably been trans people praying this sort of prayer all along, because people have been reporting that they prayed it for as long as people in our society have been even slightly open about being transgender.

There is a great deal in Jan Morris's classic memoir *Conundrum* that was unnervingly, spookily familiar to me when I first read it. In particular this passage, where Morris is recalling something from the year of my father's birth, 1935. At the time, she (or at the time, to all appearances, he) was a nine-year-old chorister in Christ Church Cathedral in Oxford:

> I began to dream of ways in which I might throw off the hide of my body and reveal myself pristine within – for ever emancipated into the state of simplicity. I prayed for it every evening. A moment of silence followed each day [at Choral Evensong] the words of the Grace – 'The Grace of our Lord Jesus Christ, and the love of God, and the fellowship of the Holy Ghost, be with us all ever more.' Into that hiatus, while my betters I suppose were asking for forgiveness or enlightenment, I inserted silently every night, year after year throughout my boyhood, an appeal less graceful but no less heartfelt: '*And please God let me be a girl. Amen.*'[2]

Jan Morris uses the phrase 'born in the wrong body' in the very first sentence of *Conundrum*. Carol Steele has the born-in-the-wrong-body idea too, in her very similar report on growing up roughly halfway between Jan Morris's childhood and my own:

> [When I was seven, in 1952] my father read out a story from *The News of the World* to my mother, and suddenly it all became clear to me. The story was ... about Christine Jorgensen, the first transgender person to receive worldwide publicity about her gender confirmation surgery. I recognised myself in that story. This was who I was too. I also remember, in chilling detail, the words my father said after he finished reading that story: 'Perverts like that need locking away in a loony-bin and the key throwing away.' That was the beginning of the shame that haunted me for a further twenty years and resulted in two attempts at suicide.
>
> From that point on, my childhood was spent every evening praying that God would put right this terrible mistake and that the following morning I would wake up a proper girl. At primary school, I used to be teased and called

---

[2] Jan Morris, *Conundrum* (New York Review Books, 1974), p. 25.

a sissy and the boys started calling me Stella. Oddly enough, even though I knew this was meant to be bullying, it gave me a sense of peace and confirmation that my peers recognised me for who I actually was.[3]

Perhaps, if we had had centuries of openness about transgender, we would have centuries of reports of the same sort. But what we actually have is just a couple of decades of the internet, where for good or ill people have been as open about being transgender as they have about everything else in human life. Before the internet everything was different; most things to do with transgender were veiled in secrecy, hidden in shame and confusion.

Why the shame? Why the confusion? Where does that come from?

1.8: The shame

As far as I can tell, the shame comes mainly from outside. And to judge by her words just quoted, Carol Steele would agree. It doesn't occur to you to be ashamed of how you are and who you are until other people tell you that you should be. You just are that way, and you're perfectly happy that way, and it seems in no way abnormal to you. It's your normal, and you carry on being normal – normal *for you*; being who you are – until other people block your path.

When I was (as I then saw it) a small boy who wanted to be a small girl, that was just how things were and who I was, as far as I was concerned. Left to my own devices I would have accepted it and built it into my ordinary life without the slightest shame or confusion or embarrassment, as naturally and as happily as I accepted and lived with the facts that I was English, ash-blond, hazel-eyed, and right-handed.

I wasn't ashamed of being who I was until I was taught to be ashamed. The shame came later – not much later, but later (it wasn't there before I started school). It came from my parents and my siblings and, well, everyone really. Over the next ten or twenty years, it came from Walter the Sissy in the *Beano* and Basil Fotherington-Thomas in *Nigel Molesworth*, from 'You'll Be a Man, My Son' in Kipling and

[3] Carol Steele, 'The formative years', in Christine Burns, *Trans Britain* (Unbound, 2018), p. 69.

the gendering of everything I read from the Famous Five to Narnia, from constant firm reminders from everywhere that Boys Do This and Girls Do That, from my schoolmates' vocabulary of derision and their playground chants. Shame about my predicament was not a natural but an acquired response. So was the very idea that it was a predicament, a problem, as opposed to simply how things were for me.

What are little boys made of?
What are little boys made of?
Frogs and snails,
And puppy-dogs' tails;
That's what little boys are made of.

What are little girls made of?
What are little girls made of?
Sugar and spice,
And everything nice;
That's what little girls are made of.

You can be chaotic, messy, dirty, rough, noisy, adventurous, an outdoors kind of person; or you can be sweet, tasty, orderly, tidy, pretty, demure, an indoors kind of person – a classroom or library or nursery kind of person. But you can't be both: you have to be one or the other. If you are frogs and snails, then you aren't sugar and spice. If you are sugar and spice, then you aren't frogs and snails. And you don't choose which to be – it's not up to you to decide which you are. As people now like to say, 'Being a woman is not a feeling.' If your body looks like this, that's it: no sugar and spice for you. If it looks like that, too bad: frogs and snails are off.

And if you feel any different, like I did – if you are into both frogs and snails and sugar and spice, but also think that, if you really do have to choose between them, then it's the sugar and spice that you most deeply go for – if you are like that, then you should feel ashamed of yourself, and your parents should feel ashamed of you too, and they should do something to stop you. The opposite of what they do in the Who song 'I'm a boy', where a boy child is forced into presenting as a girl because that's what his mother wants. A song that I heard much later than the nursery rhyme, of course, and sung with plenty of subversive intent to them; but even when I was fourteen, I heard the words before I noticed the subversion. To have parents who left me no choice but to be a girl instead of a boy – yes, well, I could dream. But dream was all.

1.9: And the confusion

I wasn't ashamed, then – not at first. And I wasn't confused, either – at least, not when I was four or five I wasn't. If you'd asked me when I was four or five 'Are you a boy or a girl?' I'd have said, grumpily and sadly, 'A boy, I suppose.' If you'd asked me 'What do you want to be, a boy or a girl?' I'd have said, immediately and definitely – and very hopefully – 'A girl – please.' And if you'd then asked me 'So are you really a boy or a girl?' I think I'd have scratched my head and said something like: 'I don't really know. I know I look like a boy. But that's not the way I really am… or feel… or want to be… Could we try this again, please, this which-am-I business? Please can I change?'

No one ever asked me any of these questions, unfortunately. But I don't think my hypothetical answers to them were symptomatic of confusion. Incomplete information, yes; uncertainty, yes; but confusion? I wasn't confused at all. As far as any small child can have, or could have then, I had a very clear idea of my own nature and my own situation.

I did have a certain sense that I wasn't being told everything, and that sense perhaps was part of what motivated me, as I always have been motivated, to find things out for myself rather than taking other people's word for them; to find different ways of exploring and learning things. Me all over, in pretty much every sphere: I find an unorthodox way to do something, and do it that way and feel guilty about it, and pretend I am doing it the same way as everyone else – until it dawns on me that actually there might be something to be said for my unorthodox approach. The first exam I ever took was the entrance exam to my private primary school when I was four and a half. I was asked to solve a maze, to get a mouse from the gateway to the cheese in the middle. I already knew that the easiest way to solve a maze was backwards, starting from the endpoint and going back to the beginning. But I didn't know whether I was supposed to know this, or whether doing the maze that way was cheating. So I did the maze twice in the time allowed, once furtively, backwards in my head from the cheese to the mouse, and once openly, tracing the route forward with my finger from the mouse to the cheese, as I believed I was supposed to.

I took the unorthodox route with learning to read, too. So long as my learning-to-read books were *Janet and John* and *Peter and Jane*, I hated reading and was bored rigid by the whole business and insisted vehemently that there really wasn't any need for me to learn to read. I had always got by in the past (all four and a half years of it) without being able to read, so why, I insisted, shouldn't I get by without reading in the future too?

And then, while I was staying at my grandparents' house, I got hold of a creaky, dusty old copy of *Alice in Wonderland*, probably my father's from his childhood, or maybe my grandmother's from hers, all hand-cut pages and oil-sheet-covered Tenniel illustrations, and learned to read from that instead.

I wonder what it was about the contrast between dreary, monosyllabic, large-font prose involving faceless, cardboard-cut-out, gender-binary figurines, and a riotous explosion of a book about a subversive, solitary girl in a Victorian dress who finds herself magicked away into a world of giddy mathematical imaginings, that can possibly have made the difference for me.

But on the topic of boys who wish they were girls all the time, I didn't even know what I didn't know. I didn't have the first idea whether anyone else had ever been like me in this way. I hadn't a clue how I might tell if they were, or what to look for in others to try and read them or clock them or work them out. Nor did I have the slightest clue what, if anything, could be done about my constant, deep, haunting longing to turn into a girl.

Another thing that happened when I was about four was that I had my tonsils out. In some vague way I had high hopes of this operation, especially since I was dressed for it beforehand in what looked to me pretty much like a girl's nightie. Secretly, I was deeply disappointed when I came round afterwards with a very sore throat – and a boy's body still.

Like the shame, the confusion came from outside. I wasn't confused about being who I was until I was taught to be confused – until I was taught that being a boy who wanted to be a girl was being a problem, an anomaly, a freak of some sort. It was being someone who deserved to be laughed at, someone who was mixed-up and weird, and had a duty to keep their weirdness to themselves. Whether or not it seemed that way to me, I was taught that being a boy who wanted to be a girl was being someone who was both confused and shameful.

I am not in the least angry or bitter about how my life has gone. My life has gone *great*, thanks, so far, and provided it doesn't end with me getting knifed in the park by some lunatic transphobe, or with us all getting blown up by some lunatic tyrant. But even if my life hadn't been good, I would still believe in forgiveness. The autobiographical aspect of this book wouldn't be there unless I thought that there were things that can be learned from it, things to reflect on, things that might prompt course-corrections for others besides me. Still, this is not a denunciation or a charge sheet; nor an exercise in self-justification or revenge. It is a memoir. Maybe it is even, in the end, a celebration.

So I don't want to blame anyone for anything.

And anyway, truth to tell, the person in my family who gave me the hardest time for being transgender was, by far, me myself.

Still, I really don't think that it should have happened like it did. I really don't think that children should be taught to feel confused, and ashamed, and guilty, and wrong, just for being the way that they naturally are. I don't think it's right for any attempt they make to say who they are, and be who they are, to be met with anger, aggression, hostility, repression, ridicule, denial, bullying, browbeating, threats, enforcement, punishment, sanctions, deprivations, surveillance, policing, gaslighting, ideological brainwashing, demands for desistance, Praying Away The Sissy – and the patronising accusations that the children in question are 'confused'.

In fact – and especially if we focus on the effects that follow this sort of behaviour, rather than the intentions preceding it – I'd call it child abuse.

'You can be whatever you want. But you can't be *that*.'

1.10: Why there is no such thing as 'gender confusion' – or at least, not the kind you meant

In this context, of course, 'confusion' is a loaded word now. It's being used these days as a weapon in a culture war, as in the wearily familiar talking point that 'young children are being confused by being exposed to gender ideology'. We'll come on to 'gender ideology'; let's start by dealing with this idea of 'gender confusion'.

It really needs to be dealt with, because there's no such thing. At least not in the sense usually intended. The idea behind the phrase is evidently that 'normal people' (the non-freaks; the 'cis'; the natural people, including the ones who rage about being described as 'cis') have a common-sensical feel for what it is for them to be a boy, or a girl. This sense is strong and clear, though it might not be an inner feeling of any kind; perhaps it just derives from noticing the shape of your own body. And this sense guides 'normal people' into the correct two paths of the 'gender binary': each of us is either a boy with no doubts about it, or a girl with no doubts about it.

However (the idea is), this clear strong sense of what it is for them to be a boy (or a girl) can be disrupted! People can be infected by doubt and confusion about their doubt-free, unconfused sense of what it is to be a boy (or a girl)! Bad people who want to harm our society – and our children!! – are busy spreading this doubt and confusion! Transgender is an 'irreversibly damaging' 'craze' that is 'seducing our daughters'!

(Alert readers will spot which book I am referencing here. I hope all readers will understand why, if it's all the same to you, I'd rather not spell out the reference. This sort of talk deserves obscurity, not amplification. First, it is factually wrong to describe transgender as a 'craze'. Transgender is not a merely recent or local phenomenon (see 2.6 below), and realising that one is transgender is not like suddenly deciding to go in for hula-hoops or Wordle; it might be more closely compared to facing up to the fact that one is gay. Secondly, there is certainly 'irreversible damage' being done to transgender people; but – as I know to my own cost – the vast majority of it is being done by those who submit us to intimidation, browbeating, harassment, and sometimes outright psychological or physical torture, with a view to preventing us from existing as transgender people at all. So from someone with violently trans-exclusionary views, these words are, shall we say, a bit much. They are also, thirdly, irresponsibly inflammatory. To begin a discussion of transgender with the claim that 'our daughters' are being 'seduced' is to resort to the kind of moral-panic rhetoric that is used, and I speak literally here, to whip up lynch mobs. In a world that is increasingly threatening for transgender people, where transgender children are routinely bullied and brainwashed to deny their own nature, where an increasing number of US states are making snoopy-neighbour informers' witch hunts against the families of transgender children part of their law, and where lethal transphobic violence is by no means just the dark imaginings of offline anxiety, such dangerous language deserves, not the oxygen of publicity, but what a certain author would call an invisibility-cloak.)[4]

When you lay out this train of alarmist thought about 'gender confusion' like this, it shouldn't be hard to see how, well, confused it is. If this sense of what it is for someone to be a boy, or a girl, is so strong and clear, how come it is also so fragile, so easily disrupted by 'confusion'? And how come there are counterexamples to it? Both cases of people who aren't sure about their own gender, and maybe wish they didn't have a gender at all, and also cases like mine: cases of people who are sure which of the two genders they belong in, but are sure that it's the other one from the one they were 'assigned at birth'.

And anyway, what exactly is so harmful about having one's sense of one's own gender disrupted? Maybe our society's norms of femininity and masculinity are oppressive, and could do with a bit of disruption and subversion. Or even if it is confusion we're talking about, well, is it always such a terrible thing to be confused? Cocksure ignoramuses are hardly ever confused. Speculative research scientists are confused all the time.

Keep it in mind that we're talking about cases where someone is perfectly well aware of the biological facts about their own body (at least in its original form), but decides for whatever reason that they'd like to live in a way that flouts normal expectations about the lifestyle of people (who at least started out) with that shape of body – in what is sometimes called, jocularly or scornfully, a gender-bending way. In cases like this, why speak about confusion at all? Why not speak instead of, say, exploration? What's the confusion here? What are gender-bending people supposed to be confused *about*?

Or consider, again, the language of 'seduction' that has (as above) so reprehensibly been inveigled into this discussion. 'Seduction' implies deception of some kind. (It also implies sexual abuse and non-consensual

---

[4] Plenty more reasons to worry about this sort of discourse: https://xtramagazine .com/power/far-right-feminist-fascist-220810.

sex; like I say, it's a pretty despicable move to invoke the word at all.)
But usually, when someone chooses to bend gender norms, there *is* no
deception. And there *is* no deceiver.

'The rich man in his castle, the poor man at his gate; God made them
high and lowly, and ordered their estate.' Suppose we voluntarily chose to
live together in a community where everyone's basic physical needs were
provided for by an elected organising committee, and, beyond those needs,
everyone had exactly the same amount of money to spend on whatever
they wanted. Such communities exist; kibbutzim, monasteries, anarchist
collectives, and nunneries are organised in something like this way.

Does a community like this involve its members in 'confusion' about
the God-given 'estates' of 'high and lowly'? What would the confusion
be, exactly? Confusion presumably means false or incoherent beliefs; but
where is the falsehood, or the incoherence, in communal living?

Or even if there *were* some confusion involved – say, an undermining
or a compromising of some people's previously firm conviction that the
estates of rich and poor are in fact God-given – would that be so terrible?

In any area you like (wealth or gender or sexuality or anything really),
would it actually be worse to be confused about society's norms, than to
be totally clear what they are and utterly distressed by them?

1.11: Purity and danger

When people talk about 'gender confusion' in this way, as a taint or
infection that you can catch from other people, they are talking the
language of purity and danger. *Purity and Danger* is, as you may or
may not know, an important book by the famous anthropologist Mary
Douglas. Central to her argument is the thesis that much of our religious,
ethical, and political thinking is really thinking about hygiene and
infection, often disguised as tabooistic or religious or moralised ideas
of sanctity or purity. Alas, this is exactly how a lot of people now think
about transgender people: as a contagious virus. (It is also how white
racists think about black people, and how anti-Semites think about Jews.)

In the UK and the US, mainstream media has for years been spreading
propaganda about how awful we trans people are. Propaganda that is
generally extremely good at never allowing actual trans people to show
up as *people*; we are always carefully depicted as a faceless, shadowy,

threatening mob. Both metaphorically and literally, you never see our *faces*. If someone gives you the Pavlovian prompt 'Gay people', I bet it triggers in your head an image of a gay person. But what if they give you the Pavlovian prompt 'Trans people'? I wonder whose image pops into your head then. Is it even someone transgender at all? How did we get to the point where our national 'debate about trans people' *simply bypasses actual trans people*? Where people who are at the very least equivocal about trans people, and in many cases actively hostile to them, have succeeded in making our 'conversation about trans people' a conversation that is *all about them*?

Such, sadly, is contemporary anti-trans propaganda. And thanks in part to this propaganda, people think of us, if at all, as a plague, a dangerous infection, perhaps as a taint on the nation's racial purity. (This last suggestion is rife in places like Uganda and Iran and Russia, where it is commonplace to claim that trans people, and/or gay people, may exist elsewhere, but simply don't exist at all in their pure nation. Despicably, the very same insinuation is now being repeated by leading members of the transphobic side of the Scottish independence movement.) Racists think that you can catch terrible things from other races; homophobes think that you can catch AIDS, or being gay, from gay people. Likewise, for transphobes, transgender is a frightening contagion, a threat to 'our' women and children. And 'confusion' about gender is something that can be spread, and it is spread – well, by people like me, I suppose, and by books like this one. (Step away from the tranny-lit, readers! Now wash your minds! Whoop whoop, DANGER, here be *pollutions*!)

An earlier generation was accustomed to tabloid headlines about 'the gay plague' – that is, to the stigmatisation of homosexual attraction as something dangerous and toxic that is caught from others, and indeed is sometimes deliberately spread by intentional propagators. 'The gay plague' meme cruelly conflates this idea of infectious ideology with the devastating scourge of AIDS, a disease that has no intrinsic connection whatever with being gay.[5]

---

[5] 'In the past LGBTI+ people were widely accused of spreading HIV/Aids (see HRC report from 2015). Today such disinformation is being rephrased within the current COVID-19 pandemic.' https://www.europarl.europa.eu/RegData/etudes /BRIE/2021/653644/EXPO_BRI(2021)653644_EN.pdf, p. 12.

I don't think many people today still buy this gay-epidemic nonsense. Not, at least, in the UK, though unfortunately there's been a new outbreak of it in Poland and Russia. (See what I did there?) In the UK, everyone, or almost everyone, is perfectly well aware now that being gay is no more 'infectious' than being straight is. If you're a boy who fancies boys, there it is; it's a brute fact about you, and there is no converting you to fancying girls any more than you could be forced to fancy Marmite, or Marillion. ('What made you transgender?', 'What made you gay?': similar questions with similarly worrying agendas and assumptions behind them; similar, too, in that neither question really needs answering at all, beyond '*I just am*'.)

Yes, you might experiment, and try things out, just as you might with Marmite or Marillion. And yes, experiments of this sort might be revelatory: you might find yourself saying 'This is what I really like! This is who I really am! If only I'd realised before!' But none of this experimenting will stick unless it finds something real in you to catch on to. And whether or not it sticks, whether or not it finds something in you to catch on to, whether or not you are in fact mistaken about your own nature (and mistakes are certainly possible in principle) – notwithstanding all of this, there is a crucial freedom here. Namely, the freedom to be allowed to discover for yourself, in the sexual or the gender aspect of your nature as in every other aspect, who you really are.

Today in the UK, the ubiquitous (and iniquitous) media rhetoric of 'gender confusion' usually targets transgender people instead of gay and bisexual people. (Usually, though, the homophobes are now being increasingly re-emboldened by the apparent successes of transphobia.) But the pattern of thought is patently the same. It's a plague, there's an epidemic of people declaring themselves transgender or non-binary – in public too! Shall we say they're 'shoving it down our throats'? There are superspreaders of transness! There are people spreading it *deliberately*! And the only way to extirpate it is to extirpate them. In a remarkably sinister phrase that has sometimes been used, we need to 'eliminate transgenderism'.[6]

To this alarmist and sometimes eliminationist rhetoric about transgender people, the correct reply is the same as it was to the

[6] https://www.pinknews.co.uk/2021/01/27/womens-human-rights-campaign -gender-recognition-act-inquiry-trans-transphobia/.

alarmist and eliminationist rhetoric about gay people. Being gay is no more 'infectious' than being straight is; likewise, being transgender is no more 'infectious' than being cisgender is. We may also point out, again in parallel with the gay case, the terrible consequences of this sort of rhetoric: 'Get people to believe absurdities, and you will get them to commit atrocities' (as Voltaire allegedly[7] said). There is a very short and direct route whereby ridiculous alarmism, based on palpably false and indeed nonsensical descriptive claims, leads to fear, hatred, violence, and witch-hunting prejudice against a small, marginalised, and essentially harmless minority. And that minority are seen not as what they are, simply humans who live a bit differently from other humans, but as advocates of an ideology. Not as transgender *people*, but as transgender*ists*.

We've been here before, too. Remember when gay people were described as *homosexualists*?

1.12: Back to the Fifties

'Homosexualism' used to be a thing – a thing that was vilified as unnatural. 'Apart from *homo sapiens*, there isn't another species in the whole of nature', a friend who was reading medicine earnestly informed me in the first week after our arrival at college in 1984, 'that goes in for homosexuality.' He is still a friend today, and he still does medicine, but he was spectacularly wrong about this.[8] And since he was reading medicine, he probably never did come across the bit in *Nicomachean Ethics*, Book 1 (1097b22–1098a20), where Aristotle argues that anything that 'only humans do' is not specially *un*natural, but specially natural (for us): it is, in fact, the crowning glory of human life. So, being gay is the human *ergon*? Maybe the homophobes should read more Aristotle.

Likewise, today, transgender people are vilified as unnatural. To make this vilification stick is one of the main functions of the 'gender

---

[7] But not, it seems, actually: Voltaire on Capitol Hill: 'Anyone who can make you believe absurdities can make you commit atrocities.' Voltaire Foundation. https://voltairefoundation.wordpress.com/2021/02/16/voltaire-on-capitol-hill-anyone-who-can-make-you-believe-absurdities-can-make-you-commit-atrocities/.

[8] https://en.wikipedia.org/wiki/List_of_animals_displaying_homosexual_behavior.

confusion' rhetoric. It presupposes that there is a natural order of things that is the opposite of 'gender confusion'.

The more you look into this, the stranger it gets. Typically, the people who use this rhetoric seem to be dreaming of a 1950s graphic novel world, a world where men are real men, women are real women, boys are real boys, girls are real girls, and (if you'll forgive the Douglas Adams steal) small green furry creatures from Alpha Centauri are real small green furry creatures from Alpha Centauri.

The men: tense and curt and urgent, never a trace of irony or even of humour (unless it's at someone else's expense), strong-clenched shaving-shadowed jaws, Brylcreemed crew cuts under jaunty but resolute trilbies, shiny black leather brogues, Zippo cigarette lighters, sharp-cut suits in endless ever-so-important business meetings... with other men.

The women: frivolously complex beehive hairdos, floaty floral frilly rockabilly skirts, full-on mascara and sheer nylon stockings and un-runnable-in stiletto heels... checking their lipstick in the driving mirror of an enormous dream-car twenty-foot long, or footling around at Tupperware parties with other women, unless they're swooning into the men's arms. ('Oh, Brad!')

The boys: smaller and rosier-cheeked versions of their fathers without the Brylcreem and the Zippo, in grey flannel shorts and with baseball bats or model Mustangs instead of rolled-up umbrellas.

The girls: smaller and rosier-cheeked versions of their mothers without the nylons and the mascara, in shorter and even frillier skirts, and with dolls instead of rolling-pins.

This is the natural order of things? The one and only natural order of things? It's hard to imagine a more consciously and deliberately engineered condition of affairs than 1950s American gender politics. Or a more particular and culturally specific condition. And this hit-parade of straitjacket stereotypes, this bizarre set of folkways, this howlingly peculiar and heavily policed social construction – you want us to believe that it is not only uniquely natural, but also entirely unconfused? And that something else called 'gender confusion' threatens it? And that it's only the advocates of this terrible, threatening, shadowy thing called 'gender confusion', and not at all the advocates of this 1950s vision of 'the natural order of things', who have something worth calling a gender ideology?

The ironies in this background narrative are simply dazzling.

1.13: Why there is no such thing as 'gender ideology' – or at least, not the kind you meant

But it's one of those irregularly conjugated verbs, isn't it? 'I talk plain, down-to-earth, honest-to-goodness common sense'; 'You respect scientific fact'; but 'They have a gender ideology.'[9]

I am a trans woman. I am a philosopher who reads and writes about the philosophy of transgender. (Sometimes; though I actually spend most of my time on other things.) So I must have a gender ideology, right?

Wrong. I don't have a gender ideology. I don't even know what a gender ideology is. Or at least... almost not. But depending what exactly you mean by 'gender ideology', maybe that's not quite literally true.

The word 'ideology' is a little tricky, in the way that 'accent' or 'smell' is. Saying that someone has an accent – or has a smell – is usually pejorative: it picks up a restricted sense of these words, meaning that someone has a *noticeable* accent or a *bad* smell. But there is also, obviously enough, a wider sense of these words in which everyone has an accent, or a smell; intonation patterns and odours occur on continuums, and everyone is somewhere on those continuums. Same with 'ideology': we say that someone is 'driven by ideology' when we mean by *bad* ideology. But everyone has some ideas that form their view of things; in the wide inclusive sense, everyone has an ideology, including me.

With this noted, we can turn to the narrower sense, and note that one increasingly prominent use for the phrase 'gender ideology' is simply for the purposes of blanket dismissal. It's a kind of catch-22 for trans people and their allies. If we say nothing in our own defence, or if we challenge the terms of the debate or the very idea that our rights and our being should be up for debate, then we are denounced for refusing to engage rationally with our adversaries. But if we *do* engage – like I am engaging

---

[9] A perfect example of what I'm talking about is in the *Observer*, a piece unaccountably given the gravitas of lead-article anonymity. 'Ideology has no place in medicine', it solemnly begins, and then treats us to eight paragraphs of pure and undiluted imposition of 'gender critical' ideology upon medicine, up to and including the outright false and repeatedly debunked claims that trans people are just confused gays and that puberty blockers are experimental medicine. https://www.theguardian.com/commentisfree/2022/mar/20/observer-view-cass-review-gender-identity-services-young-people.

in this book – then the experiential evidence and the rational arguments that we present are simply dismissed as 'gender ideology'. Accused of never explaining our way of being or defending where we're at, we come up with explanations and defences of how we are and where we're at. Which are then not engaged with rationally, but treated as if they were a cloud of infection, as if we were trying to brainwash others with our 'woke ideology'. This refusal to engage is obviously disingenuous when it comes allied with a demand for rational arguments from us. It's not that we don't present rational arguments. We do, but when we do they are simply ignored, or dismissed as 'gender ideology'.

Another way that the phrase 'gender ideology' is used quite often seems to be simply to mean 'what Judith Butler says about gender'. Now Butler is an ingenious, often revelatory, sometimes baffling, theorist of sex and gender; but the idea that their views are somehow canonical for all transgender people does no favours at all either to Butler or to us. Obviously enough, the vast majority of transgender people have never read a word of Butler; fourteen-year-old trans boys and trans girls in rural Kansas are (forgive me, Judith) *totally not* quoting *Gender Trouble* everywhere they go. And in any case, Butler's is hardly the only view of gender on the market. So even if someone succeeded in knocking down Butler's views about transgender, that would prove precisely nothing about transgender itself.

I do have some ideas about gender and sex – of course I do – and one point of writing this book is to think them through, to get them straight in my own head, and to present them to others to see what they think. Do these ideas of mine add up to an ideology? Well, see for yourself; but I don't think so. I don't think they are organised enough, systematic enough – or far-out enough – to constitute a *theory* of sex or gender, let alone an ideology. Though of course, it might just be that I have high standards about what it takes for something to count as a theory, or an ideology; more about that in 1.15 below.

A fortiori, then, since I don't have a theory of gender, I don't have a theory of gender identity either. Maybe this book should have a section headed 'Why there is no such thing as gender identity'.[10] At any rate, I

---

[10] See my article 'Trans without the gender (well, almost): A response to Rich Rowland.' https://www.researchgate.net/publication/365873193_Trans_without_the _gender_well_almost_a_response_to_Rich_Rowland#fullTextFileContent.

don't think we *need* any very substantive notion of gender identity. There is certainly the experience of finding that you are physically shaped like one sex and wanting to be physically shaped like the other; and there is certainly the experience of finding that you are socially treated like one gender, and wanting to be socially treated like the other. But 'a theory of gender identity' seems to be a name for a view that offers to *explain* these experiences. Like I said above, I don't really see why these experiences *need* explaining, any more than the experience of finding that you're same-sex-attracted needs explaining.

Some people just are gay; some people just are transgender. What's to explain here? And anyway, what counts as explaining? You can say if you like that you have a Mystical Feminine Essence. But that isn't an explanation of the experience of being embodied one way and deeply longing to be embodied the other way. It's just dressing that experience up in pretentious language that doesn't really explain anything. (It is like saying that a drug puts people to sleep because it has a dormitive virtue.) Or you could say that you are a trans woman in this life because you are the reincarnation of someone who was a woman in a previous life. But then, who was *she* a reincarnation of?

Explanation is one supposed purpose of such theories of gender; another is, of course, political and psychological control. If you want to see a theory of gender being ideologised – imposed on real-world people as a way of controlling them – then turn back to the 1950s graphic novel world of 1.12. Now *that's* a gender ideology, at least when it's supposed to be the, or even a, 'natural order of things'. Sweeping claims about what men and women must be like, about 'the essence of masculinity' or 'the essence of femininity': that's all gender ideology. Our society is absolutely awash with it today. In an updated version, to be sure, because the fashion industry needs the way we dress to change in order to keep on selling us new clothes. But still in a version that would be entirely recognisable to the people from the 1950s graphic novels. It's a key part of this gender ideology that 'the female role' and 'the male role' in society are fixed and separate, and that if you are born male then you should (or must, or cannot help but) take on the male role, whereas if you are born female then you should (or must, or cannot help but) take on the female role, and that anyone who blurs the boundaries between these two roles is some kind of threat. All of this most certainly is gender ideology. And imposing it on children is, as I said, child abuse.

So in fact, strictly speaking, it is true that I, and most transgender people, have undergone 'child abuse', and grown up 'confused by gender ideology'. But not as these words are intended when right-wing tabloids and trans-exclusionary commentators use them.

> The term 'Gender Ideology' is an empty signifier which allows a diverse range of religious and far-right actors to team up to fight women's equality, sex education and the rights of LGBTI+ people such as same-sex marriage … opponents [of these things] are transnationally interconnected, notwith-standing the fact that they proclaim their local embeddedness and support for national sovereignty; their declared aims are fighting against morally corrupt elites – notably represented by the EU and UN – that attempt to 'colonise' them by propagating liberal ideals. More recently, also the term 'LGBT ideology' has been repeatedly used derogatorily, notably by Polish politicians, to attack and dehumanise LGBTI+ people. (In response, the Commission President Ursula von der Leyen and others, including the European Parliament, have replied that it is not an ideology, it is an identity.) Since 'Gender Ideology' is a construction by outsiders opposing gender and LGBTI+ equality, in cases where the term is spread intentionally to deceive the public this falls into the category of disinformation. However, it seems from the reviewed literature that many opponents of a 'Gender Ideology' actually believe in this as an intentional 'ideology', probably [confusing] it with 'Gender Theory' in feminist studies.[11]

---

[11] https://www.europarl.europa.eu/RegData/etudes/BRIE/2021/653644/EXPO_BRI (2021)653644_EN.pdf, p. 12. Later in the same report (p. 16), the unsettling role of the Vatican in all this becomes clear: 'A case of anti-LGBTI+ campaign is the "Gender ideology" opposition campaign that started in conservative wings of the Vatican in the 1990s, in reaction to UN conferences in Cairo (1994, on population and development) and Beijing (1995, on women) believed to spread a so-called "Gender Ideology". Kuhar and Paternotte (2017: 9) therefore claim that the "Gender Ideology" was a Catholic invention, with the Catholic Church its chief "discourse producer" (p. 262). The Vatican feared that sexual and reproductive rights would become a vehicle for recognising abortion, undermining traditional motherhood and legitimising homosexuality. Opposition to "Gender Ideology" is thus a clear case of supporting and advocating for unfavourable treatment and discrimination against LGBTI+ people. Theologies of the woman and of the body (insisting on

The ideology that has been in my face, most of my life, is not some imaginary 'transgender ideology'. (If only.) No: it is the tedious, unimaginative, tabloid spite of the dominant public ideology of gender in my society, which tells me that I shouldn't be a trans woman. That since I was born in a male body, I should – or must or cannot help but – live in the male gender role, and that there is something seriously wrong (and/ or deluded, wicked, sinful, unnatural, sexually perverted, etc.) about me if I don't.

'Confused by gender ideology'? I'll show you someone caught in the very moment of being confused by gender ideology: Carol Steele, as I quoted her in 1.7, hearing her father's bigoted dismissiveness about Christine Jorgensen. Till then she wasn't confused or ashamed. Till then she didn't even have an ideology.

The same happened to me. Till I ran smack, headlong, into other people's expectations of me, I didn't have anything like a theory of gender. I just had my own experience, and the way I knew I was – however vaguely and dimly, given I was only a small child. From then on – from then until pretty recently in my life – I most certainly was confused, indeed brainwashed, by a gender ideology. But not my own gender ideology; rather, the gender ideology that society imposed on me.

Not that everything before that was rosy. Even pretty early on, and well before I was exposed to the full force of my society's dominant gender ideology, there was already pain, and – well yes – one kind of confusion too; just because of the deeply unsettling feeling of mismatch between my body and my self-perception, and because I had been given no way of making any kind of sense of that mismatch, not even a name for it.

---

the difference and complementarity of the sexes) and the Vatican's idea of a "new feminism", together with different publications from the former Pontifical Council for the Family, seem to have played a particular role. These ideas have persisted in the Vatican, evident in statements that gender is eliminating "the anthropological basis of the family" (cited in Kuhar & Paternotte 2017: 5). The reason anti-gender campaigns gained momentum in the 2010s was because of crucial encounters with right-wing populism (Paternotte & Kuhar 2018). The term "LGBT ideology" is also more and more used by right-wing conservative political figures connected to various religions and religious figures.' As an instinctive pro-Catholic, I find this all very saddening.

1.14: *The claustrophobia of the body*

For the pain and confusion that I did feel as a transgender child, a fairly suitable name – if we didn't like 'gender dysphoria' or 'dysmorphia' – would be 'the claustrophobia of the body'. You look at your body in the mirror and you think something very like: *Tear it all down and start again.*

Start again where? Start again how? Tear what down? You're eight years old. This is your body. What can you do about it? What can you do about anything, at eight years old? How could you possibly start again? What would that even mean?

You can't change your body. But here's what you can change: your clothes.

The thing is, the dressing-up box was right there in my bedroom. That happened to be where it lived – if memory serves, I insisted on that – and we made full use of it, all three of us: my older brother, my younger sister, and me in the middle. But I made even more use of it when I was on my own, away from self-conscious feelings and teasing from my siblings and parents and anyone else.

There were soldier and policeman and cowboy and tiger costumes in there that I happily wore. There were also various shipwrecked ball-gowns and worn-out party dresses and net petticoats of my mother's, and a bridesmaid's dress from when her best friend had married her brother, and various other frilly bits and pieces of girl-toddler stuff, and, best of all, a white ballet tutu.

The girls' clothes in the dressing-up box I wore even more happily than the boys' clothes, though naturally some of them were a bit too small and others were a lot too big. Sometimes I slept in them overnight (overnight being, after all, the longest stretch of undisturbed hours alone in all the twenty-four). I don't clearly remember my mother finding me wearing a ballet tutu when she woke me in the morning for school; but I do have vague inklings that that happened, and that I hoped she'd be pleased, and she wasn't. (I think it must have happened, and fairly often too.)

Like I said, there never was a time before I did this, not that I know of anyway. As soon as I could dress myself at all, I dressed myself as a girl sometimes, and I had no idea why.

If I'd been articulate enough to muster an explanation – and I was a very articulate and indeed mouthy child, but not yet that articulate – I would have said: 'This is something I can change.' In everyday language, to 'get changed' is to change your clothes. And that's the point of dressing up, right? You change yourself, at least as far as you can. Into a tiger, or a policeman – or a girl. (Not that I cared in the slightest about being a tiger or a policeman; but, for various reasons, it became convenient to pretend that I cared about the three transformations equally; to hide in plain sight; to act nonchalant.)

My body was there, and boy-shaped, and at some deep and inexplicable level I didn't like that, and never had liked it. From the moment I was aware of my own body at all, I wanted to change myself. I wanted to be a girl, not a boy; so I wanted my body to be a girl's body, not a boy's. I couldn't actually fix that. But I could fix my clothes. And I could try to use a change of clothes as a way of asking (but asking who?) for a change of body as well.

I did what I could about my body as well, of course; not that that was much. If I had had a magic wand to wave, I most certainly would have waved it, and turned my boy's body into a girl's body. But I was eight years old. I didn't have a magic wand. I just had some tattered old clothes.

So the thing to do was wear the girliest ones possible; because, to repeat, they were all I had. And tattered and ill-fitting though they were, I did look like a girl in them; or at least, more like a girl. Wearing them made me feel so happy that it made me go all woozy; it made me float away on a wave of blissed-out contentment; it brought out of me all sorts of fun and laughter and creativity; it made me feel playful, and dreamy, and light-headed, and giggly, and special, and pure – and relieved to get free of the stifling, cramping, suffocating imprisonment of being clothed and gendered as male. And once I was dressed as a girl, I wanted to be seen as a girl; I wanted others' seal of approval. I didn't get it, of course.

But it wasn't just that I used feminine clothing to escape from being male. It was also that I had magical beliefs about clothing. I was reasonably convinced that the more I dressed as a girl, the more of a girl I would become. It certainly felt that way: dressing as a girl certainly made me feel like a girl. (Whatever that means. Yes, I see the problems. Still.) And the more emphatically 'feminine' the clothing was – by which I meant: the pinker, the frillier, the prettier, the girlier – the more power

I believed it would have to make me female. Putting it on was, in all sorts of senses, magical. Like Frodo putting on a Ring of Power, I became my invisible self, the me that, despite my longing to be recognised, no one could ever be allowed to see. Dressing feminine defined me, I then believed, as feminine. After all, I thought, that was how it worked for my sister: didn't my parents define her as a girl by the way they dressed her? But, as we've seen, I had little or no hope that my parents would ever do the same for me. So, I thought, I'd better try to do it for myself. It wasn't like I had any other magic wand to wave.

Secret time spent dressed feminine was time off from public being masculine. But as it got clearer and clearer (as it already had, for starters, when I began school) that no seal of approval was forthcoming, it did have to be secret. This is one of the first things that being transgender did to me: it taught me inwardness, it made me secretive, it taught me how to hide, it made me want to be capable of vanishing every now and then when I felt I needed to – like a hobbit with a fine gold ring; it taught me that whatever The Team was, I wasn't quite on it.

Whether visibly or not, being dressed feminine was always a huge relief. Dressing masculine was a weariness to the spirit: it made me feel tired, ugly, constrained, trapped, strained, awkward, wrong. It still does. But dressing feminine was, simply, a delight: it brought a sense of serene, calm, happy, relaxed, floating-away euphoria that nothing else gave me, a simple and straightforward innocent childlike joy; just a sense of rightness. It still does.

Except that, as time went on, I had less and less chance to play like that, and less and less, at least in this area of my life, to laugh about. One day the dressing-up box got mysteriously purged. The petticoats and ballgowns and the ballet tutu and the frilly girly stuff just disappeared and I never saw them again, though for years and years I went on looking for them: in the house, in shop displays, in book illustrations, on the television…

'You can be whoever you want. But you can't be a she.'

1.15: 'When ideology meets reality' – the reality of experience

I hope to get a wider, or at any rate a more diverse, audience with this book than a philosophy professor might normally expect for most of her writings. But who knows: you yourself, dear reader, might have read some of my more conventional writings in philosophical ethics. (My *much* more conventional writings in philosophical ethics – though still not that conventional.) And if you have, you may know this about me as a philosopher: that I agree with Dr Johnson that 'Human experience, which is constantly contradicting theory, is the great test of truth'.[12] Let me say a little bit about why.

One of my favourite philosophers is Bernard Williams.[13] At the outset of his writing career, Williams took for his own 'a phrase of D.H. Lawrence's in his splendid commentary on the complacent moral utterances of Benjamin Franklin: "Find your deepest impulse, and follow that".'[14] Thirty years later he added, when looking back over his career, 'If there's one theme in all my work it's about authenticity and self-expression … It's the idea that some things are in some real sense really you, or express what you are and others aren't … The whole thing has been about spelling out the notion of inner necessity.'

Yes, that; very much that, about me and transgender. 'I just want to', but in capitals. An inner necessity, a need to be authentically and above all openly who I actually am, and to be known as who I am by those around me, and accepted and, yes, loved, even so. That is exactly what it's all been about. In many ways, being recognised and known as a trans woman and accepted nonetheless is the most important thing of all to me, even more important than presenting as a woman.

But as I said in 1.13, that doesn't mean that I have a theory of transgender to offer. I doubt I do. I tend to steer away from philosophical theories of anything, at least in those parts of philosophy that aren't best understood as handmaids of science. And even in science, I think the real truth of things often resists systematisation. Resisting systematisation is very much my thing; after all, what is being transgender but resisting systematisation?

[12] See Boswell's *Life of Johnson*, for 28 July 1763.
[13] For more from me on Bernard Williams, see https://plato.stanford.edu /entries/williams-bernard/.
[14] Bernard Williams, *Morality: An Introduction to Ethics* (Cambridge University Press, 1972), p. 93.

What theory is so certain as this, That all theories, were they never so earnest, painfully elaborated, are, and, by the very conditions of them, must be incomplete, questionable, and even false? Thou shalt know that this Universe is, what it professes to be, an infinite one. Attempt not to swallow it, for thy logical digestion; be thankful, if skilfully planting down this and the other fixed pillar in the chaos, thou prevent its swallowing thee.[15]

Like Carlyle, I am never quite sure what a theory of anything outside strict science is supposed to do. Ever since Plato's *Meno*, philosophers have been saying, and rightly, that the point of philosophy is to change true belief into knowledge: into a state where you don't just think true things, but also understand, deeply, why they are true. Fine. But is it obvious that constructing a philosophical theory always helps with this? Can we really not have a deep understanding, and an explanatory understanding, that (for example) murder is at least typically and maybe always wrong, or that love is usually a good thing, or that flowers are generally beautiful, or that paedophilia is profoundly wrong, until we have a philosophical theory's kind of explanation of why this is so? Why is some set of words, arranged in propositions with inferential relations between them, the sole kind of explanation that we need to understand the goodness of love or the badness of murder? For most ethical cases, that seems to me an oddly inappropriate picture of understanding and explanation. In ethical matters, understanding can be verbal and articulate, but quite often it isn't at all; oftener still, the propositional bit isn't the only bit – and not the most important bit, either. And likewise for explanation: explanations don't have to be verbal, and often are better if they're not. (Think of explaining how to do something – by doing it. Or of explaining the wonders of a landscape – by taking your friends for a walk, and mutely gesturing at it. Or by writing music about it, like 'Appalachian Spring'.)

Science limns the structure of reality, as Quine says in *Word and Object*. Sure it does, at least if it's any good. But so does poetry, if *it's* any good. There isn't just one correct way to grasp the deep structure of things. There are lots, because there are lots of things that we might call 'the deep structure of things'. Propositional structures are great for

---

[15] Thomas Carlyle, *The French Revolution*, Book 1, Chapter 2.

the understanding, but experience matters too, and experience is no less cognitive for being, sometimes, non-discursive and not expressible in propositions. All these general considerations about theorising apply in the particular case of transgender: here too it should be experience first, theory later – if at all. In Nietzsche's famous words, 'the will to a system betrays a lack of integrity'.

In any case, and also with particular reference to transgender: trans people don't owe cis people, or anyone else, an explanation of why they are who they are. No more than gay people do, for instance, or black people or Jewish people or neuro-diverse people, or any other historically stigmatised minority. There is a genuine and unsettling analogy between the way hatred leads people to demand justifications from these other groups, and the hostile and often scornful way transgender people are interrogated in the UK today – when, that is, we are not simply ignored. But our right to exist as transgender people is not conditional on our being able to prove that right, say by demonstrating the truth of something called 'gender ideology'. (Our gender ideology, that is, not some hostile cis society's: see 1.13 above.) The onus of proof is not on us transgender people at all. It is on those who want to exclude us. By what right do they discriminate against us? By what right do they demonise us, marginalise us, gaslight us, ridicule us, patronise us, in ways that no one would accept for a minute of any other minority?

Round here we confront the kind of demand of which I think it's right to say that there should be no 'transgender debate'. We shouldn't be refused admission to society until we've won some abstract rhetorical cage-fight, or arrived at a Grand Unified Theory Of Transgender that is 'satisfactory' (to whom?). Our right to be ourselves, without apology and without explanation, is simply not up for discussion, any more than anyone else's. We don't get kindly admitted to equal status once we have satisfied our critics. Nor are transgender people's civil rights conditional on the crime statistics for transgender people. Trans people are actually a very law-abiding bunch, by and large. But as with any other minority, even if we weren't, it would be outrageous to exclude us for not being, and probably counterproductive too. Like everyone else, we have equal status from the start. Or should have.

This no-debate demand is often misunderstood as a refusal to engage in philosophical argument. That *is* a misunderstanding, and the reasons why it is a misunderstanding go rather deep. G.K. Chesterton says this:

> If you argue with a madman, it is extremely probable that you will get the worst of it; for in many ways his mind moves all the quicker for not being delayed by things that go with good judgement. He is not hampered by a sense of humour or by clarity, or by the dumb certainties of experience. He is the more logical for losing certain sane affections. Indeed, the common phrase for insanity is in this respect a misleading one. The madman is not the man who has lost his reason. The madman is the man who has lost everything except his reason.[16]

There is a scene in the fine 2016 film *Denial* where Deborah Lipstadt and her lawyers are constructing their defence to a libel action brought against her by the Holocaust denier David Irving. To show, against Irving, that there was nothing fake about the Nazis' mass murders in 1941–5, Lipstadt wants to go into the witness box herself, and she wants Holocaust survivors to testify too. Her lawyers dissuade her. It is not that she and the survivors do not have a convincing story, and one that any decent interlocutor would be ashamed and embarrassed to deny, dispute or question. The point is that *Irving* will not be convinced – nor ashamed, nor embarrassed – to carry on with an aggressive and sceptical cross-examination of frail and vulnerable old people who, both psychologically and physically, have lived out the rest of their lives in the shadow of the hellish nightmare of Auschwitz.

In Wittgenstein's famous phrase, 'see how much stage-setting must already be in place' before a 'rational debate' can even begin.[17] See, too, how some of the key stage-setting is ethical. We presuppose certain minimal standards of truth, rationality, and openness to evidence in our interlocutors. And these are *moral* presuppositions.

It is a relatively familiar point that it is very difficult to discuss proofs of the reality of anything with people who will not accept the same standards of proof as any reasonable person accepts in any other debate. It is perhaps a less familiar point, but an equally important one, that it

[16] G.K. Chesterton, *Orthodoxy* (New York, 1909), p. 32.
[17] Ludwig Wittgenstein, *Philosophical Investigations* I, 257.

is also very difficult to debate with people who do not accept the same standards of *shame*. People who are not ashamed to browbeat, jeer, and heckle the venerable survivors of the worst genocide in human history – such people are argumentatively inaccessible to us. And this is because of a difference not in 'morally neutral' rationality, if there is such a thing, but in their sense of what is shameful.

Just this double lack, both of epistemic responsibility in the narrow, 'non-ethical' sense, and also of shame, is all too evident in all too many people who come at transgender people and their allies waving the much-misused banner of 'free and open debate'. Take, for example, those campaigners who complain that they themselves are being 'silenced' by harassment and mockery and intimidation, but are entirely happy to harass and mock and intimidate anyone who attends a pro-trans rally in clothing that they don't approve of, or who tries even to run a conference that they don't like the look of. Very often these campaigners' immediate response to the harrowing statistics for transgender suicide and transgender assault is not to express sympathy and solidarity, but to cast doubt on the reliability of those statistics. And among them are supposedly respectable journalists and academics who are perfectly happy to describe trans people as 'parasites' or to promulgate bizarre myths about 'transgenderism being bankrolled by Jewish billionaires' – myths that strikingly close the gap between transphobia and anti-Semitism, and sometimes between both of those and conspiracy theories like Q-Anon as well.

Such claims get us into the territory of what Raimond Gaita calls 'the crank':

> 'Cranks' is an interesting word... it is not just a term of abuse. It refers to someone who has so radically lost his capacity for judgement that his views are not even worth considering. Like those who are severely mentally ill, the most interesting thing about cranks – about what makes someone a crank – does not show itself when they declaim what they believe. It does so when they do not rule certain things out of consideration. They suffer from something far more serious than ignorance. Knowledge and understanding – and therefore, all serious radical critique – depend upon the exercise of sound judgement about what counts as evidence, about when authorities can be relied upon, when they are justifiably discredited, and so on... Reason is not

what determines what it is to be 'in touch with reality'. Rather, being in touch with reality is a condition for the sober exercise of those critical concepts which mark our sense of what it is to think well or badly, concepts whose proper application is what we call the exercise of 'reason'.[18]

Among other things, Gaita is writing here about how we should do philosophy – a question on which I have myself learned a great deal from him. I am almost echoing Gaita when I say that I think philosophy should not be a bureaucratic pigeonhole within a university's administrative structure, kept 'pure' of 'non-philosophical' material by vigilant gatekeeping (and outgrouping). Rather, philosophy should be a loose-bordered range of enquiries that are kept rigorous, maybe even a little bit austere, by the rather different but very much complementary requirements of two things: first of logic, and second of a grown-up, and open-minded, and kind, and humane, and humorous, and inquisitive, and unfanatical, and tolerant, and mature – and sensible – sensibility.

There are (at least) two kinds of quality-controlling challenge that philosophers should push each other hard with. One is: 'That is logically inconsistent'; the other is: 'Come off it.' In the academy today, partly because of the bureaucratic pressure to stake out – I am tempted to say, to scent-mark – research territory, we hear plenty about inconsistency, but rather less about 'Come off it'. In an age of perversely brilliant research programmes, for example about whether we're living in a computer simulation – and also, in an age of conspiracy theories, many of which are, among other things, transphobic – 'Come off it' is an important challenge too.

'Come off it' matters both within and beyond philosophy. Quite often in both contexts, another way to put it is: 'Do not feed the trolls.' And sometimes 'Come off it' also signals that, to think clearly and fruitfully about transgender, we philosophers need to be doing something other than moral theory.

It isn't only being transgender that has led my thoughts in this anti-theory direction. All sorts of events and experiences have had that effect

[18] Raimond Gaita, *A Common Humanity: Thinking about Love and Truth and Justice* (Routledge, 2002), pp. 160, 165–6. Gaita too quotes Chesterton. For my review of Gaita's fine book, see *Mind* (2002): 411–413.

on me. For instance, I started writing a book in 2007 that was supposed to be an introduction to moral philosophy, following up on the general introduction to philosophy, especially epistemology, that I'd published in 2005, *The Inescapable Self.* My plan was to put the case for and against the usual menu of alternative moral theories, then end up in the final chapter advocating my own preferred moral theory, which at the time was roughly the liberal, non-doctrinaire natural-law theory that I'd argued for in 1998.[19] Then halfway through writing the new book, I had a serious climbing accident on Zero Gully on Ben Nevis. In the light of that near-death experience,[20] the competition of the theories that I was writing about in the book – it began to look to me a bit frivolous, a bit trivial, a bit of a philosopher's parlour game; compared with the real stuff of life, the hard realities of experience. That was why the book ended up being called *Ethics and Experience*, and ended up not presenting my own pet moral theory, but as my first shot at offering new arguments in a campaign against the very idea of pet moral theories.[21]

I don't want to give unnecessary offence here to my many good friends and deeply respected colleagues who are moral theorists in the sense that I tend to target. Of course, you can be a deeply morally serious person and be a systematising moral theorist; no doubt it's moral seriousness that makes most philosophers into systematisers in the first place. But it came to seem to me that there was a mismatch between that seriousness, and the theories that it was seriousness about. To be blunt, the theories didn't deserve to be taken that seriously; the seriousness was admirable,

---

[19] *Understanding Human Goods* (Edinburgh University Press, 1998). A natural-law theory of ethics says, roughly, that the shape of ethics for humans is determined by the fact that we are zoological creatures of a certain kind; that fact, and lots of more detailed facts implied by it, give the ultimate natural grounding for the way things are normatively. I still think this is roughly correct; but I don't think that seriously and sincerely following out this route of enquiry gets us anything like a neat or tidy moral theory, and I'd be more cautious now than I was in 1998 about claiming that the basis of ethics is specifically zoological, as opposed, say, to sociological or political or institutional. Insofar as there is any such thing as the basis of ethics or a 'grounding' for ethics, it is all of those. It lies in our life together – in our 'form of life', as Wittgenstein would say.

[20] I wrote about it here: https://www.academia.edu/1336147/the_fear_of_death.

[21] The campaign continues: see my *Knowing What To Do* (Oxford University Press, 2014) and *Epiphanies* (Oxford University Press, 2022).

its object not so much. Indeed, I sometimes think this about religious commitment and doctrinal theory as well. With at least some believers, I am awestruck, humbled, and deeply moved by their devotion to their God – at the very same time as I am decidedly underwhelmed by the God that they're devoted to. I am a Christian, but I get this with Christianity too.

As one of the epigraphs to *Understanding Human Goods* – so these things were already beginning to worry me in the 1990s – I'd quoted a wonderful line from Yeats's notes on his own poem 'The Dolls': 'I noticed once again how all thought among us had become "something other than human life".' When utilitarians go on in a perfectly abstracted and seminar-room sort of way about whether to divert a runaway trolley by throwing a fat man underneath it, or about whether there is anything really wrong with murdering babies or buggering dogs except that it tends to upset people (or dogs), and when Kantians turn the question whether you should lie to the SS-man at your door about the Jews in your cellar into a kind of three-card-trick of practical rationality, and when natural-law theorists get into solemn debates about whether cutting off a breeched baby's head to save its mother's life is a case of action or omission... then something other than human life, it seems to me, is what we're getting, and I would just rather be talking about something else. Or if we do need to talk about these questions – and there may be times when we do, but too often we fail to ask first why we need to talk about them, what makes them into pressing practical issues for us – then I don't want to talk about them in those ways.

1.16: What is it like to be a human being?

The question that I think philosophical ethicists should be starting from (or one such question, anyway) is one that stands alongside Thomas Nagel's famous question 'What is it like to be a bat?'. The question I mean is: 'What is it like to be a human being?'[22]

Start with that. Don't start with a moral theory, start with where you actually are. Start with what it's like to be you, with your subjectivity here and now, with what looks serious and real and important and

---

[22] I use this question as the title of Chapter 4 in *Epiphanies*.

beautiful and (yes, why not?) fun to you just as you are, from your own viewpoint. Because actually that's the only place you ever can start from, really, and one tendency of systematising theories is to obscure this truth. And when you end up ignoring aspects of your experience because they don't fit your theory, then you've fallen into a kind of inauthenticity, a kind of Procrusteanism. If theory and experience don't match, then it is almost always theory that needs to give way; not experience. At bottom, thinking well about the ethics of such matters is all about authenticity.

So I am not an advocate for transgender people, and their rights to be respected, to be treated equally with other citizens – and also, to be left alone and not harassed or bullied or humiliated or threatened or silenced – because I have a 'gender ideology', or any kind of nice neat theory about gender or sex. That wouldn't be like me. I don't have a nice neat theory about anything.

And I am not here to do balloon debates with 'gender critical' people. The reality of transgender people is not a debating point, any more than global warming is, or the dangers of COVID, or the historical fact of the Holocaust, or the untruth of the Q-Anon conspiracy theory, or apologias for Putin's illegal aggressions in Chechnya, Syria, and Ukraine. I am not prepared to give denialists, cranks, trolls, bigots, and conspiracy theorists the status of legitimate dialectical opponents on those four topics. Nor, then, on the topic of transgender. I will not climb gamely into the ring and treat 'Transgender theory: for or against?' as a This-House-Believes philosophical debate, another round of fun and games at the Arguments Club, where, at the beginning of the evening, for all we know, either side has an equal chance of 'winning'. It's not a matter of winning and losing, but of truth. The subject is not transgender theory; it is transgender reality, and compared with genuinely abstract debates, about the existence of universals, say, or the nature of our moral psychology, it requires a quite different treatment. That's what this book is for.

It's not that I refuse to do explaining or argument about transgender. Of course I am happy to explain and even argue about transgender; this book would not exist otherwise. But I don't start from the question 'What would a nice neat theory of all this look like?' Instead I start from the question 'What is it like to be a human being?' – and more specifically, from the question 'What is it like to be a man, or a woman, or transgender?' (On this last, see, in particular, Part III.) But I only do any of these things when I think I have some chance of actually talking to people who might be interested in listening, rather than, as I put it above, just looking for anti-trans ammunition.

I am an advocate for transgender people because we're *people*, and because we have a distinctive kind of experience of our society and our world, which deserves to have a voice. And by and large, we don't have a voice. By and large, our experience is squeezed out – by trans-exclusionary ideology.

Jesus says in the Gospel (Mark 2.27) that 'The Sabbath was made for man, not man for the Sabbath.' I see ethical philosophy that way. It's there to help human beings. It's not there to be theoretically neat, if necessary at human expense. As a value, humanity trumps pretty well everything else; it certainly trumps systematicity.

For better or worse, then, what I've got to offer in this book is experience, and some lessons from experience. I am not a psychiatrist or a child-development specialist or a sociologist or a statistician or a lawyer or a biologist. Good luck to those who are, of course, and all power to the elbows of workers in those lines who support trans people. I am an ethicist and a philosopher, and I am a trans woman: those are my qualifications to write about transgender. Both these qualifications matter, I think, which is why this book contains both autobiographical bits (mainly in Parts I and II) and also something more like straight philosophical argumentation (mainly in Parts III, IV, and V); not to mention an open letter in Part VI, and a piece of sci-fi/fantasy writing in Part VII. Who knows, maybe there's something for everyone here. But I begin, deliberately, from my own experience.

I thereby put myself at risk. At risk from you, dear reader. Unlike Iago in this book's third epigraph, I am what I am. And, especially in this book, I wear my heart upon my sleeve. I am talking about some of the things that have most deeply preoccupied me, and haunted and shamed me, throughout my life. I am talking about my own heart, my own identity – and my own sexuality. This is all going to be quite autobiographical, and to include some admissions about my own past that I still find it a little hard to talk openly about, and not very long ago, found completely impossible to go anywhere near. I could have written a more cautious book, in which I took fewer risks and exposed fewer of my own scars and vulnerabilities. But you only live once. I chose to take the risk of writing this book.

So if some of the detail of what I say here about my own experience is embarrassing to you – too – then I apologise in advance. I'm admitting at once that I still find it hard to talk about some of this stuff; I'm a little scared of your reaction. I certainly don't wish to bruise anybody's sensibilities. Nor do I aim to make a spectacle of myself. I do think that being reasonably explicit about some of this stuff might help people to understand it a bit better. Whether that means from the outside – so that people who aren't themselves trans come to know a little more about what it's like to be trans – or from the inside – so that I manage to help my trans brothers and sisters to a touch more self-understanding and self-forgiveness and self-acceptance.

Best of all, I'd like my words to make a difference to someone who is like I used to be. It breaks my heart that people still have to go through what I went through as a kid and as a young adult – and of course, many of them go through far worse than I did. Can't the bad stuff that happened to my generation at least be redeemed in this generation, by us learning not to make the same gratuitously stupid and cruel mistakes again and again and again? I'd love it if my words could reach out and touch someone who is as alienated from their own transgender nature as I used to be – and help them too to become, openly and manifestly, whoever it is they secretly dream of being.

For this to happen, there'd need to be someone reading this who is something like the fairly hard-line evangelical Christian that I used to be, or otherwise self-stiflingly moralistic. Which might seem a little unlikely (though perhaps it is likelier than it seems; I am not the only lady ever to protest too much). But when I think what it took to get me from that position to where I am now (I'm none of those things now except Christian), my heart goes out to people who are like I used to be. To anyone who is as miserably repressed and self-hating as I once was, I want to say: another world is possible. You are allowed to be happy, and you are allowed to be who you really are. Seize the day and take hold of the freedom you were born for. You're going to love it.

It isn't entirely easy for me to write about all this, then. Though in some ways, the fact that this book comes from a rather different place from anything else I've written makes it easier to write. Maybe it will make it easier to read as well; I hope so. But if my readers are sympathetic, I am worried that I might just appear to be replacing 'proper argument' with a kind of sentimental emotional blackmail. Whereas if my readers are unsympathetic – well, I haven't yet forgotten how devastating I found it, at school and elsewhere in my early life, when the response to any attempt from me to tell the truth about myself was derision, scorn, and public mockery.

Within my own lifetime in the UK, for a philosophy professor to talk openly about some of the things that I've already talked about would have been a dismissal offence – 'bringing the university into disrepute'. Long after that ceased to be true, talking openly about these things has continued to involve serious reputational damage. Perhaps it still does; just as well I don't need to be on the jobs market. Certainly, in the UK today, on this subject of all subjects, the world is not short of daws to peck. I will be saddened, but not surprised, if some readers are eager to tell me that they find the autobiographical parts of this book contemptible, or ridiculous, or self-obsessed, or merely boring.

This book is going to be (already is) quite unlike any book I've written before, and very probably quite unlike any book I will write after, in the degree of autobiography and self-revelation that it will involve. But this fits. Because transgender, at least for me, isn't just an abstract debate about 'them over there'. It is a flesh-and-blood, life-and-death issue about us right here. To get the issue straight, we have to start with the way things really are for transgender people, no matter how difficult or personal or just plain embarrassing it is to explain that.

The truth has got be told.

So I'll tell the truth.

1.17: 'Reality matters', part 1: Two baffled double-takes

Experience, I say, gets squeezed out by ideology. This squeezing-out needs to be borne in mind when you come across some of the recent books that cisgender people have written about transgender people. (Or perhaps I should say: against transgender people.) Quite often they have subtitles like 'Why reality matters for feminism', or 'When ideology meets reality'.

To either of these subtitles, it seems to me, the most appropriate response is a baffled double-take. For reasons I've just been explaining, 'When ideology meets reality' sounds like a subtitle I could have used myself for this book. Our society is absolutely stuffed, totally drenched, with an ideology that is virulently – sometimes lethally – poisonous to transgender people, to the point, at times, of denying not only their right to exist, but their very existence. (We don't even exist, yet we're a threat – how do we manage that, then?)

My aim in this book is to bring this trans-exclusionary ideology into collision with reality: the reality of trans people's lives; in particular, though not exclusively, my own. Do I intend this collision to be explosive and destructive? Yes, but then some things deserve to be exploded and destroyed. In particular, any ideology deserves to be exploded and destroyed that stunts, imprisons, constrains, poisons, abuses, and oppresses not only the people whom it targets, but also the very people who are doing the targeting. And trans-exclusionary ideology is exactly like this.

Turning to the second subtitle: how could anyone possibly need an explanation 'why reality matters', to feminists or to anyone else? To state the blindingly obvious: reality matters because, well, it's reality. And it matters to feminists because, well, it matters to everyone.

But isn't this second subtitle implying that there are feminists to whom reality doesn't matter? Apparently so; and a more careful look at the rest of the book in question makes it clear that the feminists to whom reality 'doesn't matter' are supposed to be the majority of feminists, the ones who are trans-inclusive.

This is such an intensity of straw-womaning that it is hard to know how to respond to it, or indeed if it's worth responding at all. No one thinks that 'reality doesn't matter'. How could it be a worthwhile move in a serious debate to insinuate that anyone does think that?

The question is not whether 'reality matters'. The question is what reality is. And it is a rather striking feature of much contemporary trans-exclusionary 'feminism' that it steadily denies the reality of transgender people and transgender experience – the reality of the kind of experience that I began this book by describing autobiographically, from my own case; the reality of the kind of experience that I shall be coming back to throughout the book; the reality that trans children so insistently, persistently, and consistently report to parents and other adults who, for whatever reason, simply refuse to believe them.[23]

1.18: 'Reality matters', part 2: Four silencing falsehoods

In fact, all too many trans-exclusionary 'feminists' are only too happy to deny obvious realities in the interests of keeping their ideology afloat. The people I mean seem to spend much of their time, especially online, producing and reproducing claims of a kind that I'll generically call *silencing falsehoods*. Here I'll pick out, and perhaps pick on, four particularly annoying examples of the genre.

Silencing falsehoods are claims that are made with the intention of taking away speech from, silencing and shutting down, the group they target: in this case, trans people. Typically, they are either literally false or else, while themselves literally true, they work as proxies for nearby claims that are not literally true, but that it takes a bit of leg-work to distinguish from them. Thus, those of us who spend too much time on Twitter are wearily familiar with, for instance, the two silencing falsehoods that 'There is no such thing as a trans kid' and 'No one is born in the wrong body'.

The first of these two slogans is indeed just plain false. The right response to it is: 'Oh yes there is: I was one – see above.' Transgender is not a sexual taste, so it is not something that emerges only at adolescence or later. The endless insinuation that it is 'all sexual' is one of the most recurrent, and the most carefully nurtured – and the most dangerous – falsehoods in the transphobic playbook. Kids aren't trans because they are brainwashed – or, God help us, 'groomed' – into being trans by misguided others. They are trans even when, as with me, they are brainwashed *out* of it by misguided others. That this slogan is false is a matter of experience, as obvious as anything can be, to literally millions of people past and present, including me. Anyone who claims to care about 'reality' should not be ignoring (or wishing away?) the plain and obvious fact that, while the absolute proportion of the human population is no

---

[23] One example among many (which popped up as if by magic exactly when I was writing this): https://www.theguardian.com/commentisfree/2022/feb/15/what-i-should-have-done-when-my-12-year-old-told-me-he-was-transgender.

doubt small (one in 190 seems to be about the proportion), there are plenty of trans kids, and always have been. And as it happens, I am one of them.

The second slogan is slightly more awkward to deal with. I have already talked (in 1.14) about the sense that many trans people have, including me and Jan Morris and Carol Steele, that they were in fact born in the wrong body. Is that sense to be taken literally? There is lots to say about this; on the one hand, it is of course good to be at peace with your own physical being; on the other hand, such peace can be pretty costly. But as a first, and rather terse, approximation: 'Well … it's complicated.'

And this, of course, suits the trans-exclusionary silencers just fine. It is a favourite Twitter technique to deploy apparently simple slogans that enmire others in complexities; one master of this technique is, of course, the loathsome Donald Trump. We'll come back later to some of the complexities that are swirling around here. But very briefly, there is one debate to be had about whether the slogan is literally true, and that 'No one is born in the wrong body'. There is another and separate debate to be had about why you would want to chant this slogan, loudly and repeatedly, at young vulnerable transgender people who are clearly deeply unhappy in the bodies that they were born in. The usual motive for repeating it, as far as I can see, is a silencing one: it is to deny those trans people a way of saying something that, even if they're not saying it accurately, it is important to listen to rather than to shout down.

A third silencing falsehood has the same characteristic of enmiring us in complexities. This is the trans-exclusionary article of faith that 'It is impossible to change your sex'. This one does take a bit of unpicking; hold on to your hats.

The thing is, there are a number of ways of understanding this claim, depending on what you mean by 'sex'. Some trans-exclusionaries make much of the claim that 'men have penises, women have vaginas' – and apparently don't notice that this crude statement commits them to accepting that actually some trans men *are* men, and some trans women *are* women, namely the postoperative ones. At a slightly less crass and tabloid level, many trans-exclusionaries themselves accept that sex is a 'cluster concept': what makes anyone a woman, or a man, are various criteria working together. So, for the concept 'woman', there are something like the following eight criteria, not one of which does everything on its own:

(a) being assigned female at birth;
(b) having XX chromosomes;[24]
(c) having a female phenotype and anatomy (e.g. vagina, ovaries, womb, fallopian tubes, breasts, and body-shape);
(d) playing a characteristically female reproductive role (ovulating, menstruating, getting pregnant, giving birth);
(e) having an endocrine system full of typically female hormones;
(f) being routinely identified and accepted by others as female;
(g) being socialised as female;
(h) considering oneself female.[25]

If what the trans-exclusionaries mean by 'It is impossible to change your sex' is just about (a), then of course they're right. Time travel is

---

[24] In fact there is more than one way of classifying beings as 'male' or 'female' even at the basic biological level: chromosomes are one thing, DNA another, cell characteristics a third. It is biologically possible for someone to be 'phenotypically female' but have 'male DNA' or 'male chromosomes' or 'male cell characteristics'; usually such conditions are simply not picked up, because they are indiscernible without specialised equipment, and there is no general medical need to pick them up. These complexities reinforce my main point – that male and female are cluster concepts. But I skip them here.

[25] *Technical question*: These are supposed to be defining criteria for 'female'. But all eight of them except (b) use the word 'female' that they are supposed to be defining. Isn't there a vicious circularity here?

Technical answer: With criteria (a)–(e) there is indeed a circularity here, but not a vicious one: it's just shorthand. In each case the criterion's use of 'female' could be spelled out in other terms; it would just take longer to do so, and this isn't a human physiology textbook, so I don't do it here.

With criteria (f)–(h), however, what we have is not a circularity but a recursion. For these criteria, being female is partly constituted by being considered female. This sort of recursion is logically unproblematic, and entirely familiar from the wider social life of humans: e.g. it is part of what it is to be a judge, or a philosophy professor, or a police officer, that people see you as an occupant of those roles. Clearly this sort of recursive perception can't be all there is to these roles – that would be viciously circular; but it is part of what they are.

impossible: no one can go back in time and change what sex they were assigned at birth. (Demanding as some do that female anatomy should be 'endogenous' in order to count as 'really female' comes to the same thing, since in this context 'endogenous' means 'there since birth'.)

But if what trans-exclusionaries mean by 'It is impossible to change your sex' is anything more than (a), then their claim immediately begins to run into trouble. Criterion (b) points us to chromosomes, and it is certainly hard to see how those could be changed. On the other hand, as a matter of plain scientific fact that has nothing particularly to do with transgender, not all those whom we (trans-exclusionaries included) 'naturally call women' have XX chromosomes.[26] So whether or not I can change my chromosomes, it's not actually all that obvious that criterion (b) should be in the list at all.

As for criterion (c): well, first, as with chromosomes, and quite apart from transgender, not all those whom we naturally call women have (or originally have) these anatomical features either. And secondly, it is perfectly possible to acquire female anatomy; that's what gender reassignment for trans women does. (Though see above on 'endogenous.') At least, it is perfectly possible, in the present state of science, to acquire some female anatomy. If we are actually sincere in our claim to take criterion (c) seriously, that should incline us to say that it is now more possible than it used to be to change sex, and that in the future it will probably become more possible still.

The same inclination might come, too, from thinking about criterion (d), about the reproductive role. As with (c), cis women too are sometimes 'lacking' in this sort of department; and here too, it seems quite likely that future scientific advances may well make it more possible than it used to be to change sex as marked by this criterion.

Similarly for criterion (e): I'd have thought that there is every chance that well-to-do and desperately seeking trans women – for example, Jan Morris in the late 1960s – might well have more 'female hormones' washing around their systems than typical cis women. By criterion (e), that makes them more female than those cis women.

---

[26] https://www.genome.gov/about-genomics/fact-sheets/X-Chromosome -facts#:~:text=Typically%2C%20biologically%20female%20individuals%20have ,X%20chromosome%20from%20their%20mother.

As for criteria (f), (g), and (h), it is just patently obvious that – by these tests for sex – it most certainly is 'possible to change your sex'. As a matter of plain fact, people can and do change their presentation so that they are routinely identified in their desired sex, not their birth sex; so that, over time, they come to be socialised in that sex; and so that, without any kind of self-deception or delusion, they come to see themselves as *bona fide* members of that sex. (Perhaps, of course, they always did see themselves that way.)

What sense or truth, then, can we extract from the slogan 'It is impossible to change your sex'? It was the trans-exclusionaries themselves who were saying that sex is a cluster concept, a concept rather loosely dependent on multiple criteria, no single one of which is *the* criterion; and on this, we need not disagree with them. The trouble is that the trans-exclusionaries' slogan 'It is impossible to change your sex' looks false by some of those criteria, and true by others. Relative to criteria (c)–(h), the slogan is just plain false. Relative to criterion (b), it might be true – but criterion (b) looks irrelevant. The only criterion by which the slogan comes out as unproblematically true is criterion (a). And even there the slogan is only true because backwards time travel is impossible, which is hardly something that trans people and trans allies are in the business of denying.

If the trans-exclusionary is committed both to saying that 'Sex is a cluster concept' in the sense captured by criteria (a)–(h), and also to saying that 'It is impossible to change your sex', then the trans-exclusionary is caught in a logical contradiction. If we think (as I think myself) that sex is that kind of cluster concept, then what we should say is that in some senses you can't change your sex, and in others you can. But in practice, this is not what trans-exclusionaries do say. What they do in practice is continue to chant the faith mantra 'It is impossible to change your sex' in the faces of trans people who, as a matter of fact, have changed their sex in at least some of the senses of 'sex' that the trans-exclusionaries themselves recognise.

This is an illogical muddle. But it doesn't stop the slogan being deployed; those who deploy it are apparently not much bothered about logic. The real work done by the slogan 'It is impossible to change your sex' (as philosophers say, its illocutionary force) is faith reinforcement, gatekeeping, and exclusion. Its real point is to deepen solidarity within the cult, and to send the signal to trans people: 'It doesn't matter how much you change yourselves, we will never recognise you or accept you as who you say you are.'

The slogan is a logical muddle; and a political bin-fire. Like all gatekeeping anywhere, its effects reach far beyond those it is intended to exclude. As Chandran Kukathas has argued in his wonderful book *Immigration and Freedom* (2021), the effect of all serious and consistent attempts to surveil a few is that *everyone* ends up under surveillance, *everyone* ends up an object of suspicion. (Exhibit one: bathroom bans.) And again, the slogan goes with the trans-exclusionary mentality that is unable to think of trans people and trans-inclusionary cis people as doing anything more than 'engaging in a fiction': a mentality that thinks, in short, that trans people are pretending or performing. Apart from the immense condescension and incomprehension involved in thinking any such thing – it rather reminds me of those Americans who think that 'British people' can't possibly *really* speak like that, they're just putting the accent on as a wind-up – there is a kind of irony to the 'just pretending' trope. Because being trans *can* feel like just pretending. Just as proclaiming the rule of the workers, or the independence of Scotland, might feel like just pretending if you did it against a known background of sufficiently ferocious enforcement of the status quo ante. That doesn't mean it *is* pretending. It means that trans people live under oppression and, like the revolutionary or the *independentista*, have some work to do to change their dream into reality. And it means that to come along, as some do, and tell trans people at *this* point that they're 'just pretending' is a naked and shameless way of being on the side of the status quo and the oppressors.

Similar points apply to my fourth and final silencing falsehood. This takes the form of a Gotcha, a challenge often thrust in the faces of trans people and trans allies by hostile or otherwise combative journalists. The challenge is 'How do you define "woman"?' (I suppose it could equally be 'How do you define "man"?', but by and large the focus of the usual fixation is trans women.) The required answer is 'Adult human female', and this answer is supposed to be 'a purely scientific answer' and somehow to count against 'transgender ideology'. It's supposed to involve a damaging admission that 'biology matters' and 'sex matters' (neither of which we ever denied: see above), and also a concession that trans women are 'not really women'. It's supposed to be such a Gotcha that it shows up on T-shirts and posters as if it were the ultimate triumph of trans-exclusionaries.

The trouble is that this whole line of thought is a farrago of nonsense. The entire challenge is completely misconceived, for at least three reasons.

First, as Ross Cameron has pointed out, the required answer is literally mistaken. There could be Martian women, but if there were, they would be adult Martian females, not adult human females. There most certainly were Neanderthal women, and they really were women, but their status as women does not depend on us classifying Neanderthals as humans (which is a moot point; Neanderthals weren't *homo sapiens sapiens*). So being human is apparently not essential to being a woman.

Secondly, as Robin Dembroff has pointed out, the required answer is not 'purely scientific'. 'Adult' is not a biological classification; it is a sociological one. Or if it is a biological classification, it means 'sexually mature' – which, given that ten-year-old girls can be sexually mature, is certainly not an ethically or socially acceptable understanding of 'woman'.

Thirdly, and most important of all, the point of the Gotcha is supposed to be that it shows that 'trans women aren't really women'. But if 'female' is a cluster concept – as above – then it shows nothing of the sort. The correct response to the Gotcha is to agree that women are indeed adult females, and, in our own experience so far, nearly always adult human females. But then: what are females? See above on the third silencing falsehood. As I pointed out there, there are – at the very least – plenty of trans women who will satisfy most of the criteria for 'female' as a cluster concept. Even on the trans-exclusionaries' own account of 'female', plenty of trans women will be females too. This Gotcha question isn't a Gotcha at all. Or if it is a Gotcha, then it gotchas back.

Of course, these four silencing falsehoods are by no means the worst of it. The activists I mean don't just go in for repeating their obvious or not-so-obvious falsehoods as a way of silencing trans people and their allies. There is also, all over the place on the internet, a whole slew of much more extreme silencing falsehoods: that transgender people are delusional; that we are mentally ill; that we are liars or frauds, deceptive or self-deceptive; impostors, perverts, sexual predators, paedophiles, parasites, 'doing woman-face', stooges of some massive big-pharma

Jewish conspiracy or of a 'cultural Marxist' campaign to destroy the family, or masculinity, or Western culture, or something – or as above, that trans people (or trans kids) simply don't exist at all. Absurd as these claims are, there is a burgeoning industry of trans-exclusionary voices online that are very happy to keep pumping them out the whole time; along, of course, with much activity that is merely insulting and abusive (I have an archive of such abuse; it's a very dull and wearisome document), and some activity, such as legal and procedural intimidation, that is also threatening behaviour.

Given all this manifestly terrible behaviour, perhaps people on that side of the debate who have any sense of shame might be a little less assertive about the claim that they are defending 'reality' against 'ideology'. A lot of the time, despite their deployment of the rhetoric of reality, they are doing the exact opposite: they are defending their own ideology against reality. And this activity has serious costs. Sometimes it even has costs for the trans-exclusionaries themselves and not just for those around them whom they so relentlessly attack.

As Sara Ahmed points out in a recent essay, this rhetoric of reality is as reactionary in this context as the wider rhetoric of 'common sense' is elsewhere.

> Gender conservative feminisms are part of the not-so-new conservative common sense, which has reweaponised 'reality' as a 'war against the woke', that is, as an effort to restore racial as well as gendered hierarchies by demonizing those who question them … When you enter the gender critical world as a feminist who is not used to being in that world, it is deeply disorientating. Let's take the social media world … You enter, and you will encounter twitter handles with purple and green, the suffragette colours. On the same handles, you will find utterances like *Sex not Gender* or *Sex is Real.* You might see statements like *I stand with*, and the name of such and such person who has been targeted apparently for saying something like *Sex is real.* You will encounter words like *adult human female*, or *natal woman*, or even *biological woman.* You will encounter claims that you know have been central to patriarchal logics, for instance, *women are oppressed because of their biology.*[27]

[27] https://feministkilljoys.com/2021/10/31/gender-critical-gender-conservative/.

I have already said a bit, and there is plenty more to say, about 'sex not gender', 'sex is real', 'adult human female', 'sex matters', 'biology matters', 'sex matters', etc., and about the important silencing falsehoods that are to be found in the vicinities of these catch phrases.[28] First, let me pick up on Ahmed's phrase 'gender conservative feminisms'. There is a terminological point here that I'll need to make some time soon. And the earlier the better; so I might as well make it right now. It is a terminological point, but not a merely terminological point: it gets us, as we'll see, into some interesting questions, and indeed some confusing ones. It is a point about the term 'gender critical', and why I won't be using either it or some connected terms.

While I'm on about terminology, I'll also say something about 'cis' and 'trans'. This too isn't a merely verbal point. That is, it is verbal but not merely verbal: it has some important consequences. I'll take it first.

1.19: Terminology 1: 'Cis/trans'

In ancient Roman geography, there were two Gauls: Cisalpine Gaul, the Gaul on this side of the Alps, the Italian side; and Transalpine Gaul, the Gaul on the far side of the Alps, Gaul 'over there' – roughly speaking, France. (The Gaul that Julius Caesar 'captured and divided into three parts', in the successful war of genocide that he waged there in 58–50 BC, was Transalpine Gaul; the three parts were Belgica, Celtica, and Aquitania.)

And in modern organic chemistry, if I may quote Wikipedia at you, there is this:

---

[28] There are silencing falsehoods around 'woke' too, of course. How on earth can it be a bad thing to be concerned about being respectful and kind to other people and their view of the world, which may be different from yours? What could possibly be wrong about being prepared to hold back and listen to others rather than bulldoze them with our own prejudices? Yet the idea that such humane tolerance is a bad thing is exactly the silencing falsehood at the heart of 'anti-woke' rhetoric. To make this sound bad is truly a remarkable achievement of the reactionary propagandist.
Likewise with 'virtue signalling'. This phrase implicates that anyone who acts well (or at least, anyone who acts well whom the speaker doesn't like) is motivated solely by a concern to be admired for acting well. What a dismal and implausible view of human nature. Chuck it in the bin.

Cis–trans isomerism, also known as geometric isomerism or configurational isomerism, is a term used in chemistry that concerns the spatial arrangement of atoms within molecules. The prefixes '*cis*' and '*trans*' are from Latin: 'this side of' and 'the other side of', respectively. In the context of chemistry, *cis* indicates that the functional groups (substituents) are on the same side of some plane, while *trans* conveys that they are on opposing (transverse) sides. *Cis–trans* isomers are stereoisomers, that is, pairs of molecules which have the same formula but whose functional groups are in different orientations in three-dimensional space. *Cis-trans* notation does not always correspond to *E–Z* isomerism, which is an *absolute* stereochemical description.[29]

The trans/cis distinction for people works in close analogy with these two cases. To call someone a cis man or a cis woman is to say that their psychological sense of their own body lines up with the biological nature of that body (at least in its original configuration): roughly, you are a cis woman if your consciousness is sexed and gendered female, and your biology too is sexed and gendered female. Likewise, to call someone a trans man or a trans woman is to say that their psychological sense of their own body *does not* line up with the biological nature of that body (at least in its original configuration). So roughly, you are a trans woman if your consciousness is sexed and gendered female, but your biology is (or started out) sexed and gendered male; and you are a trans man if your consciousness is sexed and gendered male, but your biology is (or started out) sexed and gendered female. (For more about sex, gender and consciousness, see Part III.)

Now, for sure, there are some complexities round the edges of this cis/trans distinction; some of them have to do with complexities that we've already explored a little (1.18), about what 'male' and 'female' actually mean. But the basic idea is pretty intuitive. To be cis is to have a sense of yourself as the sex and gender that you would naturally and traditionally be assigned to; to be trans is to have a sense of yourself as the other sex and gender. Trans people are pretty literally inhabitants of that Gary Larson realm, *The Far Side*. (And is it time we inaugurated the description 'cisatlantic accent', for firmly 'British' accents like my own,

[29] https://en.wikipedia.org/wiki/Cis%E2%80%93trans_isomerism#; the article gives cis-but-2-ene and trans-but-2-ene as an example-pair.

as the opposite of 'transatlantic'? I think it is. You know you want to join me on this.)[30]

It's not hard, then. But there are plenty of people online who seem to make heavy weather of it. People online frequently claim, unconvincingly, to find it baffling. Or to feel insulted or erased by being called 'cis': 'Don't you dare pigeonhole me! I'm not a cis woman, I'm just a woman – a normal woman!' (In this area there is also sometimes a moral-panicky pretence that 'the trans rights activists' are making out that 'woman' must always be prefixed with either 'cis' or trans', and that therefore 'women are being erased'; which is simply untrue.)

If we were to reject the distinction, presumably trans women could say just the same: 'Don't you dare pigeonhole me! I'm not a trans woman, I'm just a normal woman!' – as indeed they sometimes do. But we shouldn't reject the trans/cis distinction, any more than we reject the gay/straight distinction. And comparison with the gay/straight distinction should help us to see why not, and to notice some of the problems with the refusal to allow oneself to be described as cis. If someone said 'Don't call me straight, I'm just normal!', we would immediately see the problem with this utterance. The problem is very simple: it's an insinuation that gay people are *ab*normal. Of course, we very often don't need to specify 'gay' or 'straight': when I say, for example, 'Chris is Robin's lover', I usually convey everything I need to convey in the context, without explicitly specifying whether 'lover' here means 'gay lover' or 'straight lover' (or indeed what sex or gender either Chris or Robin is). But to refuse ever to be called 'straight' in one's sexual orientation is, in effect, to refuse to admit that there is any other legitimate way to be in one's sexual orientation. And on this view, gay people are either abnormal or invisible. Thus 'Don't call me straight' leads quickly to the erasure and delegitimising of gay people, and to depriving them of a key part of their own vocabulary for describing themselves. And, I'm afraid to say, this is not accidental: it is very usually the intended effect of the utterance.

Just as with the slogan 'Don't call me cis'. In practice, this slogan is typically deployed in bad faith anyway: it turns up in online debates

---

[30] Or there is my favourite Twitter joke of last week: 'How can Russians be gender critical when even the Siberian railway is trans?'

simply as another form of silencing falsehood; as just another method of putting psychological and expressive barriers in the way of trans people and their allies. But even when it is deployed in good faith, the slogan is deeply problematic.

One might wonder, too, whether the bit of 'transgender/cisgender' that we ought to be dropping is actually the *gender* bit, not the trans/ cis bit. As I've already said, I don't actually have a 'gender ideology' in any very definite or substantive sense. It's quite possible to gain a basic understanding of what 'transgender' is without invoking a notion of gender or gender identity at all. I think we should seriously consider going that way. But if we do, then maybe we should drop the 'gender' bit of 'transgender'. Maybe it's just causing confusion and red herrings. I won't commit firmly on this here; but I do think it's something to think about.

1.20: Terminology 2: 'Gender critical', 'transphobe', 'TERF', and 'trans-exclusionary'

A word can get so ideologically polluted, or otherwise problematic in its associations, that it needs replacement just for the sake of good PR. This happens with the names of government nuclear sites (Windscale then Calder Hall then Seascale then Sellafield, etc. – if I've got the order right); or political parties (there were markedly fewer self-declared Communist Parties in Western Europe once Stalin's reputation began to realign itself in the direction of reality after 1945); or brands (Facebook/Meta); to say nothing of Okhrana/Cheka/OGPU/NKVD/MGB/KGB/FSB... There are also the cases where a term is self-consciously reclaimed, as has for example happened with the originally pejorative terms 'Tory' and 'queer'.

The trajectory of the term 'TERF' looks like an example of this phenomenon. We sometimes hear that this acronym for 'trans-exclusionary radical feminist' was originally coined by people who wanted a term to apply to themselves. Or we hear that it was originally coined by people who were not themselves trans-exclusionary, but were interested simply in classification, not in abuse. Either way, the originally neutral, or perhaps even positively toned, acronym 'TERF' came over time to be seen as a slur; using it came to be seen as being automatically bullying and abusive, just like any other slur.

This classification of 'TERF' as a slur might seem puzzling, because those who object to it usually claim to be radical feminists, and certainly are exclusionary of trans men and trans women from at least some contexts. So they might well seem to be both trans-exclusionary and radical feminists. In which case, the acronym describes a position in a way that the position's holders themselves say is accurate. So you might wonder: what's the problem?

Well, this point about accuracy isn't the end of the story. A term can be a slur even though it's descriptively accurate. Whether some term counts as a slur depends not just on its accuracy but also on the tone with which that term is typically used. For example, the abbreviation 'Brit' from 'Briton' is not usually thought of as a racial slur, just as a cheery bit of journalese. And it just means the same as 'Briton', so it can't be descriptively inaccurate. However, there is a parallel abbreviation of 'Pakistani' that clearly is a racial slur, simply because of the term's terrible history, and the tone with which that abbreviation is typically used.

By the same reasoning, 'TERF' can still be a slur even if it's semantically innocent and descriptively accurate. And whether or not anyone agrees that it's a slur, the facts that the term is highly dispensable and that some people hear it as a slur give all of us good reason not to use the term if (like me) we're not trying to be offensive.

For at least these reasons, I won't be using 'TERF' myself, any more than I will make any, or much, use of 'transphobe'. A lot of the time these terms are mere name-calling, and just enable the people at whom the terms are thrown to distract us all from the substantive issues; getting enmired in a bust-up about the word 'TERF' is just another way for trans people and trans allies to be silenced.

But anyway, there's a further reason not to use 'TERF'. This is simply that it's descriptively inaccurate. To be a feminist is to stand up for the rights of women, meaning all women. But most of the people we're talking about do not stand up for the rights of all women. That's true on my account of what a woman is: according to me, trans women are women, and the people in question typically don't stand up for trans women's rights. But it's also true on their own account of what a woman is: according to them, trans men are women, and they typically don't stand up for trans men's rights either. So they aren't feminists at all, still less radical feminists. Neither the R nor the F of 'TERF' is descriptively accurate of them.

A different term that is sometimes applied to broadly the same group of people is 'gender critical feminists'. We've just seen the problem with the 'feminists' bit of this. As for the 'gender critical' bit: oh, the irony.

To be transgender is to be gender critical by definition. To be transgender is to spend your entire life criticising and distancing yourself from your society's prevalent gender norms and stereotypes, just by being yourself. By contrast – and here is the irony I mean – many of the people who are now most insistent on calling themselves 'gender critical' are not gender critical at all; at least not when it comes to transgender people. When it is transgender ('-ism') that is under discussion, typical 'gender critical feminists' are gender *conservative*. In this context they are as firmly insistent as it's possible to be on the reality and indispensability of the gender binary, i.e. the perceived-biological-sex binary. In their own way, they are as adamant about that binary as are the fans of Fifties graphic novels.

Consider, for example, a recent insurance advertisement that the chain store John Lewis released in the UK, which happened to feature a small boy trashing his parents' décor while wearing a dress and lipstick; this was referencing a previous advertisement of their own which featured a small girl doing similar. The previous advertisement got very little reaction at all. Yet the response of many people from the 'gender critical' end of the spectrum to a similar innocent and funny advertisement, when it happened to feature a boy, was exceedingly revealing. It was sheer hysterical rage. It was completely unhinged. Apparently when these self-described 'gender critical' people came across even such mildly gender-norm-subverting material, they couldn't cope with it at all.

Not unrelatedly, 'gender critical' people frequently claim that it is impossible (or nearly impossible) for trans people to 'pass' in their preferred gender. According to them, we humans all have an evolutionarily hard-wired sexing capability in us, and this on-board sex-radar operates infallibly, or almost infallibly. (No science is ever offered to establish this implausible claim. And there are online contexts where you can see would-be biological-sex-radar operators registering 'trans woman' as output for… Sigourney Weaver.[31]) At the same time, sometimes almost in the same breath, the very same 'gender critical feminists' insist too on the crucial importance of maintaining the gender binary, the perceived-biological-sex binary, as it already exists, and on ensuring that no one at all is ambiguous relative to that binary – precisely because we can't always tell 'who is a man and who is a woman.' It is not exactly difficult to see a logical inconsistency here. But the 'gender critical' movement don't worry their heads about that. Their defence of the gender binary on safety grounds can be taken, and quite frequently is, right up to the point of denying trans people's right to have their preferred pronouns used of them.

In the words of a rather horrible slogan, 'Pronouns are rohypnol'. That is to say: if you respect trans people's preferences about how you should refer to them, then it's like they have slipped you a date-rape drug. This is not a very pleasant proposition to spell out. On the other hand, it is important to spell it out, just to see how deeply unpleasant a proposition it is. To quote Sara Ahmed again, the core assumption here is,

> that compliance with preferred pronouns would be dangerous for women. The cognitive disadvantage for those who try and comply with pronouns will be the same … *Something that slows down the cognitive processes of women in relation to potential aggressors may turn out to have very serious ramifications for them.* Note [that] the danger here is implied to follow from compliance: by complying with preferred pronouns (pushed by 'trans activism' …), women

---

[31] See e.g. https://twitter.com/StopTweetingMia/status/1508972400091705349 /photo/1. There was also a celebrated case where a high-profile trans exclusionary signed up under a false name for a women-only dating website, then went round the website, pretending to be a woman, in order to find 'trans predators' who were pretending to be women. He then 'outed' some of them on his blog. Only trouble was, some of them were cis women, and they objected very strongly indeed to being so misidentified.

More recently, along similar lines, there have been frequent accusations (the right word in the context) that Daniel Radcliffe's partner Erin Darke is a trans woman. No she isn't.

Many seem happy to keep repeating the trope that 'we can always tell' trans women from cis women – among them many whose own track record spectacularly disproves it.

will be at a disadvantage, suffering *very serious ramifications* for their health, safety or well-being.

This association of compliance with preferred pronouns and danger suggests that safety depends upon clarity, that bodies need to line up, or be *accurately sexed.* Those who are not *clearly* men or women, who do appear how 'he' or 'she' should appear, are, in other words, dangerous. Any demand that people *clearly* be men or women, let us be clear, is the patriarchal world view. But from the view that sex is material, that biological sex is immutable, comes a requirement that bodies line up, to appear as *men* or *women*. Biological sex is used to create a social line, that we have the right, even moral duty, to enforce. Any costs become [merely] regrettable. In such a world view, deviation is seen as dangerous, even deadly. This is how, by treating the idea of two distinct biological sexes not as the product of the sex-gender system, but as before it and beyond it, 'gender critical' feminists tighten rather than loosen the hold of that system on our bodies. To breathe in feminism we have to loosen this hold.[32]

If we're going to have the slogan 'Pronouns are rohypnol', why not also the slogan 'Titles are rohypnol'? If we're supposed to be worried that transgender people might use their pronouns as a way of getting vulnerable women off their guard, why aren't we worried that people who describe themselves as doctors or police officers might use their titles that way too? After all, unlike with pronouns, there is plenty of genuinely disturbing evidence that this actually happens: google Larry Nassar, John Schneeberger or Wayne Couzens. In reality, pronouns are not 'rohypnol' (in the sense meant by the slogan). But 'Doctor' and 'Constable' can be. So where is the 'women's activist' campaign against those forms of address?

All this looks to me like a very solid case for not using the label 'gender critical feminist', or even 'gender critical'. That is still the name preferred by most people in the movement in question, though it is interesting to note that recently at least some activists of that stripe have begun to express their own disquiet with 'gender critical', precisely because they themselves can see that the name is increasingly disastrous PR.

[32] Sara Ahmed, 'Gender critical = gender conservative'. https://feministkilljoys .com/2021/10/31/gender-critical-gender-conservative/ (italics in original).

For my part, though, I will mostly just refer to trans-exclusionary views by that name – as trans-exclusionary (apart from the odd use of 'gender critical' in scare quotes). For trans-exclusionary is what they are. No one has told me yet that this term is a slur, though I have heard people make the following complaint: 'Calling us trans-exclusionaries gives the false impression that our movement is centred on trans people. But that's not the main thing we're about at all. We're not even that interested in trans people.'

As if the owner of a colour-barred hotel in 1960s Dixie should say to the African American protesters on his front steps: 'My hotel offers all sorts of attractions! And I'm not even interested in questions about civil rights. It isn't all about *you*, you know.'

So much for terminology.

1.21: *Rewinding the tape*

One familiar psychotherapist's exercise is to try and rerun a conversation, and imagine how it could have turned out better: how the story would have gone if it had gone as you wish it had. And an important constraint on this exercise is something like psychological realism. The alternative reality that you try to visualise is indeed alternative, so it's not actual reality. But the closer to reality it is, the better. The more the exchange that you imagine is something that really could have happened, the more good the exercise does you.

That conversation with my mother that I began this book with: sometimes I try to rerun it in my head. But when I try to do this under the constraint of psychological realism, I get lost. How, realistically, could that conversation have gone better? How could it have gone otherwise at all?

I do know that, in Lancashire in 1969 or whenever it was, she couldn't have just shrugged and said: 'Sure, go to school as a girl if you like.' That might be all right today, at least in some places. But if she had said that then and there, it wouldn't have been better for me. It would have called my bluff, pulled the rug out from under me, and left me floundering with the practicalities. (I was under five.) And I would have drowned in a whirlpool of derision, and she would have been vilified for letting me.

A better reply, maybe the best reply, for her to give to me would have been this: 'If you want to try being a girl sometimes, why not just be a girl at home first? Like you already do, only without hiding away – and see how you like that?'

Now to imagine my mother saying that is a very happy imagining. I naturally want to go further, and imagine her following up with: 'So what do you want to wear as a girl? Oh, that? And these? We'd better get some in your size, then.'

Or I can go further still, and imagine where these concessions might have led me. I suspect they could have led me to something like a double identity. I'd have quickly established a girl identity at home. Maybe – at least till adolescence, anyway – I would have settled for that.

Interesting, by the way, that for me it was always home that seemed like the relatively safe environment, compared with school. For thousands of trans kids today, it's the other way round. School is the only place they feel safe to be themselves; coming out to their parents is simply not an option. To have even that safety taken away by ignorant government ideologues is inexpressibly sad. The cruel results of such policies – which are increasingly popular now not only in the more judgemental parts of the US, but in England too – are entirely predictable: more childhood distress, more absenteeism from school, and more self-harm. But when you look at the basis of misinformation, prejudice, tabloid panic, and sheer vindictiveness that underlies such policies, it is hard not to conclude that the cruelty is the point.

Thinking my way into the double-identity scenario that might have developed in my own life, I can imagine how much I would have hated having to pretend at school, and having to switch from girl mode to boy mode every morning. Still, maybe it would have been enough (and of course better than nothing). Maybe that double-identity approach would have enabled me to bear the trials of life at school in a boy identity, and survey them with more or less complete detachment and sangfroid. Because even in the worst moments I'd have been thinking: 'At 4pm I disappear. I am out of here, and you are no longer in my face. And by 5pm I'm going to have not a single trace of school stuff or a single item of boy clothing upon me, anywhere about my person. Nope, I'm going to be snuggling up on the sofa at home in a rustly blue satin dress with white net petticoats, eating chocolate digestives and drinking a glass of milk, and tying polka-dot ribbons in the ringlets in my hair while I watch *Blue Peter*.'

I'd have wanted a girl's name too, before long. *Call me by my name* – my real name, the one that shows that you too recognise my reality; at least in my home identity... And I wonder, idly no doubt, what that name would have been, if I'd chosen at that age? If I'd had the chance, I would have pursued this question very seriously indeed – I've already talked about my attempt to find the correlative term to 'Tom-boy'. But supposing I had then hit on the name I chose in 1998: '*When I come home from school, I'm not HIM any more. I am ME. And me is SHE, and I have a NAME. Sophie Grace Chappell: call me by my name. Admit that I exist.*'

Yes, well, we can all dream.

These follow-up imaginings are even happier ones. The trouble is that they are completely unrealistic. They're nothing like adjacent to reality. There was no way on earth that my mother was ever going to allow me within a hundred miles of any of this.

Deprived of these possibilities, I was, nonetheless, always fascinated by male–female pairings of any kind. When I arrived at secondary school it had a Boys' Division and a Girls' Division, both rather grand in style, and they were architecturally mirror images of each other. And because, as soon as I could, I did unusual subjects (Greek, Latin, Classical Studies, as many languages as the timetable would allow), this meant joint classes with the Girls' Division. And so, almost every school day, I used to pass from the Boys' Side to the Girls' Side: through the stairway and the shared room, at the arch over the central court; then back again after the lesson.

In ways I wasn't really articulating at the time, this back and forth fascinated and delighted me. So did the shared room, the in-between room beyond the Library, straight above the arch dividing the two sides and therefore the only room in the whole building that was not strictly speaking in either Division – unless of course it was in both. For some reason this was my favourite place in the whole school.

Much earlier in life the phenomenon of brother–sister twins already intrigued me deeply. I realised as soon as I encountered it that it actually was an answer to another secret question of my own: what a boy would look like if he was a girl, and what a girl would look like if she was a boy.

There was the story that I wanted to tell about myself. It was about me being a girl, and not being a boy. And at the level of clothing – which, like I say, was pretty much the only level that I could see was available to me, apart from the naming level – this was all about occasional visions of delight like Wimbledon, or *Gone with the Wind,* or *Swan Lake,* or the illustrations in *Alice in Wonderland,* or what some girls whom I actually knew sometimes got to wear.

But – at the clothing level, and at any other level – all of this was absolutely forbidden. Not partly sidelined, not tolerated in some contexts but not all, not put-up-with with tolerant if condescending eye-rolls. Just forbidden. All of it. Completely and totally and universally forbidden, full stop.

When I wrote all this down for the first time in my life, in the fag-end of December 2020, I wondered – as I wonder still – if in fact I can now unearth a little more of the memory of what actually happened in that conversation that I began with. When I asked if I could go to school as a girl, maybe my mother said not only 'Why?' but also 'And what would happen then?' And maybe I shrugged and said 'I don't know.' And maybe my mother said 'People would laugh at you.' And maybe I replied 'Why should they laugh at me?' And maybe she said 'But they would laugh at you. I'm not having it. You're a boy, not a girl, and you're not going to do that.'

Did this happen? I can't tell. I just know that the whole area got shut down, somehow; *I* got shut down. And maybe something like this exchange was part of that shutting-down.

Not that I was constrained, of course (I think my parents might have said). I was perfectly free to tell all sorts of stories about who I was. Just so long as I didn't try telling that one.

'You can be whoever you want to be. Just not a girl.'

That part of me was to be silenced, erased, bulldozed away, made like it had never existed, tarmacked over like the previous world in *1984.* From the mid-Seventies on, it pretty much was.

1.22: Shoulda coulda woulda

How should it have gone – that conversation, and my life thereafter? How do I wish it had gone otherwise? How could it have gone otherwise?

As a certain lion says in a certain children's book: 'No one is ever told what *would* have happened.' But I do know this (and again – this isn't blaming anyone, and is not meant as an emotional blackmail appeal for sympathy, just as a statement of the truth): what did happen hurt and damaged me. It did me lasting harm to be told that I couldn't express that side of my being in any context at all. It did me lasting harm to have it repressed and denied by others, and to learn to repress it and deny it myself. It would have been far better if my parents had said: 'All right then, be a girl at home, and see how it goes.'

That sort of response didn't happen much then, certainly not where I grew up. Maybe it happened in liberated bits of California, or wherever. Or maybe it happened in 1970s Lancashire too – but only in top secret. It does happen nowadays, all over the place, and pretty openly. You hear about it from friends, or online, or in the media: there are kids whose parents *do* let them live in their preferred gender expression, even if that is trans. It happens at school too: these days there are even kids in school who get to be who they really are gender-wise, without it being much of a big deal or trouble to anyone.

Here are two anonymised examples from recent correspondence with Facebook friends: let's call their subjects Leonie and Christine.[33] The usual convention is for me to say 'I apologise for their length', but actually, no: the length adds depth and detail.

(1) Leonie
My first grandchild was born in Texas in July 2016, into a melting-pot family, and named Leo. His parents moved to France in 2017. His mother was one of the very many people who said that if Trump won the election, she would leave the US, and also one of the very few who actually meant it. For two

---

[33] Thanks to those who told me about the originals of 'Leonie' and 'Christine', for permission to tell these fragments of their stories here. Unfortunately, it is not for nothing that I anonymise the cases. One English transgender child who was recently in the public eye, Emily Williams from Liverpool, has now sadly become the object of an extraordinary hate campaign on Twitter and elsewhere, to the extent that Emily's mother has had to restrict access to her Twitter feed to deter 'gender critical' trolls.

Emily Williams is a thirteen-year-old child. She is a little girl. Some people really do need, at the very minimum, to learn to mind their own business.

years after that, they lived in my house near Carcassonne. There was born Leo's brother, Marc, in 2018. In 2019, they moved to London, a few months before the outbreak of the pandemic, and rented a pleasant, small house about a quarter of a mile from where I had had piano lessons as a boy.

In December of 2020, I finally managed to escape COVID captivity, and went back to London, expecting to spend a week or so at most there with my family before returning to my house in France. Things didn't work out that way. COVID cases were surging, and France was about to close its borders again. I ended up staying in London until March before returning to the US – I never got back to France.

So I spent quite a lot of time in fairly close confinement with my family. Some time towards the beginning of January, my daughter said to me, in the kitchen: 'Leo thinks he's a girl' (we had problems with pronouns for quite a while). At first I had to make sure that she meant it literally, descriptively. My initial reaction after that was sceptical. Are you sure? How can he know? Yes I know he likes dressing up in girls' clothes, but so does Marc (their mother used to make them for them). I suppose that at first it seemed so implausible to me that someone that young really could have such a sense of themselves that they knew, at least on this very important axis, who they were.

I think my reaction was normal, and not just in a statistical sense – and I'm not ashamed of it (and in general I don't think it's a bad idea for people to reflect on whether something is something that they really mean, or are committed to). But it did derive from a profound ignorance about the lived experience of the people who exist, and always have existed, who question their gender assignments from a very early age.

As I said before, I was lucky to be living in very close – claustrophobically close after a while – quarters with my family, so that I could observe how Leo behaved, utterly unselfconsciously, as she gradually adopted a more and more female external persona. It was also, in retrospect, hugely fortunate that we were all locked down – no one, myself included, was going to school, and although Leo's school tried heroically to maintain school contact by Zoom, it was very patchy – and Leo didn't like it at all (to be fair, neither did I, as I tried to run university classes in the US in the afternoon online from London in the evening). It also gave Leo and his mother time, and space, to be in touch with the school, at all levels from his teachers up to the principal, about what was going on, and what they should expect. The school was, without

66

exception, understanding and accommodating, even though, as one of them said, they'd never actually had a case like this before.

The week before school reopened was the week before I returned to the US. Leo – who was shortly to become Leonie – received her new, schoolgirl clothes. The day before school started, my daughter, myself, and the two kids went out for our regular lockdown 'treat', a walk to the local railway station to have coffee, chocolate and cakes outside the platform café. Leonie wore her new clothes – and that was the moment that I was finally, utterly convinced that this was real. Because, wholly naturally, without affectation, she skipped ahead of us down the pavement – she was light, airy, happy, carefree. She was, as the French say, *bien dans sa peau*, fine in her skin, at ease with herself. It was, for me, one of those rare moments when you can just, immediately, see the truth. An epiphany, if you like.

The following day, my last in London, I walked with Leonie on her way back to school for the first time in months, in her new clothes. She didn't seem nervous or apprehensive, although I was a little on her behalf – not so much because of the possible reaction of kids, who at that age have no preconceived prejudices, but because of that, possibly, of their parents. In the event, so far as I know, nothing bad has happened, or at any rate not as a result of Leonie's acknowledgement that she is Leonie. She is very lucky, all things considered, to be living in London in 2022. It could be a lot worse – it could be Texas, or some other twisted theocracy, for God's sake (Leonie's mother will never go back there for that reason – not, to be fair, that she ever likely would have anyway).

Leonie has also had, for the most part, supportive and understanding people around her (although the fact that one has to emphasise that, rather than it simply being something that goes without saying, is of course significant). There have, of course, been exceptions to this rule – and it is lucky that they are exceptions. I will make no further comment, and certainly will not identify them, other than to say that one is a born-again Christian, and another a flat-earther. It is now more than a year since the beginning of this story (or rather, the beginning for us – for Leonie it began a lot earlier). I have, I think, learned quite a lot since then.

Very shortly after I got back to the US, I was visited by an old friend, whom I hadn't seen in forty years, who happened to be coming to town. I had known (via mutual friends with whom I was more in touch) that he was a very high-powered academic doctor. I hadn't known that his main specialism was paediatric endocrinology – including the physiology, and psychology, of child gender-identification. Talking to him was both enlightening and reassuring. He said – something which by now really only confirmed my own raw and untutored impressions – that, in general, the earlier people recognised that they were, biologically speaking, transgender, the more likely it was to be a completely settled disposition (at the same time, he was quick to point out that gender, and gender-identity, can be fluid); and the earlier people make up their minds – if they do – to undertake specific chemical and/or surgical routes to confirming these facts, the easier it is for them, if their parents are willing to help (unless of course you live in Texas, where your parents will be prosecuted for child abuse).

One last thing. People often say that young children engage in make-believe all the time, and for this reason cannot be trusted to know – or at least to speak truly about – what they actually believe. Independently of the obvious fact that adults are far more adept at, and far more unconscious of the fact that they engage in, make-believe, it is obviously false that children can't tell the difference. If they couldn't, then no child would ever be upset to be told that Santa Claus wasn't real. You can't be upset about a difference you can't recognise. On the contrary, it is precisely because children have such a robust sense of reality that sometimes they retreat into make-believe as a way of avoiding, or trying to avoid, the pain of that reality (as of course adults do too, and for exactly the same reasons). But they do so only when they have to. I'm very happy that Leonie will no longer have to make believe, and make others believe, that she is something that she isn't.

(2) Christine

My 5-yr-old MtF daughter started her new preschool today. All instructors are aware of how she identifies, and a few of the kids know too. Last night, she told me she was nervous because she was afraid of getting teased for having a penis. (Note: she's super open about her identity, she doesn't hide it, so other kids are likely to find out even just through casual convo.) We had a nice long talk about what to do if she's teased for any reason at all (even if it's a dumb one, like the fact her dress wasn't a pure green colour), and how she should also always be nice to other kids too.

Today when I picked her up, I asked if she had made any friends and she said 'Mmm, I don't know yet. Nobody picked on me, but there was one kid who was getting picked on and these two kids just kept yelling at him. So I went over and asked them to stop, but they didn't. So I turned to the kid and said "You run along, I can handle this." So he left, and I tried to get them to stop yelling and finally they did.'

I am such a proud mama bear that my baby cub stood up for another child who she didn't even know, on her first day of school. I'm very impressed, and my heart is swollen and bursting with immense joy. She doesn't want to be picked on and knows what it would feel like, so she wants to make sure other kids don't have to experience it either – for any reason. That's how change happens. That's how we progress. And I'm glad she sees that at such a young age. I'm proud that not only is she brave enough to be herself, she's brave enough to stand up for others too.

[Update, Christine seven years later]:
She is now 12, and we find out soon if she can start puberty blockers like she wants. Her whole life, I've listened to her and followed her lead and let her dictate the way she wants her journey to be played out; it is her life, not mine. At no point has she ever wavered in her confidence of knowledge in who she is, and for that I am immensely proud. There are adults who struggle with discovering who they are (even cishet adults) and so she's miles ahead of even them.

I hope that as she grows older, she continues to trust me enough to share these things with me and let me continue cheering her on and supporting her in whatever paths she takes.

What these wonderful stories tell us is that very often, these days, young people get to be openly transgender without the slightest trouble. And when there is trouble, it is, usually, not the kids who get worked up about transgender. It is, usually, the parents who get scared and angry and convinced that something terrible is happening that really needs to be stopped.

Yes, sometimes the kids are bullies too, unfortunately. But as a rule, the kids get their relaxed view of their transgender classmates from seeing them every day; whereas the parents get their alarmed and uptight view of those trans kids, whom they usually don't know personally, from reading the tabloids or watching certain TV channels. (And the 'gender ideology' at work here is the pro trans view? And the 'mainstream media' is full of 'trans propaganda'? Come off it. See 2.8 below.)

For me, these tales of free and happy transgender kids are a delight to read. It's exhilarating to see that such freedom and such happiness is possible for them – at an age where for me neither freedom nor happiness was possible, at least in this respect. But just for that reason, they also make me miserably envious. *Shoulda coulda woulda.* 'Why couldn't it have been like that for me?', I wistfully wonder. Or at any rate: 'How much like that could it have been for me?'

Suppose that my parents had allowed me, as I put it above, to 'establish a girl identity at home'. Like I said, maybe that would have enabled me to bear the trials of life at school in a boy identity – at least till adolescence. But what then? If I had been offered puberty-blockers when I was twelve or thirteen, would I have wanted them? If I'd had the chance to press Pause, pharmaceutically, on male adolescence, would I have taken it? And would I have understood what I was doing?

I think the answers come out in reverse order, actually. I would only have gone for it if I had been sure in my own mind that I understood what I was doing. But brought up where, and when, and how I was brought up, there was no chance of my understanding what it is to take puberty-blockers – which in any case were not yet on the pharmaceutical scene then (they appeared in the early 1980s).

If I were a twelve-year-old child now, and one who was not hemmed in by spiteful, hostile, lying, scaremongering propaganda, then I would have a chance of understanding – in a way perfectly legally adequate for exactly the same level of 'informed consent' that a twelve-year-old can show to any other medical procedure – that puberty-blockers do not prevent but pause the physical processes of puberty. I would know that I was not making an irreversible decision, but one that I could review later, and largely, though perhaps not completely, reverse if I chose. I would know that puberty-blockers are (despite much online propaganda) not risky or dangerous or experimental medicine, but well-trialled drugs with a long and uneventful track record that have been around for more than forty years.[34] By now, for example, they are far less 'experimental'

---

[34] In the words of Jason Klein, a paediatric endocrinologist: 'Puberty blockers have been used for decades in cisgender kids who either are going through puberty too early, or, in some instances, kids who are going through puberty very quickly. Their use has been FDA [US Federal Drugs Administration] approved,

than COVID vaccines. So if anyone wants to oppose puberty-blockers for being 'experimental', they should in consistency be even more fanatically anti-vax. There is a certain sad dark humour in the fact that some anti-trans campaigners who get worked up about puberty-blockers have actually bitten this bullet.[35]

They also like to go on about trans-affirming medicine being a way of 'subjecting a child to a lifetime of medication'. Well, I take latanoprost eyedrops to keep my eyeball-pressure down. This prevents me from getting glaucoma and going blind. Should my ophthalmologist have been deterred from diagnosing my high eyeball-pressure, and prescribing eyedrops to control the problem, by the consideration that the result for me would be 'a lifetime of medication'? She should not. And thankfully she wasn't. But gender dysphoria causes a lot more deaths than glaucoma.

Or take another case: Bruce Springsteen, by his own confession in *Born to Run* (2016), has been in and out of depression for most of his adult life, and would have struggled even more than he has without anti-depressant drugs. Is that being subject to a 'lifetime of medication'? Even if it is, does anyone really want to say – to Bruce? to his face? – that that means it's a deal not worth making?

So if I was a kid now, and living under trans-favourable conditions – yes, I think I would very probably want to take the pharmaceutical option. As things were, it caused me considerable distress to go through male puberty. I felt like I was changing from a charming, cheeky little monkey – who looked pretty good in a green satin ball-gown, even if it was way too big for me – into a lumpen, ugly, stubbly, smelly oaf. I hated

---

well-studied, well-documented, and well-tolerated for a long time now. And it's the exact same medication that we use in trans or non-binary children to basically put a pause on pubertal development. Exactly the same medications, at exactly the same doses.' https://www.vice.com/en/article/epnzjk/no-one-had-a-problem-with-puberty-blockers-when-only-cis-kids-took-them.
[35] And if they want to oppose the use of, e.g., Androcur for trans women beginning transition, they should also oppose the use of Androcur to repress facial-hair growth in cis women who have 'too much' testosterone. In this latter context Androcur is unproblematically, routinely, and immediately prescribed by specialists; whereas a trans woman who requests it to help her transition is likely to have to wait five years and jump through a whole succession of hoops. The double standard here is flagrant, and a direct and seriously harmful consequence of the demonisation of trans people.

it. It added to my sense of alienation from my own physical being in the world. Having the option of not going that way would have been a huge relief. And yes, having the option of pharmaceutical help to go positively in a feminine direction, at the earliest possible opportunity, would have been better still.

But that isn't what happened. That isn't my story. I was stuck with what I had. I didn't even know what I wanted so badly. All I knew was how badly I wanted it.

Both when I was quite small, and when I was rather bigger too, this made me cross.

1.23: The cross-dresser

Men get coarse black jeans,
scratching catching-crotched,
B.O.-armpit suits,
boxers, sweaty socks.

Women get silken skirts
that rustle and flow from the waist,
sheer stockings, cream-cotton shirts
soft with shimmering lace.

For boys there's the winded jockstrap
and the rugby boot's muddy cleats;
for girls the miraculous tutu
and tennis's frills and pleats.

But taboo says do not complain.
Even cross feelings are banned.
You are stuck in the stubble-chinned strain
and the drudge of being a man.

On the other hand, though. On the other hand: if things had gone that way at some early stage, then many of the very best things in my actual story – above all, my wife and my children – would never have happened. And I certainly wouldn't wish them away even if I could, not now they're here, and perhaps not even before that. One of the things that I wanted most badly as a child was to have a family one day. And I couldn't see how that could happen if I got turned (or turned myself) into a girl – unless I really did turn completely into a girl, and into one who could get pregnant and have babies, which I'd have been perfectly prepared to do if it had been an option. But as I found out fairly quickly, that definitely seemed not to be possible without magic.

I get lost when I try to reimagine my own story, because some of the possibilities that I am trying to consider are so very, very counterfactual. I also sometimes feel a certain duty (incumbent on me at least) to stand in solidarity with the past. There have only been puberty-blockers and hormone therapies – or anything, really, in the way of pharmaceutical or surgical help – for the past sixty years or so. But as far as I can make out, there have always been transgender people. (For more about the history, see 2.6 below.)

My heart goes out to the transgender people of the past. With no prospect of medical or therapeutic support, they had to find other ways of coping. (The way things are going with the present transphobic moral panic, the transgender people of the future will have to find other ways of coping too. Another good reason why some trans people don't take the presently available medical help is because it is fenced in by such heavy gatekeeping already – and at the moment the situation is getting worse by the day. Why should someone else get to decide who I am, and what life choices I should be allowed to make?)

And no doubt people of the past also experienced the crises of morale that I too experience sometimes (only it must have been worse for them): a sense of total exhaustion, a sense of total despair at *ever* being able to be the way you want to be; a feeling that it would be easier to run away and hide, to 'fade far away, dissolve, and quite forget'; to disappear from all view, rather than even try to present as the person you know you are inside.

The urge to find peace, if necessary by vanishing completely.

I have desired to go
Where springs not fail,
To fields where flies no sharp and sided hail
And a few lilies blow.

And I have asked to be
Where no storms come,
Where the green swell is in the havens dumb,
And out of the swing of the sea.

Such must have been the struggles of transgender people in the past. And at times, I feel that at least some of us transgender people today should simply stand with them.

But like the lion also says: No one is ever told any story but their own.

1.24: Je ne regrette not very much

It is easy to regret the lives we aren't living. Easy to wish we'd developed other talents, said yes to different offers. Easy to wish we'd worked harder, loved better, handled our finances more astutely, been more popular, stayed in the band…

It takes no effort to miss the friends we didn't make the work we didn't do and the people we didn't marry and the children we didn't have. It is not difficult to see yourself through the lens of other people and to wish you were all the different kaleidoscopic versions of you they wanted you to be. it is easy to regret, and keep regretting, ad infinitum, until our time runs out.

But it is not the lives we regret not living that are the real problem. It is the regret itself. It's the regret that makes us shrivel and wither and feel like our own and other people's worst enemy.

We can't tell if any of those other versions would have been better or worse. Those lives are happening, it is true, but you are happening as well, and that is the happening we have to focus on.[36]

Matt Haig hits the nail on the head here, I think. All the way down the line I wanted to be a girl, or a woman, and all the way down the line that was going to be possible, if at all, in only some senses (see again 1.18 above on sex as a cluster concept). So every choice I could have made – and every choice that others could have made for me, too – would have been a compromise in one way or another. I don't suppose I am the

---

[36] Matt Haig, *The Midnight Library* (Canongate, 2020), p. 277.

only transgender person for whom that is true, or even the only person; compromise is a fact of life for everyone.

I wouldn't say that I have no regrets. Of course I have *some* regrets; I certainly think there are ways that things could have gone better for me, and maybe some of those ways were closer to reality than they seemed to be at the time. And there are certainly ways I could have behaved better; could have been fairer and kinder to those around me who have also had to deal, whether or not they realised it, with me being transgender. And I do think it's important, and worthwhile, to reflect on those regrets sometimes, and the lost possibilities that they correspond to. That needn't mean being consumed by the regrets, or distracted by the possibilities, from getting on with my actual life, like someone at a cocktail party who constantly keeps hearing snippets of other conversations that sound so much more interesting than the conversation she's actually in. Quite generally, human understanding is irreducibly modal: a key part of understanding what has happened is understanding what else might have happened, instead. And that's what I'm trying to do here.

In the past – not, I'm glad to say, the very recent past – there certainly have been times when the regret has been close to all-consuming and close to unbearable, especially while I was still trying to fight down this side of my nature. There were certain things on television, for instance, that I could not allow myself to watch, because I knew the kind of longings they would set off in me. You wouldn't believe the amount of inner turmoil that *The Sound of Music* used to cause me in the first two decades of my life: 'Why can't I look like that? Why do I have to be this shape and not that shape? What can I do about this, how can I fix it? Will this ever change, or is it all too late for me now, and I'll never get there?'

Another example, though I was a good deal older (I was twenty-eight in fact) when this appeared: that extremely twee old Yellow Pages advert with the boy who is too short to give an under-the-mistletoe kiss to the girl in the tartan-and-white-lace Christmas frock.[37] I'm sorry to tell the advertising company that the advert didn't at all make me want to go out and buy Yellow Pages. But however cheesy and icky and ridiculous this may sound to you, it really did make me wish desperately (yes, even when I was twenty-eight) that I could look like (that I could be, or have

---

[37] https://www.youtube.com/watch?v=786sCIp8iXg.

been) that girl; and it made me desperately sad and regretful that I didn't, and never had, and for all I knew never would.

If my response was any of the seven deadly sins, it was – to be totally clear about this – not lust. It was envy and despair. In words, it was: 'I so want to look like that, and I never have looked like that, and now I am trapped until I die inside this loathsome, laboursome dragon-hide, this hideous, heavy, smothering encasement of adult maleness... so I never will look like that. It's all much too late, and it's all much, much too far away for me.'

With a stinging and self-loathing side-order of: '"I want to look like that"? What the hell is wrong with me? How can I be responding like this, for God's sake, to a small girl in a tartan dress in a trivial, saccharine, thirty-second TV advert? I am so shameful. I am so pathetic.'

> The feelings that hurt most, the emotions that sting most, are those that are absurd – the longing for impossible things, precisely because they are impossible; nostalgia for what never was; the desire for what could have been; dissatisfaction with the world's existence. All these half-tones of the soul's consciousness create in us a painful landscape, an eternal sunset of what we are.[38]

Every time that ad came on the telly I would get out of the room as fast as possible, because I knew if I watched it, it would make me feel miserable and desperate and ashamed and regretful, all over again. That was a late example, as I say (the ad came out in 1992). But all through my life, until I finally began to make peace with my own nature from May 1998 on, there were loads of things like that, and I censored all of them as much as possible. I would do anything then to keep (what I regarded as) temptation at bay; to keep my skeletons in their cupboard; to keep my own dark side – as I took it to be – thoroughly in the dark.

1.25: A quick blast against the 'non-affirmation model'

Let's go back for a moment, though, to the contemporary transgender kids that I was talking about in 1.22, and about how they are telling their

---

[38] Fernando Pessoa, *The Book of Disquiet*, ed. Richard Zenith (Penguin Modern Classics, 2002).

own stories, in how they present at home and even at school, today. I salute their courage and their honesty – while also devoutly wishing, of course, for a time when honesty needs no courage.

About what happens to us trans people, notice again: (1) it happens spontaneously; (2) it happens forcefully; and (3) it happens early.

The trans kids we're talking about are acting out of an inner necessity, just as I was. Just as with me, it comes from inside, not from outside. Just like me, they're transgender because it comes naturally, not because someone else brainwashes them into being transgender. (Indeed, they're transgender even if someone tries to brainwash them into not being transgender; even if they try to brainwash *themselves* into not being transgender; that is precisely my story here.) And though of course there are some experimenters, typically the kids who say they're transgender are transgender. They mean it. It's not a whim or a fad or a fashion. It's who they are, and attempts to get them to 'desist' are pointless, counter-productive, and mind-bendingly cruel.

('But what about the sudden upsurge in young people identifying as trans?' Insofar as there has been such an upsurge, a lot of it has to do with destigmatisation. When schools stopped trying to beat left-handedness out of their pupils, there was a 'sudden upsurge' of people identifying as left-handed. Things settled down when the left-handers reached their natural level, which is about 10 per cent. The same is very likely to be true with transgender. But even if it wasn't: what of that? Suppose lots more people find that they are trans now than happened in any other era. So what? If it was a fact that there are *suddenly lots of them now*, why would that fact be a reason not to treat them respectfully and compassionately? Why would the fact that there are *suddenly lots of them now* throw any suspicion on the validity of what they find to be true about themselves – unless we were casting around for justification for a suspicion that, for underexamined reasons of our own, we felt anyway?)

Being trans happens spontaneously; it happens forcefully; and it happens early. We are that way from the beginning, and in particular from well before adolescence. Deployed as an anti-trans slogan, that phrase I mentioned in 1.4, 'Let kids be kids', is not only horridly sentimental. It also encapsulates the serious misunderstanding that transgender is something sexual that only kicks in at puberty – something alien and external that shouldn't be allowed to interfere with a child's childhood.

This is completely upside-down. If you're transgender, being trans *is* your childhood, and it is the exclusion of your trans side from your childhood that constitutes the interference.

As everywhere in this book, I can speak from experience here. But not only my own experience:

> I am in deep despair about the future of my daughter, an 11-year-old who is absolutely sure about her gender. As Dr David Bell[39] insists (Letters, 27 January), children and teenagers really are vulnerable. I'm not sure why this leads him to conclude that they should therefore be forced through puberty to become something they dread, which means that at the very inception of their adult life they may never be able to live without discrimination.
>
> I fear that removing all hope of being medicated will lead to needless suffering for my daughter and other young trans people like her, as indeed we are already seeing for trans people of all ages relying on the shameful NHS provision.
>
> I understand that a tiny minority do detransition, not least because they are abused or socially pressed into doing so. Why should the vast majority suffer to facilitate this?
>
> As an aside, the suggestion that autistic people are unable to understand the implications of their own actions in this space is also abominable. I write as an autistic professional myself, with a family and a good education.
>
> The way that trans people are treated in this country is a disgrace. It isn't uncommon for them to have a detailed personal plan to leave the country if things get even worse. Sadly, I can't in all conscience say that it won't.[40]

There's been a lot of talk recently about 'non-affirmation models' of talk therapy for transgender kids. The advocates of these so-called 'non-affirmation models' typically seem rather keen to keep vague, at

---

[39] One of the so-called 'whistle-blowers' at the Tavistock Centre in London in 2019; a person who seems firmly, and antecedently, committed to the view that at least most of his trans-presenting patients while he worked there 'did not mean it', no matter how insistent, consistent and persistent they were, and also to the view that at least many of them were 'really confused gays'. As I have already noted, there seems to be a close correlation between such views and overt transphobia.

[40] https://www.theguardian.com/society/2023/jan/31/i-fear-for-my-trans-daughters-future-in-the-uk.

least in public, just exactly what they have in mind. So let's help them out. Here's a bit of clarity: at least much of the time, 'non-affirmation models' means 'conversion therapy'. What non-affirmation models generally involve is telling their subjects – or victims – that 'No one is born in the wrong body', that 'No one can change their sex', that 'It's all right to cross-dress if you like but that isn't the same as changing sex, which no one can do anyway'. In short, 'non-affirmation models' mean subjecting transgender people, and by definition typically young and vulnerable transgender people, to a lecture course in trans-exclusionary ideology.

But that's not all. Alongside the lecture series come 'exploration' and 'challenging' of the transgender person's sense of themselves. And not in a good way. Of course a therapist has a duty to push their client a bit about such an important issue, and part of the propaganda against the 'affirmation model' consists precisely in the false assertion that affirming someone's gender identity means *unquestioningly* affirming it. Nothing of the sort is true, and no responsible practitioner would go that way. But neither would they use their time with the client to try and talk them into 'desisting'.

'Are you sure you're transgender?', 'Is this perhaps just a phase?', 'Haven't you picked this up from your peer group?', 'Aren't you just trying to get attention, to look cool?', 'Don't you think you're making yourself a bit ridiculous?', 'Can't you just accept your own body as it is?', 'Are you sure you're not really just gay?' (I have been confronted with all these questions myself.) The 'non-affirmation model' means using questions like these to instil self-doubt and undermine the self-confidence of transgender people. It means gaslighting them, telling them that they don't understand themselves and that someone else understands them better. And it means barraging transgender people with some of the most tediously shop-worn transphobic tropes on the market.

Just imagine the uproar if someone tried proposing 'non-affirmation models' for gay kids.[41] 'Heterosexuality is normal', you'd tell them, 'heterosexuality is mandated by biology'; 'Feel dirty urges towards other boys if

---

[41] In the UK, I mean. In the USA this happens already, if you are unlucky enough to be a young gay person in the wrong state. The situation elsewhere in the world is often even worse.

you must, but that's no basis for a lifelong commitment'; 'Two men can't fit together psychologically the way a man and a woman can'; 'God made Adam and Eve, not Adam and Steve – that's evolution' (see the power of these 'debates'! They make even creationists keen on evolution); 'The family is central to society – and if you go that way you can never have a family.' Plus, of course, 'Are you sure you're gay?', 'Isn't this just a phase?', 'Aren't you just copying your peer group?', 'Are you sure you won't regret this, like all the other detransitioners?',[42] 'Aren't you just trying to look cool?' – not to mention, 'Maybe you just haven't found the right girl yet.' This is, patently, just a string of pernicious nonsense, degenerating towards the end into the hoariest clichés in the homophobic playbook.

[42] Amidst all the manifold horrors of the current public debate about transgender, the discourse about detransition is perhaps the cruellest, nastiest, most mendacious and manipulative bit of all. On the whole I think I'd rather skip it. But very quickly: of course we should give our sympathy and support to those who sincerely regret transitioning, and want to reverse it. We should also recognise that detransitioners are statistically a tiny minority of transitioners (regret after gender-confirmation surgery runs at about 1%, way below the regret rate for most other surgical procedures); that in many cases, the decision to detransition is driven not by someone's realisation that they aren't transgender after all, but by an inability to cope with the storms of bigotry and abuse that can assail anyone who does transition; that alongside detransitioners, there are also *re*transitioners; and that the whole narrative about detransition has been hijacked and politicised by those whose real aim is not merely to get trans people to detransition, but to desist – that is, to make themselves invisible, to eliminate themselves.

There are interesting philosophical questions about the whole idea of detransition. In particular: understood a certain way, it seems to challenge the Hegelian narrative of irreversible enlightenment. We still have today the idea, which we inherit from Hegel, that there are certain changes in our consciousness, our self-understanding, that are irreversible: once they have happened, they can't be reversed. The idea of transition might seem to be a Hegelian enlightenment in just this sense; and irreversible in just this sense. *De*transition, the reversing of this kind of enlightenment about one's own nature, seems impossible on such a Hegelian view. But as we now see – just look at the US – enlightenments are, alas, not irreversible.

The whole subject is of enormous interest and importance. But I can't do it justice here. It needs a paper of its own. I'll write it as soon as I can.

https://journals.lww.com/prsgo/fulltext/2021/03000/regret_after_gender _affirmation_surgery__a.22.aspx. https://metro.co.uk/2019/10/23/dont-believe -what-you-read-about-transition-regret-10961836/.

But that's what the 'non-affirmation model' would be for gay kids. Why think it's any better for trans kids?

> [G]ender health is defined as a child's opportunity to live in the gender that feels most real or comfortable to that child and to express that gender with freedom from restriction, aspersion, or rejection. Children not allowed these freedoms by agents within their developmental systems (e.g., family, peers, school) are at later risk for developing a downward cascade of psychosocial adversities including depressive symptoms, low life satisfaction, self-harm, isolation, homelessness, incarceration, posttraumatic stress, and suicide ideation and attempts ... gender-nonconforming children are [likely to be] negatively impacted when given the message by therapists, doctors, or families that their gender expression must conform to traditional gender roles associated with their birth-assigned gender ... Psychotherapies attempting to tweak[43] a child's gender identity or expressions have been shown to suppress authentic gender expression and create psychological symptoms ... these psychotherapies are unsuccessful because they aim to alter a child's emerging gender identity (i.e., an internal sense of self) by attempting to change the child's nonconforming gender expression (i.e., a behaviour). Similar behavioural efforts to change aspects of *sexual* identity (i.e., reparative psychotherapies for homosexuality) have also proven unsuccessful, deleterious, and lacking in efficacy... Professional health organizations, including the American Academy of Pediatrics (AAP), the American Psychiatric Association (APA), and the American Psychological Association, recommend against implementing such change efforts in clinical care.[44]

1.26: Epiphanies

To say it again – I want this to be totally clear: I was not a miserable child, and my parents were not monsters, and I am not writing this 'to get my own back on them'. On the contrary, they were wonderful parents, generous, warm, protective, supportive, hospitable, engaged, intellectually stimulating, kind, ambitious, and encouraging, and I'm

---

[43] Here 'tweak' would seem to be a euphemism for 'smash into pieces'.
[44] Marco A. Hidalgo et al., 'The gender affirmative model: what we know and what we aim to learn', *Human Development* 56 (2013): 285–290.

deeply grateful to them. They are the dedicatees of this book; and they absolutely deserve to be.

Yes, there was something crucial to who I was that went missing over time – that got buried and erased for decades after – because they thought that was what ought to happen. And yes, they were dead wrong about that. And yes, that burying and erasing caused me serious unhappiness and damage.

But as we've seen, the question 'So what should they have done instead, in that time and place?' is not an easy one to answer. And after all, everyone has something wrong in their lives; no parent is ever perfect (I should know, I am a parent). In most ways, I had an extremely happy childhood, and my relationships with my parents were both happy and loving.

Once we children reached the age of reason, if my father had a fault with us it was that he talked too much, not too little – we would ask him questions like 'Where does the rain come from?', and he would explain and explain until our little brains exploded. As for my mother, I have still to this day met hardly anyone with an aptitude anything like equal to hers for listening – really listening – to other people, for being interested in them.

If there were miserable parts to my life, there were happy parts too, and probably more of them. Including some glorious days of utter epiphany that would still have been exactly what they were, no matter whether I was a boy, or a girl, or something in between, or something nowhere near any of these categories. Like climbing Pen-y-Ghent at Christmas time in 1977, I think it was, in the deepest snow and the most brilliant sunshine I had ever seen in all my thirteen years: up from the pinewood-scented, mince-pie-sofa-ed, spaniel-draped firesides of Ribblesdale, up through the coniferous forests past the little jagged-silver-limestone escarpments, swimming through the powder drifts and crunching through the ice, up onto the sweeping icy moors and into the cold clear curlew-haunted air at the trig point: a foretaste of Alpine light and Alpine cold, twenty years before I ever set foot on a glaciated mountain.

Human experience is indefinitely complicated, and there are indefinitely many stories that we might pull out of it. To find any pattern at all in experience is to be selective, and to be selective is to risk falsifying. No story taken from experience can be the truth; but it can be a truth.

For sure, my parents loved me and wanted the best story for me. Just not that story, just not the one that I wanted to tell about myself.

And were they wrong? Was that even a story that could have been told, in a harshly respectable, middle-class north-of-England society in the 1970s? When I asked my mother to let me go to school as a girl, what was she supposed to say?

The whole gender business – it was just too dangerous, too risky, too unknown, too unpredictable. My parents' challenge to me – everyone's challenge to me, apparently – was to give up that, and look for other stories to tell about myself.

So I looked.

1.27: The lethality of rural life

I used to go and sing to the cows while they were being milked. We lived in Hawkshaw in the Lancashire Pennines, in a house that my father had built around the time I was born, fifty yards from the dairy farmers from whom, I suppose, he had bought the land. (House-building was the family business, like it said on the side of his company's vans and JCBs: William Chappell & Sons Ltd, Builders. Apparently my father hoped that my brother and I, his sons, would take it over from him, as he had from his father, and his father from his grandfather. We didn't.)

To get to Clifford's farm you turned right out of our back-garden gate, down the muddy lane under the wizened little hawthorn trees, across the brook on the big brick bridge, and right again into the farmyard. At the farm, besides entertaining the Friesians (dancing round their sharp-hooved, mire-splattered rear ends, squeezing between their crushing flanks), I also collected hens' eggs (salmonella-encrusted, no doubt) from the coops and the hedgerows, talked to the pigs (with no tetanus jab), and did high-dives out of the haystacks, twelve or fifteen feet into the straw below, where fortunately there never turned out to be a lurking pitchfork or an iron-framed 1940s Acme mangle hidden under the straw.

But singing to the cows was the safe bit, because almost all our child's play in Hawkshaw was, by modern standards, staggeringly dangerous. (It was 1970–2.) Of course, there were the usual trees to climb (and fall out of), brooks to dam (and fall into), traffic to play chicken with (and fall under), Forestry Commission plantations to get lost in (and fall on you when the gales had blown them half down), and hayfields to make secret tunnels in (and risk getting mown down with the hay, or shot for a rabbit by the farmer). Moreover, the village was surrounded by abandoned paper and cotton mills. So we, a bunch of boys and girls all under eight, would sneak in through the shattered windows and dance across the rotting floor joists three floors up, climbing right out onto the ragged-holed Coniston-slate roofs through cobwebbed iron skylights 'to get the lead'. (What for? We didn't even know. If we had been ten years older and from a less innocent part of Lancashire, we might have.) On the wet green hillsides above the mill ruins there were mill chimneys, built up there 'for the draw' – for the air currents that brightened the furnaces. We would crawl up along the shaft tunnel between the mill and the chimney, and back down along it too if there turned out to be no breach in the base of the tower when we got up to the tunnel end. And there were dripping abandoned oil tanks twelve feet deep to jump down into through the hatchway if you dared. (If we ever had dared, God alone knows how we, four feet tall at most and unequipped with ropes, would have climbed out again.) And little fishing lodges and mill-wheel reservoirs with slurping whirlpool culverts that would have swallowed a child without any fuss at all, and next to them rusty steel dams three inches thick; the dare, of course, was to tightrope-walk the dam from one side to the other.

All of this was bloody brilliant and I absolutely loved it.

Funny how it was all right to expose us all to this sort of risk... yet allowing kids to experiment with gender was, and is, seen as far too dangerous.

Middle Earth
Witches lived by the pond in the Forestry once:
no bomb-site then, but ancient, unplumbed, elven.
Those summer-meadows' hay, those stands of spruce,
tangled and dry-scented, were our warren:

filled with our stealth, held monsters and sharp wonders,
strange painted devils for the eye of childhood,
held magic, black or white, or of as many colours
as Saruman's cloak in the story.

So for us
green hills and hillsides, Lancashire rain and wind,
gained faces of our fantasy, were turned into
the battleplace of armies long ago:
and chimneys, roads, and rooftops there below
became a makebelieve scarce worth our glances
while marvellous the runes and cognizances
of intricately-patterned dense-wrought shields
shone and flashed upon our empty fields.

'Life is freedom', wrote Vasily Grossman,[45] and consciousness is 'the flame of freedom'; 'what constitutes the freedom, the soul, of an individual life, is its uniqueness', 'The reflection of the universe in somebody's consciousness'. Each of us 'exists as a whole world that has never been repeated in all eternity'. And that is as true of trans people as of anyone else. Like everyone else, trans people have a unique perspective to offer on the world. That shouldn't be lost, just because some cis people 'have a problem with us'.

1.28: Things visible and invisible

My grandfather had four grandsons, if we count me. A thing he used to do with the four of us was roll up his own sleeve, flex his own considerable bicep, and say to us all: 'Right, lads, let's see your muscles.' At which we would all cackle, roll up our own sleeves, and flex our own puny little forearms alongside his; Grandpa would squeeze our biceps between his thumb and forefinger, purse his lips dubiously, shake his head definitively, and (lapsing into broadest Yorkshire) pronounce the inevitable verdict: 'Nay, lad, nay, yon's niver mooscles, tha's got mooscles like knots in cotton.' And we would all laugh aloud together, and think to ourselves that we needed to do better on the manliness front.

I don't know if my brother or my two male cousins started doing ten press-ups a night as a result of this little routine. But I certainly did. (And then twenty. And then thirty. At one stage I could do 150.) If I have

---

[45] Vasily Grossman, *Life and Fate*, trans. Robert Chandler (New York Review Books, 2006).

to go that way at all, I thought, if I have to go at being male, I suppose I might as well go at it hard. And in any case, I was a physical child who loved rough and tumble; and who grew up watching the majestic Welsh rugby sides of the mid-Seventies hammer everybody, including the England side that my father supported and I was supposed to support as well.

So there was rugby, which I was pretty good at (I was quick and I was forceful and I was combative). And there was climbing hills, something that I had been doing all along, but which I now realised could be done as a mark and an exercise of toughness, bravery, and 'mooscles', and not in the rather dreamy, hello-clouds-hello-sky sort of way that I naturally climbed hills (and still do). I tried out manliness because that was clearly expected of me, and because I hadn't, really, been left with any other way to go. I was funnelled into it, like a ewe-lamb into the rams' pen.

My grandfather helped me learn to love hill-walking, and story-telling, by taking me on (small-scale) hill walks while telling me stories. He also helped me to understand, as Eli helped Samuel to understand, who the Presence was that I was aware of from the beginning: he helped me give a name to that aspect of my world, my sense of the divine.

But the aspect of my world in which I was feminine? My sense of myself as, in some way that I could make no sense of, a girl really? No, that was absolutely off limits. As far as I can make out, it would have been nonsense to him too. He wouldn't have approved or understood at all.

The story in which I got turned into a girl, or got to live as a girl, or got to be a girl, openly, in at least some contexts: I was taught by my parents, and everyone else, that that was a story that was simply not to be told. And I was taught that I needed to look for other stories to tell about myself. And I went along with this.

From then on, whichever way you looked at it, being myself was always and inevitably going to involve *not* being myself. Everything became codes, everything became masks, everything became a foreign language or a secret script or a hidden cipher or a forced diversion; all expression became a matter of indirection and redirection.

I looked for other worlds, other imaginaries, other languages. I looked for ways of being that would provide me with an otherwhere, and with stories of otherwhere: stories that were *of otherwhere*, but that I was allowed to tell. And the more different they were from the ordinary world around me, the better.

I got drawn in to ancient Greece or Rome, and before them to Tutankhamen's Egypt too. I spent my imaginary life in Tolkien's Middle Earth, in C.S. Lewis's Narnia, in Ursula Le Guin's Earthsea. I invented languages and alphabets in imitation of Quenya or Sindarin. I discovered othernesses like Welshness, and the Welsh language: the secret Celtic underlay to the Anglo-Saxon (then Norman) world around me, its real but so-hidden-it-was-almost-lost identity. And I pored over maps to find the names that gave away Roman towns (Rochester, Alcester, Wroxeter, Caistor, Hincaster), and the straight lines of Roman roads between them (Stainforth, Spittal, Walgate, Watling Street – one branch of which went straight past Hawkshaw). Or like the characters in Alan Garner's wizardry-in-Cheshire novels, I looked for the roots and the foundations of things, for the underground networks that grown-ups weren't telling me about, for the magical deeper world that was, surely, hidden under the face of the prosaic everyday ordinary world. In the places that I knew best that were not strictly speaking home, in Kents Bank or in Hampshire for instance, I would walk out of the door into the cold and damp of the wood-scented night, and hear the owl call, and sense something deep and dark and thrilling at large in the icy blackness, almost within my touch, and be overwhelmed by an adrenalin-charged romantic longing for some kind of deeper secrets, something dark, deep, uncanny, unknowable, some kind of ghostly world that I could vanish into.

For vanish is in one sense exactly what I wanted to do with myself. Off the rugby pitch, I am not drawn to any kind of violence at all (I usually detest violent films, for example). So I am not drawn to violence against myself, either. At bad times, I did (and do) sometimes have what psychiatrists call suicidal ideations. But even at my most cornered and desperate, I have always remembered something else from Tolkien – namely Sam Gamgee at his darkest hour, lost and alone in the stinking, deadly blackness of Cirith Ungol, when he thinks that his beloved master Frodo is dead.

He looked on the bright point of his sword. He thought of the places behind where there was a black brink and an empty fall into nothingness. There was no escape that way. That was to do nothing, not even to mourn. That was not what he had set out to do. 'What am I to do then?' he cried again, and now he seemed plainly to know the hard answer: *See it through.*[46]

Like Sam, I have never, or hardly ever, been actually suicidal. In the times I am talking about here, that wasn't it. But what I *did* want to do was to vanish; to disappear; to become invisible. I wanted to erase myself from the world, like Frodo does when he puts on his ring. I wanted to stop being me. Being me simply felt too complicated; and I had a deep and persistent sense of the censure and disapproval of others. So I wanted, somehow, to get to a space where I was *simpler*, and where I was safe from that disapproval: a mountain top, perhaps. And how deeply I envied other and, as they seemed to me, less complicated people.

Sometimes I prayed like this.

Had enough
I'm tired of myself and my moods,
Of being controlled by my rages;
By old sorrow that festers and broods,
By the baggage of ages and ages;
My own spite that *must* settle its scores,
My stale repertoire of poses and masks.
I don't think I want to be me any more.
Please can you give me an easier task?

If I hadn't been me
I'd not have hurt B
Or offended A
Or driven C away;

If I hadn't been me
I'd have made it with D
Not split up with E
Thawed the cold war with F;
Almost certainly G
Would never have left;

[46] J.R.R. Tolkien, *The Lord of the Rings*, Book 2, Ch. 10.

My friendship with H would be just as before
Had my struggles with I not now led me to ask:
I don't think I want to be me any more.
Couldn't you give me an easier task?

Somewhere out there is a character simple,
A straight-up persona with no traps or wrinkles,
A cold shower of simplicity in which I'd bask,
All complexes kicked off outside the door:
Can't I be that, and not me any more?
Wouldn't I find that an easier task?

All the time, as a way to evade the ever-present danger that I would actually be myself, I would be myself by not being myself. Even when I wanted to draw attention to myself – and contradictorily, I wanted to do that too – it was as an actor. (I let out my gerontophilic side – the side of me that hero worshipped my grandfather, and Gandalf, and Merlyn, and Socrates, and the Badger in *Wind in the Willows*, and Professor Digory Kirke – as Scrooge; I might have expressed something of my transgender side as Teiresias, but at that time I didn't know the myths about his gender ambiguity.)

And somewhere in the gap between the everyday me and the deeper ghostly me, I lost all my four-year-old unreflective optimism and happiness about my own ability to present myself as I wanted to present, to be at home and comfortable in my own skin, to find a way of living happily in my own body despite the mismatch between the way it actually was and my private image of how I wanted it to be. As I turned teen, I began to find it unbearable even to look in a mirror, to make myself smart or present myself 'well-turned-out'. (If I am a scruff, I suspect it is, so to speak, motivated scruffiness.) Even trying to brush my own hair set off a kind of tantrum of impatience and frustration in my head, at the impossibility and unmanageability of it all. At the impossibility of *what* all, though? By now I had almost forgotten.

Because this is what I'm telling you, in case you're beginning to wonder. I'm telling you what it's like to be taught deliberately – and really quite successfully – that you aren't transgender at all.

Not malevolently or cruelly. On the contrary. This teaching, this conditioning, this *erasing*, was done with the very best of intentions. And not altogether nonconsensually. I wasn't a legally competent consenter, because I was too young. And I wasn't a psychologically competent consenter, because I didn't have a clear grasp on what was going on. (That was the whole point, to *subvert* my grasp on what was going on.) But I didn't resist the teaching. In fact I actively, and strenuously, aided it. I was a good little Christian soldier. I really wanted to please God, and to please my parents and teacher. So insofar as I was able, it was what I taught myself.

It can happen to you that you are not just repressed as a transgender person, but actually switched off: got into a condition where you don't even know any more that you are transgender.

Yes, this can happen. I know it can, because it happened to me. And to anyone observing me from outside, it would have looked like I had 'desisted' or 'detransitioned' – if I had ever transitioned in the first place, of course. It would have looked like I had been successfully deprogrammed from being transgender. But – well, that wasn't exactly the case.

> At school they taught me how to be
> So pure in thought and word and deed
> They didn't quite succeed ...

My transgender side was still there – but I was pretty secretive, and very much in denial, about it. Certainly, a trans-sympathetic psychotherapist, if there had been one around, would have had to go a long way down into my psyche to find the evidence that I was in fact transgender. And I wouldn't have thanked them for the diagnosis, any more than my parents would have. Any such psychotherapist would have been at severe risk of being charged with 'conversion therapy' – taking hold of a non-trans child, and 'turning them trans'.

And yet – the diagnosis would have been correct.

1.29: Role models

It was all impossible, and the whole world around me was telling me that it was impossible. In my family, where my parents and grandparents were all (relatively gently) insisting that boys were meant to be big and strong and brave. At school, where with every week that passed the same norms of boyhood were ever less gently, and ever more rigorously, imposed – by everyone including me, on everyone including me.

'You can be anything you like. Just not *that*.'

It was exactly the same message every time I switched on the TV or went to the theatre. For a boy who wanted to be a girl – or who had once wanted that, but was now so far from recognising the want in himself that he could barely even name it – what were the role models or icons in 1975 or '76?

There was the preposterous sequinned over-the-top-ness of Danny La Rue and Liberace. There was the spiteful, mean-spirited parading of stereotypes that was Dick Emery's stock in trade. The mincing, lisping, face-painted, limp-wristed queeniness of Gloria in *It Ain't Half Hot Mum* and the pert double-entendre campness of Mr Humphries in *Are You Being Served?* There were brash panto dames of various depressingly loud and vulgar kinds. There were one or two contemptuous swipes in *Monty Python*, most obviously in 'The Lumberjack Song'. There was a running gag about Tim Brooke-Taylor in *The Goodies*. At least Les Dawson's lugubrious mill-worker beldames, Cissy and Ada, were a genuine Lancashire type that I recognised from a hundred bus stops, church jumble sales, and village shop counters, and could happily laugh at and almost empathise with. But I didn't want to *be* Cissy or Ada, any more than I wanted to be a panto dame or Bombardier Beaumont or Tim Brooke-Taylor as Queen Victoria.

Nowhere in all of this was there anything like a positive image of what it might be like to be a boy who wanted to be a girl. There simply were – for all I knew – no stories of the kind I needed to be able to tell. Everything I saw told me loud and clear that to be a boy who wanted to be a girl was to be at least absurd, and probably despicable too. And under no circumstances could someone like that be *beautiful*. Without exception, the message was: everyone like that was ridiculous, and some of them were actually revolting.

Had I been more with-it musically speaking, I might have noticed the androgynousness that David Bowie and Marc Bolan and Freddie Mercury were up to; and above all, of course, Lou Reed. But I am a perpetual latecomer to happening scenes. Most of my rock music I got from my older brother, by slow and (on my side) involuntary sound-osmosis across the corridor between our bedrooms; even Bowie was barely on my radar until I got older and bolder, in the Eighties. There was something about T. Rex that I liked, especially *Metal Guru* (the first song that I ever remember hearing on *Top of the Pops*, in 1972); it had something sensual and subversive to it, but I was a bit scared to go near it in case I got caught up in it, in case I liked it too much. In case it infected me. I didn't even have the nerve (or the pocket money) to buy my first single until 1979, and that was not about self-expression, but about the murderously toxic anger of self-repression: it was *I Don't Like Mondays*.

The nearest thing to with-it that I had, and the nearest thing to affirmation too, was Kenny Everett. He looked a bit risqué to my parents, but once I was allowed to watch him I found him absolutely hilarious. And it was actually on his shows that I encountered, for the first time, an outrageous piece of cross-dressing that was apparently done without the slightest shame, with tremendous pizzazz and bravura, and with obvious enjoyment and quite possibly sexual pleasure on Kenny's own part.

So there we have it: right up to my teenage years in the early 1980s, the most positive role model I had for transgender was Kenny Everett's cross-dressing parody porn-star Cupid Stunt.

I mean, yeah. I know, right?

1.30: *The stories we have to tell*

The more society around you insists on the exclusive partition of the two genders, the more you want to cross that partition – from the 'Boys' Division' to the 'Girls' Division'; the more you want to be on the other side. The more unreachable the other side is, the more alluring it is.

Though I barely knew what I was doing – though I hid what I was doing not only from other people but even from myself – this was a story about myself that I could not help telling, despite all the discouragement, negative reinforcement, and disapproval that everyone around me told me to feel. And I did feel it; I did disapprove of myself. Yet even so, I needed that otherwise. Dressing as a girl in secret provided me with some obscure kind of psychological refuge, a bizarre little oasis of strangely tranquil happiness, utterly contradictory to the rest of my life. But the more it contradicted it, the better. Privately subverting and undercutting the dreary grey-flannel public me was deliriously exciting, a joyful secret liberation; but it was frightening too. It felt like self-harm, maybe even self-destruction.

Dressing feminine didn't just bring me tranquillity. As any reader of Tolkien might have predicted. And from the age of six onward, I was an avid reader of Tolkien. (I have read *The Lord of the Rings* perhaps forty or fifty times; I don't read it as much or as obsessively as I used to, but my Sindarin is still passable.) Being transgender may be euphoria, but it is also, as they say, dysphoria. Rings of Power are addictive, Tolkien taught me, and the addiction is evil and destructive. The more you give in to it, the more it turns you into – something different. Something wonderfully invisible, for sure; but not the beautiful girl that I longed to be. Instead, it turns you into an evil spirit either squalidly pathetic or satanically terrifying or both: into Gollum, or into a Ring-Wraith. (Given the uncanny fit between this bit of Tolkien's mythology and my own phenomenology when I was trying to extirpate my own transness, I have sometimes wondered what he had in his closet.)

It felt like sin, and maybe that feeling was addictive in itself. When I was teetering on the brink of dressing up as a girl, I would be all atremble, a bag of nerves, full of guilt but full of elation too, unsure whether to go on or to stop. I would toss a coin (repeatedly if necessary, best of seven if best of three didn't give me the answer I wanted), or riffle through the pages of the Bible to see whether I met the word Yes first, or the word No (I became quite good at knowing where in Scripture I was likeliest to find the word Yes, and how to avoid occurrences of the word No). And once I had taken the leap, jumped into it, seen myself in the mirror looking (to my delight and giggly relief) at least a bit feminine, I wanted to stay as a girl for ever and ever...

Until, within the hour, I was overcome by guilt and shame and self-disgust. And tore it all down. Again.

Travesti
Delight, then dread. Epiphany, then farce.
Crushed by his guilt at being the she he asked,

lost between masks for all his thirteen years,
his lonely compass fixed on his hated error,

a boy in a dress and his self-murdering tears.
The peacock's beak stabs at the reflex mirror.

I could get very afraid about where all this was going, what I was doing to myself, where it might be heading if I let it. And, despite the guilt, I so wanted to let it.

For most people, the teenage years are probably the high season for guilt, and they certainly were for me. But I felt guilty long before I hit adolescence, because everyone and everything around me was telling me that boys were not supposed to be the way I knew quite well I was: the way I kept finding I couldn't help being.

So I felt guilt, and I felt just plain puzzlement. Why could girls wear boring old clingy dull-coloured trousers if they liked, when boys couldn't wear pretty, floaty, primary colour frocks and dresses if they liked? Why could a girl put on my soldier outfit to play in, and get chuckles and smiles of approval and pats on the head, whereas if I put on her ballet tutu to play in, it was like I'd been caught trying to blow up Westminster Abbey?

And why, too, when girls' clothes were (as I then thought) so wonderful, did girls themselves seem so indifferent to them? Imagine (I used to think) – just imagine not only being free to dress like that; but being so free to dress like that that you don't even bother to.

Not To Miss
Why *do* so many pretty girls
dress as much like boys
as it is possible to,

preferring muffling serge
to frilled silk's noise
net petticoats' frou-frou?
If you *could* taste such clothes'
transposing joys
why *wouldn't* you?

Hmm. At this point, maybe it is time for me to say a bit about sex.

1.31: Bizarre and unpleasant accusations, part 1: 'Fetishists'

A number of bizarre and unpleasant accusations are routinely made, especially online, about transgender people, especially trans women. I've seen them made against myself. In 1.31–1.33, I am going to tackle three of them head-on.

First I need to explain first why these are unpleasant accusations. There's nothing morally wrong, per se, with being either a sexual fetishist or a confused homosexual. (There is with being a narcissist, of course, but put that aside for now.) Some people are into the fetish scene in all its strangeness and variety, and – provided they don't hurt anyone, it's in private, between consulting adults, it's not some psychopathology speaking, etc. – good luck to them. As a rule, I don't share their tastes (I just find it bizarre and comical that anyone would want to do... *that*, let alone get turned on by doing it); but then, thank goodness, no one's asking me to. And some other people are, certainly, 'confused homosexuals': that is, they think they're something else, but homosexual is what they really are. Such people have my sympathy. They certainly don't have my moral condemnation, nor should they have anyone's. A bit of help talking it through might be more apposite.

So why are 'merely fetishists' and 'merely confused gays' unpleasant accusations? The weight is on the word 'merely'. What is the point of saying these obviously false things about trans women? (And notice that, once again, these false accusations are made against trans *women*; trans men are either erased – again – or subjected to other kinds of misrepresentation.)

What is the point? The point is a kind of glibly cynical, armchair-Freudian reductionism: 'Get you with your fancy claims about identity, we know all you're really after is sexual gratification.' It is to insinuate that trans women are, as a class, self-deceptive, perhaps dishonest with themselves: they claim (to want) to be women, but in truth they're just blokes who want to get their rocks off. In saying these things, the accuser denies trans women's own reports about themselves, and sets himself on the way to claiming that trans women don't even exist (not at least as what they claim to be); for more about this claim, see 2.3 below. Simultaneously he equates trans women, as a class, with two other classes of people, both of whom the accuser evidently takes a rather dim and moralistic view of. (It is a remarkable feature of so much transphobic discourse, how quickly it joins hands with the most conventional kinds of puritanism.)

So, to begin with the fetishism accusation. Maybe some self-described trans women are 'merely' fetishists, and/or 'just' people who are (in the sexual sense) 'into' cross-dressing or cosplay, and/or get their kicks by dressing up as a French maid or Bo Peep or whatever. Like I say: nothing wrong with that, provided they're honest about what they're really like.

However: that isn't what I am really like. I certainly go for a particular kind of look, a certain approach, that I wear because I like it and because I think it suits me, and/or is as near suiting me as anything is likely to be. But for one thing, so do some cis women: no one accuses them of fetishism simply because they enjoy dressing a particular way.

Round about this point in the argument, transphobes like to throw around the scientifically dubious term 'autogynephilia', a long word meaning the kink of getting sexual pleasure out of thinking of oneself as a woman. Whether or not we decide to call it a kink, there certainly is such a pleasure. But the thing is, it's not only trans women who experience it. At least some cis women get this sexual pleasure too: they find it sexy to be feminine. When exactly did being sexually fulfilled in your own femininity become a bad thing?

Oh, and men also do this, and not just the gay ones: they find it sexy to look in the mirror and see how masculine they are. So will they be accused of (shock horror) autoandrophilia? When exactly did being sexually fulfilled in your own masculinity become a bad thing? Of course, going too far with this kind of feeling could be 'narcissistic' (another standard accusation against trans people – see below). But why should we believe that any manifestation at all of this feeling is automatically 'going too far'? A remarkable feature of so much transphobic discourse is just how quickly it turns into middle-class moralising.

For my own part, I wasted far too many decades thinking I was as ugly as could be to pass up any opportunity that I get today to be as close to beautiful as I can possibly manage. I think that given my own particular story, the story that I am telling here, and all the sadness and repression and desperation and self-hatred that there was in it because I was trying so hard for nearly three decades to be not transgender – given all that baggage, it's kind-of-politically important for me, not to mention psychologically healing, to affirm to myself that it's perfectly okay (indeed not just perfectly okay, but perfectly brilliant) for me to dress just a little bit… celebratory. And the best way to affirm that is to do it.

And I suspect, anyway, that people who throw around the 'fetishism' and 'autogynephilia' accusations have just not reflected sufficiently on the simple practicalities of being a trans woman. For anyone at all, deciding how to dress, how to present in public, is a matter of finding a compromise between the look I like and the look I can carry off. Cis women have to sort this out; trans women and trans men have to sort it out as well. So, in fact, do cis men, though in our society men are less policed than women are about their presentation.

But if, like me, you are a trans woman who is not all that likely to pass as a cis woman, then if you want to be out of the closet at all, you will need to find a reasonably dignified and graceful way of presenting yourself that (a) is fun, and (b) makes best use of what you've got. And that, in case you're wondering, is exactly what I try to do. To the 'gender critical' people online who repeatedly jeer and snark at my looks, I can't think of much to say beyond these three things: (1) I don't know why you imagine that you can think of a single criticism of my appearance that I haven't thought of myself; (2) criticising trans women for 'looking like men' while refusing trans girls any kind of healthcare that might help them *not* to 'look like men' is a pretty emphatic case of having it both ways; and (3): Keep it classy, guys.

Is this exactly how I want to look? Of course it isn't, nowhere near. But a lot of cis women – and cis men – would say that too. And short of a great deal of very expensive, painful, and time-consuming intervention, it's my best shot. And it's not *so* terrible. And being able to go at any rate this far towards 'a measureless consummation that she dreamt' is profoundly healing and liberating.

Like anyone sensible, I am after no less than perfection. And like anyone mortal, I don't get there. So? Can the people who jeer really not see that we are all of us in the same basic predicament, them too – just by being mortal and imperfect?

If I make the lashes dark
And the eyes more bright
And the lips more scarlet,

Or ask if all be right
From mirror after mirror,
No vanity's displayed:
I'm looking for the face I had
Before the world was made.

What if I look upon a man
As though on my beloved,
And my blood be cold the while
And my heart unmoved?
Why should he think me cruel
Or that he is betrayed?
I'd have him love the thing that was
Before the world was made.

It's also true, of course, that the further a trans woman's dress sense (or any woman's dress sense) goes in the direction of personal idiosyncrasy, the less plausible it sounds to claim that that woman is 'reinforcing stereotypes' or otherwise somehow compelling other women to dress like her. Fashion is an aesthetic language; and in that language, as in any other, both cliché and originality, both prefab sloganeering and pure poetry, are possibilities. I like to think that I'm actually fairly creative in the way I present myself. I certainly don't have any expectation at all that I am setting a norm, playing a lead, that anyone else is obliged to follow. (Nor do they follow it.)

I hate gender stereotypes too, actually. In particular, I find 'blokeyness' unbearable. I never could stand being 'one of the boys', even when I apparently was one of the boys: 'So many false assumptions about who I am here', I used to think, 'and every one of them mandatory till I get out of this hell-scene.' (This accidental hell-scene; there was nothing malicious about the blokeyness usually; it was just so very, very blokey.) But I also think it's possible to play with such stereotypes, whether masculine or feminine: to subvert them by, for example, gentle mockery. It is possible, too, to make the stereotypes your servants, not your masters: to use those forms in novel and surprising ways that take us beyond cliché and deadness of mind into new territories. And that is what I try to do in my own ways of presenting myself.

Given my physiological history, I am never going to fade into the background. Well, then, I might as well try to be something reasonably pleasant to look at in the foreground.

In any case, being a trans woman – at least in my case – has never been just about the clothes. It isn't even, believe it or not, primarily about the clothes. And – with the usual cautions about generalising from my own case – I'd say that, as far as I can see, that's how it is for most trans women. It's more about acceptance: it's about being seen and known as who you really are, without indignity or derision or contempt.

It's true, of course, that there are quite a lot of different things that someone could want here. You could just want women's clothing – in general, or particular kinds of women's clothing, more or less 'practical' or more or less 'sexy' – and you could want it for sexual reasons, or because you feel it expresses your personality better than men's clothing, or for both these reasons, or for other reasons again. You could just want to be girly rather than boyish (and certainly I want to be girly). You could just want to have a woman's viewpoint on the world, whatever you take that to be. Or again, distinct from all these possibilities, you could want a woman's gender role, whatever that might be in the society you happen to live in. That's certainly possible – though in our society, I'm not sure anyone has reason to want that, and perhaps they couldn't have in any likely society where gender roles exist at all.

I will say more about gender roles later. For now, I will just say this: *pace* the 'gender critical feminists', I don't think gender roles are necessarily oppressive. I do think that we can and should play with them sometimes, and that playing with them can be subversive. Still, on the whole, I agree with those 'gender criticals' that gender roles *in our society* are a bad and oppressive thing, and consequently that a healthy way of being transgender can't be mainly about taking on the female gender role as it is, unquestioningly and uncritically. (The word 'transgender' is itself less helpful here than the older term 'transsexual', which has been seen as problematic because it is heard as saying that transsexuality is – 'merely' – about sexuality.)

But there's another possibility, different from all the above, and this I think is the key one. You could want to have a woman's body: to be a woman not (or not just) sartorially or socially or psychologically, but physically. Whatever else other people may want, and like I say there are probably all sorts of things, it seems to me that this last – the bodily want – is the real and most basic want, in me and in other trans women: to be physically a woman. I like women's clothes, and I like being girly as well. But ultimately being transgender, at least for me, is about having a body that is the one shape, and wanting a body that is the other shape.

Like I said in 1.14: as a child, as soon as I saw myself naked in a mirror I disliked what I saw. Right from the beginning I felt disappointment, irritation, frustration, anxiety, and a mild but abiding revulsion that, with my clothes off, I was roughly the same shape as my brother, and not at all the same shape as my sister. And right from the beginning I was trying to do something about that. (Here we are back at the myth that transgender is learned behaviour: long before anyone might have even permitted me to fix my appearance, let alone encouraged me or taught me how, I worked it out – or worked a bit of it out – for myself.)

But then, if being a trans woman is all about wanting a female body, why might you want the other things too? Well, first, you might not: I know some trans women, and more trans men, who really aren't inter-ested in anything much except the bodily transformation. But, secondly, you might want the other things because you think they go with a female body; you might think that they're (social or sartorial or psychological or whateverological) markers of being female: you want to be female, so you want the markers. Thirdly, if having a male body causes you distress, as it does me, then you might want to use feminine clothing to hide or change the shape of a basically male body, e.g. by enhancing the hips and the chest and tucking in the waist and the crotch. And then the clothing and the look just become ways of expressing (and coping with) the longing to be physically a woman. They can of course also be straightforwardly fun – as I find they are myself: I am not so blasé about dressing this way that I no longer find it a complete giggle. Dressing feminine – as feminine as possible – has always made me very simply happy, at least when I am not smashing myself up feeling guilty for doing it. It still does: it is still a relief and a liberation. These things matter more if you aren't prepared – for health or age or whatever other reasons – to go in for hormones and surgery.

(According to the online bigots, there is another double bind for trans people here: if they don't go in for medical interventions then clearly 'they don't really mean it', whereas if they do go for medical interventions then they are 'mutilating themselves' and 'putting themselves in the hands of Zionist big pharma'. It's amazing what people can be got to say sometimes.)

You might also think that these other things, clothing and look and so on, are easier to achieve than the literal – surgical – bodily transformation from male to female. And this last thought, I submit, is just obviously true. It is easier to put on the right makeup and the right clothes, so that (if you're lucky enough to have the right physique) you come out of the changing room looking exactly like a natural-born woman, or as much like one as you want to look, and so get treated in social interactions as if you are a natural-born woman – in nice ways, I mean, accepting ways, not oppressive ones. All of this is far easier than it is to undergo gender-reassignment surgery. The latter is a major undertaking, and you might not know it was even a possibility; if you were born long enough ago, like me, it might barely even be a possibility. A five-year-old kid in a village in Lancashire in 1970 has no access to hormones or surgery or anything like that (not even to decent hair or makeup). What he does have access to is the dressing-up box, and his mother's and sister's clothing cupboards. It's hardly surprising if he expresses his desperate desire to be a girl by taking the simplest and quickest route available to him towards being a girl: namely, dressing as a girl.

So picture that five-year-old, seeing himself in the bedroom mirror dressed in clothes that are as girly as he can manage with the resources available to him, for what no doubt wasn't the first time, but is the first time he later remembers, and feeling a deep happiness spreading right through him like the warmth of the sun; a happiness he's never known from anywhere else, a happiness that puts butterflies in his stomach and a huge grin on his face and the desire to dance in his toes, a happiness that is both excitement and peace, both exhilaration and relief, both a giggle and a sigh of contentment, at the same time. If you picture him in what it actually was, a white ballet tutu and a broken plastic tiara, maybe he looks ridiculous to you. But I can tell you for sure that he didn't feel ridiculous, not at all. Because for me this is not something I need to picture; for me it's a memory, it really happened, and it was really beautiful. And these days, now I've finally made peace with myself and let myself be what I am, getting dressed in the morning can still feel just that beautiful.

Is that little kid a fetishist, then? About the small child that I was in 1970, that doesn't seem to me an apposite question, for at least two reasons. First, five-year-olds are five-year-olds: small children. We shouldn't be at all quick to call a five-year-old child a fetishist – if it even makes sense to do that. From asking around among other trans women, I know that being a trans woman often manifests itself in adolescence in ways that look like fetishism. But any such development is way off in the future for a five-year-old.

But anyway, secondly, what is a fetish? There have been some ingenious and frankly rather bizarre theories about that; for example, Freud's view that the fetish-object is there because the little boy has been traumatised by discovering that his mother has no penis, and tries to replace her 'missing penis' (but why does he want to?) with some other object which then becomes his fetish. My own view of what a fetish is is much simpler, and I think less counterintuitive. It doesn't, for instance, imply that a fetish has to be an object; as far as I can see, it's just as likely to be a look, or, come to that, a feel. And my own view doesn't imply that only men can be fetishists, which seems to me a clear, and clearly false, implication of Freud's account.

On my view, a fetish is simply a dissociated particular sexual taste. To see what I mean by that, think about tastes in a more general sense: in particular about the relation between large- and small-scale tastes. We might watch a film, and love the way the heroine walks across the street in some particular scene in it. We might then come to see the heroine's walk as just one part of what we love about the film overall. Or we might buy the DVD of the film, just in order to focus in on that ten-second sashay, and play it again and again and again; we might lose all interest altogether in the rest of the film, and become obsessed just by that sequence. Likewise with music: we might love (as in fact I do love) the final deep octave chord of the baritone aria *Omnia sol temperat* from Carmina Burana. And here too, we might either see that chord as just one component of the oratorio's overall magic; or we might decide it's the only thing in the whole work that we really care about.

Now focusing in in this way on one bit of a work of art is clearly something that we might do to a greater or lesser degree. I might replay the heroine's sashay twenty times today, but thereafter be no more interested in it than in the rest of the film; on the other hand, I might permanently lose interest in anything else in the film except the sashay. And whatever degree I do it to, this focusing in on one bit might or might not be aesthetically perverse. For some possible oratorio, there is a deep octave-chord in it which genuinely is the one thing in the whole work that's actually musically good. In many cases, though, including Carmina Burana, such an obsessiveness about one moment would be a kind of mistake – not least because, as usual in music, the moment depends constitutively upon its context.

Likewise, then, with sexual tastes. Obsessive focus on one particular bit or aspect of some sexual experience, or some experience that is sexual for you, might happen to one degree or another; might be more or less permanent; and might be more or less justified and reasonable, relative to the merits or demerits of the larger whole of which it is part. (Where merits and demerits are assessed by reference to whatever standards apply in the area of sexual taste. And there most certainly are such standards; the central distinctive ones are sort-of-aesthetic.)

We may now perhaps be able to see why 'fetish' is such a condemnatory word in our society. It is because we use 'fetishism' in a sexual context as we use 'idolatry' in a religious context; it's because we use 'fetishism' exclusively of a sexual focusing that is particular, obsessive, and detached from the rest of the wider spectrum of available experience to a degree that we have decided to condemn.

The opposite of fetishism is integration. Fetishism is, as I said, essentially dissociative; and dissociation is usually (though not always or necessarily) a bad thing, just as integration is usually (though not always or necessarily) a good one.

Now in a society like ours, and like the one I grew up in, transgender people tend to find themselves under severe social, psychological, religious, and ethical pressures. The tendency of those pressures is, whether visibly or invisibly, to make pariahs of transgender people; and one thing that this means is a pressure towards dissociation (along with secrecy, shame, and self-abomination). In such a society, transgender self-expression is overwhelmed by a tsunami of contempt and disapproval. What that tsunami tends to leave behind is battered little islands that are really relics of a submerged continent: disconnected fragments of what might become integrated in transgender people, if they were ever given a chance to integrate it. Without that chance, no wonder trans people (trans women in particular) sometimes look to society at large like fetishists. And no wonder they do sometimes take things to extremes. They haven't been left anywhere else to take them.

The cure for a fetish, when one is needed (and it isn't always; it depends on circumstances, context, and what the fetish actually involves), is integration. An obsession with one particular object or look or way of dressing, whether pre-sexual as it will be in a five-year-old, or sexual as it is likely to be in a fifteen-year-old, can be the only part showing above the surface of something that goes much wider and deeper in the libido, but which has been driven below the surface by the social and moral pressure of anger, shame, disgrace, and condemnation. Once those pressures are removed, the dissociated obsession can, given time and healing, become part of a broader and deeper integration not just of the libido, but of the entire psyche. It can turn out that what appeared just to be an isolated and inexplicable sexual kink was actually a sign of an entire sexual orientation; indeed, not just of a sexual orientation, but of an orientation of the whole being.

And this means that the best answer to those who say that being a trans woman is 'really sexual' is not 'No no *NO*, it's not sexual, it's something else.' Rather it is: 'Of course it's sexual. Being transgender touches everything there is in the psyche, and sexuality is one of the things that are there in the psyche. It includes that because it includes *everything*.'

1.32: Bizarre and unpleasant accusations, part 2: 'Narcissists'

They leave trans people with nowhere else to turn except in on themselves.

Then they call them narcissists.

Being transgender is not narcissism. Being transgender is about everything that we are; so it is about our inwardness and self-understanding, too. And when the whole world 'out there' is hostile to a trans person's being honest about who they are, it's hardly surprising if that trans person looks away from the world 'out there'. When there is nothing that we are allowed to do to work on our outward expressions of our being, is it really so surprising if we turn to the inward expressions? The charge of narcissism is just another form of victim-blaming.

I feel like cracking the old joke: 'Of course I talk to myself; it's the only way of getting an intelligent conversation.' But the unfunny truth

here is that it's not even like the trans person in our society is necessarily guaranteed a safe space, even inside their own head. Even the trans
person's self-understanding can be subverted and distorted; you can be so
thoroughly indoctrinated by the world out there that, even inside your
head, you can reject and despise yourself. This happened to me. That's
what I'm talking about.

But if we really have to talk about narcissism, then what should we say
about the trans-exclusionary people – who I know for a fact exist – whose
engagement with this very book will probably consist mainly in thumbing
through these pages to see if I mention them at all?[47] Perhaps, too, in
concluding that, if I talk about 'narcissists' without naming names, then I
must be talking about them; an almost comically self-fulfilling conclusion.
A startlingly high proportion of trans-exclusionary activists have this
extraordinary knack for making 'the transgender debate' all about them.
I don't doubt for a moment that they'll try to do it with this book too.

1.33: Bizarre and unpleasant accusations, part 3: 'Confused gays'

Being transgender is not narcissism. And it's not a sexual fetish either.
But being transgender modulates and conditions pretty much every
aspect of your being; so it modulates and conditions your sexuality, too.
There is a specifically transgender way to be a sexual being; or, no doubt,
a whole range of ways.

But sometimes, trans-exclusionaries – still intent on their mission
to make out the preposterous claim that trans people don't really exist,

---

[47] Spoiler: nope. As a matter of deliberate policy (see 1.10, paragraph 4), and partly
to make legal vexatiousness less likely (see 1.18), in this book I don't name *any* trans-
exclusionary activists, as such.

Trans-exclusionary activists do, at any rate, have one talent: they're quite brilliant
at making the existence of trans people *all about them*. I am interested in reversing
this, because you know what? The existence of trans people is *not* all about the
people who don't much like us, and apparently (sometimes by their own avowal)
wish we didn't exist. It's about *us*: ourselves, the actual trans people.

So, no names. Not one, not once – unless Patriarch Kirill counts, or unless Part
VI furnishes an exception.

Bad luck, chaps. Keep fishing for things to be offended by. You will find plenty
if I have done my job.

at least not as what they claim to be – tell us that we trans women are really confused gays: we only pretend to be transgender because we're too ashamed to admit that we're really homosexuals. At other times, trans-exclusionaries tell us that we trans women are really heterosexuals, 'cosplaying as the opposite sex and as "gay"' (to quote one particularly nasty online troll). There is also, of course, the wearily familiar charge that trans people erase gay people by redefining what it is to be a man or a woman in a way that makes it impossible to talk about same-sex attraction…

This is a muddle, of course. These three accusations can't all be true, not at any rate of the same trans women. As a matter of fact, not even one of them is true.

As I've already pointed out in 1.18, trans people don't deny that 'sex is real' or that 'biology is real' or that 'sex matters' (to quote once more the threadbare trans-exclusionary slogans). How ironic to imagine that we do, given that trans people, by definition, spend their whole lives preoccupied with the reality and the significance of their own sex and biology. So neither do we deny the reality or the significance of same-sex attraction. As far as I'm concerned, odd cases aside, the people who are lesbian or gay are the people who *say* they are lesbian or gay. In this area, the key criterion is self-identification, it seems to me. (And notice by the way that no one questions gay people's right to self-identify as gay or lesbian: despite the real possibility of dangerous imposture, no one thinks that the procedure of being confirmed as gay or lesbian should be medicalised. The contrast with trans people's experience is, unfortunately, glaring.)

Nor, while we're on this sub-topic, do trans people say that it is automatically transphobic to prefer to have a cisgender person as a sexual partner – any more than it is automatically cisphobic to prefer a transgender partner. When it comes to choosing sexual partners, it's a matter of taste. Some people prefer blondes, some people prefer Brummies; and they are perfectly at liberty to have whatever sexual tastes they like, and are not automatically criticisable for those tastes. The same applies to trans and cis.

Of course there are some other kinds of possible cases around here, where some people do seem to display some kind of prejudice. Suppose you find out, having never known before, that your wife of twenty years had a Jewish maternal grandmother. Therefore she is, technically speaking, Jewish herself, and so are the children you have brought into the world together. If you find this out and somehow it changes everything for you – all of a sudden you don't find her attractive, and you can't bear the sight of your own children either – then maybe you shouldn't just put this down as a harmless matter of taste; maybe you should be worried about your own implicit attitudes. Similarly, if you find out, having never known before, that your wife of twenty years was born a man. If that puts you off her, why does it put you off? What does your sudden aversion to her say about you?

(Notice, incidentally, that both cases are perfectly possible. Trans-exclusionaries seem to have great difficulty accepting the plain and manifest fact that not all transgender people are obviously transgender, or even detectably transgender without specialised equipment and/or access to their medical records. Yet so it is, as a multitude of cases from history shows. It is really important to remember how wide a range of transgender presentations there are; again, compare some other minorities. Some of us stick out like a sore thumb; probably me, for instance. But don't tell me you 'haven't noticed that there are transgender people who don't stick out like a sore thumb'. Because of course you haven't, because they don't.)

I say that 'being transgender modulates and conditions pretty much every aspect of your being; so it modulates and conditions your sexuality, too'. All right, then: how – to get really personal – does it modulate and condition mine?

You may be relieved to hear that I can define my sexual orientation in a single word. The word is *picky*. I have a keen eye for, and a strong sense of, beauty in human beings, and where I find it it haunts me and inflames me. And I am by no means exclusive in what types of human beings I find sexually attractive – both male and female, both trans and cis, both gay and straight, and all the boundary cases too. I also, however, have rather high standards. I am distinctly critical, a tough judge of beauty. And sometimes, unfortunately, I turn these weapons on myself: I am not such a bad-looking human being, but I have never looked as good as I'd like to. (But then, who does?)

Alongside *picky*, I am also *reticent* and *bumbling*. Articulate though I am about most things, I am, let's face it, absolutely hopeless at chatting people up, or at talking to them in any way about the flame that I burn for them. (On the relatively rare occasions when I do burn a flame for someone. But like I say, I'm picky.)

So how does my being a trans woman play into this? Well, it makes a difference between how I am sexually attracted to men, and how I am sexually attracted to women. When I am attracted to either, and when people notice that I'm attracted to them. But as well as being picky, reticent, and bumbling, I am also married – I have been since 1988: I am therefore 'not in the game', and very grateful not to be, given how bad I am at playing it.

Now if someone wants to come along and tell me either that I don't really mean the bit about my being attracted to women, or that I don't really mean the bit about my being attracted to men, then my instinct in both cases is the same. It's to shrug and smile and say 'Sure, you tell yourself that if you like.' *How would they know what's going on inside me?* Why should I believe their misinterpretation of my experience, or even take it remotely seriously, when I know about my own experience directly – from experience?

Of all the ridiculous lies that trans-exclusionaries tell about transgender people, I think the one about us being gay really, but too embarrassed to admit it, is perhaps the most extraordinary. But they really do retail this nonsense, even though they sometimes retract it or walk it back or try to deny it. I have had some of the UK's most high-profile trans-exclusionaries of all say exactly this to me, plain as daylight, face to face, and then afterwards they fervently deny that they ever said it, and call me a liar for reminding them that they did… And then a bit later than that, they're saying it again.

Where on earth did these people grow up? Where is this mythical society where being transgender is not a hundred times more embarrassing and shameful than being gay? It's certainly not Britain, at any point in the last sixty years, or probably ever. Didn't these people even go to school?

Here I'll get narrative again. One moral of the next bit of narrative, in case you're wondering, is going to be this: if typical trans women are anything like me, then typical trans women would make absolutely rubbish sexual predators. They wouldn't know where to begin even on being pushy towards anyone else. They don't even know how to ask for a date.

And another moral will be the following: being trans and being gay, or (more accurately in my case) bisexual, are different things. You can be both. They might even be connected in some ways; but they're not the same thing. They're not two settings of the same dial; they're different dials. Each is its own thing. Neither is a 'confused' version of the other: you could be either, without that meaning you had to be the other as well.

And how do I know this? Same answer as before: I know it from my own case. Hence the narrative.

1.34: *Doing completely the right thing, completely by accident*

I was walking down the stairs at school on a usual wet Tuesday in about 1980, bowed down and burdened with the usual woes and worries of school, dreading the upcoming Double Games period (it was going to be football, not rugby, and I hated football). And I saw coming up the stairs past me another boy in my year whom I didn't know very well. A rather beautiful boy, I'd always thought. (And it was the *rather* beautiful ones, not the extravagantly beautiful ones, that in my picky way particularly got to me. I secretly liked – and I still do secretly like – things to be subtle, not brassy or OTT or in-your-face. It's always the quiet ones. But it's like having a stone in your shoe. You feel attracted to them, and then you instantly feel guilty for feeling attracted to them, and try not to feel attracted to them, and fail wretchedly; and round and round the psychological carousel you go, feeling worse and worse.)

He was slightly built and slender, straight auburn hair, bright blue eyes, smooth pale complexion, little round gold glasses that gave him a delightfully studious look. As he went past he said casually to me 'I just heard games are off'. And without thinking about it at all, in my relief and elation I leant over and kissed him loudly on the cheek. And he went white as a sheet, and put his hand on the place where I'd just kissed him, and carried on up the stairs saying nothing. And I did a double take, thrilled with horror at the utter, utter giveaway I'd just committed, called myself a bloody idiot, and carried on down the stairs saying nothing.

I was indeed appalled at myself for doing that. But I was also, secretly, totally delighted by it. For one moment, just one moment, of pure subversion, I had managed to break free of the grinding, crushing, enslaving constraints of the dour, sour, ugly, jeering, puritanical, Testosterone-Police State that he and I both had the misfortune to live in. For just one moment, I had managed to do something that said 'It doesn't have to be like this. Gentleness, kindness, delight in each other's company – and each other's appearance – is possible. Displays of affection are possible, even (oh my God!) between two teenage boys. Love is possible.'

> Everybody screamed
> when I kissed the pupil
> and they must have thought they dreamed
> when I kissed the pupil...

I just hope I didn't embarrass him too much; I'm pretty sure no one saw us.

I have no idea how being kissed by me felt for him. But for me, kissing him felt unbelievably wonderful. And it was so funny; such an impossible, surreal, drunken moment, yet it actually happened. It was, in fact, the first time I had ever romantically kissed anyone.

For me the afterglow of happiness from this ridiculous, extravagant transgression lasted a whole week. But naturally, after that, he and I could never ever EVER speak a single word to each other. And naturally, neither he nor I ever ever EVER said a word about it afterwards, not to anyone, not under any circumstances. Until just now.

I wonder how he's getting on these days. I wonder if he remembers that reckless impulse of mine as vividly as I do. I bet I didn't 'turn him gay'; he was always going to be whatever he was going to be, the same as the rest of us. The moment didn't *change* anything in me, either. Not *change*, as opposed to *show up what was there already.*

Whether he remembers it or not, I hope he's happy, and well; and I hope he's well-loved.

I can't even remember his name. Not his first name, though I do remember his surname, and I'm not telling. (Oh wait – writing this has brought his first name back to me too. Still not telling.)

Wherever and whoever he is now, my very best wishes to him.

1.35: A secret specialist in unrequited love, part 1

But that was, unfortunately, an almost complete one-off. Most of the time I was far too reticent and bumbling to do anything of the sort, even when (despite my pickiness) I wanted to.

Throughout my time at secondary school I was still asking that old, old question of mine (I still didn't know the word 'transgender'): what is the word for a boy who wants to be a girl? My peers at secondary school answered my question for me, bluntly and in chorus and repeatedly, for seven and a half long years.

They didn't know about me, of course. Not officially. But then, by this point in my programme of self-erasure I hardly knew myself. And I didn't have the words to tell them, even if I'd been kamikaze enough to want them to know; and no doubt they didn't have the words either (not the correct words anyway). Yet their tranny-radars, and their gaydars, were in full working order. They both knew and didn't know. And I both wanted them to know, and wanted them not to know. Like Carol Steele in 1.7, of course I hated the abuse they gave me – yet at some level, I was also glad to be recognised, even in that way.

What the kids at school told me was that the word I was looking for was sissy, or queer, or Jeremy (after the late lamented Liberal leader), or bender, or fairy, or pansy, or big girl's blouse, or gay boy, or RAVING POOF, or mincing limp-wristed lisping GREAT SCREAMING NANCY BOY, or… plenty of other things.

OK, I thought, so they do have words for what I'm like. And they have hand gestures and tones of voice and funny walks and mime routines as well. And it's just as bad as it is on the telly. Every single one of their ways of talking about people like me is charged with hatred and contempt.

I would say school was consistently awful. Except it wasn't: it got worse as I went up the years. In some ways (my inner divisions got more and more intense); in others, better (we all became a bit less barbaric with each other, a bit less routinely boorish and insulting).

There were consolations, of a number of different kinds. There were consolations that I was prepared to admit to, like the Latin and Greek that everyone else including most of the teachers ridiculed me for specialising in. And there were consolations that I absolutely wasn't admitting to, even to myself, consolations that in some ways only made things worse. Consolations like that stolen kiss on the stairs that I've just talked about. Consolations like beautiful boys in football kit in the winter, and beautiful boys in cricket whites in the summer. (I liked girls too: certainly. And I fancied girls too: for sure. But I wasn't surrounded by girls all day long: unfortunately.)

Boys will be boys, they say, and girls will be girls; and did I object to boys Doing Boy? No; on the contrary, I loved it. I fell (furtively and silently) in love with boys for the way they Did Boy. I just didn't want to Do Boy myself. I wanted them to Do Boy, and I wanted to Do Girl – for them; and be loved for it, by them. I wanted boys to have crushes on me; me as a girl. They hardly ever did, of course.

I became a secret specialist in unrequited love. This added a new – and, to say it again, a quite different – level of shame to my life. I had been ashamed for years of wanting to be a girl, not a boy. And now I found that I had to be ashamed as well of having romantic (and well, yes, let's face it, sexual) crushes on boys.

But – and underline this in red if you will, it's the crucial evidential point – I was less ashamed of the gay thing than of the trans thing. At least with the gay feelings, there was clear evidence that some other boys had those feelings too.

Oh yeah? And what evidence was that, then? Never you mind.

Well, OK, one thing. There was one case – and only one – where a boy of my own age at school came on to me.

('Came on to me'? To be clear: a quick surreptitious grope is all we are talking about here.)

I was flattered and thrilled. But his approach was altogether too crude and direct for my liking. I didn't want a quick surreptitious grope, I wanted romance. I didn't want him for five minutes of hot-and-bothered. I wanted him for six months of sitting on the terrace in the sunshine drinking cold white wine together.

Like I say, I wasn't after anything quick and dirty. I was after something slow and pure. I was after *love*. I wanted to be Juliet to some Romeo (only with a happier ending). And not for five minutes, or even for one term. But for ever.

1.36: Ugly, and inarticulate

Underline this in red, too: on the rare occasions when I tried to find someone to talk to about all this inner turmoil, it happened more than once that I steeled myself to admit to the wanting-to-be-a-girl thing, then chickened out at the last moment because it was too difficult to explain and I was too ashamed of it. So I talked about the gay thing instead. Which was there too, but not so hard to admit to. (On at least one toe-curlingly farcical occasion, I tried outing myself to a middle-aged confidant whose baffled response to my clumsily chosen words was, 'Uh… what's a transvestite?' I fled immediately. And I immediately downgraded my already-low confidence that, if I tried talking about All That ever again, I would find anyone at all who had the faintest idea what I was on about.)

Meanwhile, most of my contemporaries, including the boys I had crushes on, were overt specialists in insult. That was our culture. That was how it was. It was the kind of school where everyone randomly gives unthinking abuse to everyone else, all the time (that is to say: a 1970s north of England boys' school). And I, being who I was and being how I was, was exceedingly vulnerable to insult. I was the kind of child who showed it when I was hurt, and showing you're hurt was feeding the pigeons; the more you show it, the more they abuse you.

'Don't react', my parents told me, 'don't react.' Don't react? When everyone around you all day every day, including the ones you secretly fancy, is telling you the worst and most negative things about your own body and appearance that you can think of? When your entire outer world is insisting on how male and how ugly you are, when inside – so far down inside you can barely even say it yourself – all you want to be is female, and beautiful?

Children and parents naturally decrease their physical contact, the hugs and kisses and the sitting on the knee, as the children grow. Withdrawal probably happens sooner, and goes further, with boys that with girls. Another reason why I wanted to be in the other gender: I was pleading for that reassurance without even knowing I was asking for it. Perhaps, too, I felt a little lost with my parents about which gender they wanted me to be; perhaps, at some level, I felt I was failing to be either the son or the daughter that they wanted.

And the more my parents' physical reassurance was withdrawn, the more I was reassured every day by my classmates at school that I was lumpen, awkward, physically contemptible, ridiculous to look at. In a word, ugly.

1.37: A secret specialist in unrequited love, part 2

By the time I was an adolescent I saw myself, firmly and decidedly, as hopelessly ugly and unappealing. I mean, I had zits. And stubble. And a croaking bullfrog half-broken voice. What else could I be but ugly? Monsters and freaks and grotesques came naturally to me: the Ugly Duckling not the Swan, the Beast not Beauty, Rigoletto not Gilda, Cyrano not Roxanne. (And, we may add from some years later, Shrek not Princess Fiona.) So I naturally expected to be unappealing to anyone else – either a boy or a girl. Why would they want 'to go out with' me? And anyway, how did one go about 'chatting someone up'? For all my secret unrequited passions, and despite that one brief episode of being clumsily fondled by someone even more confused and lost than I was myself, I didn't have a clue how to do that. It just looked outright impossible. (I mean impossible with a girl. It was, of course, even more impossible with a boy.)

My mother was at that time a secondary-school teacher, and one day she happened to bring home a confiscated diary from the school she was teaching in. It was a dated desk-diary belonging to some boy of my own age, called Darren or whatever. I thumbed through it when she wasn't looking. There was nothing in it at all, except every two or three weeks an entry like this: 'Started with Lorraine', 'Broke up with L', 'Started with Paula', 'Broke up with P'. I counted them up. In a mere six months this Darren character had, ahem, gone through about nine girlfriends. I still hadn't had one girlfriend (nor, obviously, boyfriend); just an endless and rather painful series of secret unrequited passions.

There was a lot more going on in Darren's love-life than in mine. Outside my own family, there was, for instance, still only one person in the entire world that I had ever kissed: see above. (And once I had kissed him, I hardly ever spoke to him again, nor he to me, precisely *because* I had kissed him.) On the other hand – at least to go by his diary – there was nothing else whatever going on in Darren's head except his love-life.

And on this evidence, when you thought about it, his love-life looked about as interesting and fun as a wet afternoon spent watching buses go in and out of Bolton Central Bus Station.

Believe it or not, a kind of private arrogance overcame me, and a kind of scorn and maybe even pity for poor old Darren. Because my own head was absolutely alive with romantic imaginings. OK, admittedly hardly any of my stuff, unlike Darren's, was actual real life. (Like I said: in my love-life I am three things in particular: picky, reticent, and bumbling.) But never mind the real life, feel the fantasy. My romantic headspace was in glorious technicolour, full of poetry and pizzazz and sensual grace and mystery and depth; and beauty and purity too.

Everything was in my head, everything was ideal and remote and imaginary. The loved one was not someone that you talk to, for heaven's sake, but a distant dream, an ambition that you work towards by conquering kingdoms first: like Arwen is for Aragorn in *The Lord of the Rings*, or Beatrice for Dante. And because it was ideal, it was all immune to let-down, disenchantment, sullying, impurity. Maybe I even preferred it like that?

There was a family, friends of my parents, who lived just a little too far away for visiting them to be easy or routine. I had known them better before they moved away, and I was kind of in love with them as a family – in love with them collectively I mean, in love with them as a family, as you might fall in love with the Rostovs in *War and Peace*. I saw them as a kind of perfection of gaiety and grace and kindness and creativity and harmony; I imagined that everything I found difficult in my own family was easy in theirs. And lovely people though they certainly were (and are), this was no doubt just as much an illusion as it would be about the Rostovs.

Well, we went over to visit them and catch up with them one Sunday. In the course of that Sunday visit – so in the space of about seven hours – I fell, particularly and extravagantly and with painfully precise clarity and sharpness, in love (or at any rate in infatuation) with the youngest daughter in the family, a delightful girl who was perhaps three years my junior.

I didn't kiss her. I never even said a word to her about my feelings, not at least out loud. I wouldn't have known what to say. But she seemed to like me back. And because she seemed to like me back, out of those seven hours I got a romantic glow that lasted me four whole years. Whatever else was going on with me – and as I've said already, various other crushes on other girls and other boys did come and go – I was still burning a secret flame for her nearly half a decade later. I even thought I had a divine mandate to burn it; though I now think the point was more about an encounter with my own anima than with my life partner.

In all that time, my parents never paid a return visit to the family in question. (Perhaps deliberately? Had they twigged?) So for four years I never saw her again, though there was a little footling correspondence between us, and a couple of times I tried and failed to get over there on a bicycle. (Probably just as well that I never made it.) And when we finally did revisit them, she had moved on. Well, of course she had. If indeed she'd ever realised that I was besotted with her in the first place.

(But no, I suspect she did realise. After all, she did go to the trouble, for that revisit, of writing her then-boyfriend's name up with her own, and a heart with an arrow through, on the whiteboard in her bedroom. At a sticky moment in the conversation with me on that revisit, she asked me what music I'd like next. The way I felt at the time, *For Crying Out Loud* about covered it. If she hadn't copped on before, she surely did then.)

So then there was let-down and disenchantment, of a kind that Beatrice never caused Dante. But on the upside: for all that time I had managed to find a way to keep my romantic reveries pure, even if the cost of purity was living in a dream world. And I had managed to school myself to focus on an attachment both heterosexual and gender-unambiguous… or so I supposed. Above all, I had managed to avoid, or at least postpone, the question of how on earth to ask somebody out. Explicitly, overtly, I had never made a single move with my Dream Girl, never said a single word to her about how dramatically I felt about her. Because I still didn't have a single clue how to do that.

I did similar things with my gay romantic crushes, too. The most intense of those were as far away from school as possible; boys I met during the holidays, at other-worlds like summer camps in Wales, who lived way off in unreachable places like Buckinghamshire. Here too the intensity was ideal, and pure, and all in my head, and hardly ever communicated directly: not even in the six-page letters that I would write, and hope vainly for answers to. Because for the most part – for all my supposed articulacy – I simply didn't know what to say. Not about that.

Similar; except of course that with the gay crushes I berated myself for having them at all. Just as I did with the gay crushes that I kept blundering into at school. Like acne, these just kept on popping up, and I would do almost anything to try and shake them off. As I silently adored from afar, I did my best to tell myself that each of the boys in question wasn't really that good-looking, that I could see imperfections in him, that his looks and charm would soon fade anyway and he'd turn into just another greasy-haired, pustule-ridden, foul-mouthed, foul-minded orc rampaging down a school corridor in a grimy grey shirt waving his BO all over the place.

Anything to get it to stop. But even when I was right in such predictions, they didn't really work. They just dirtied and diseased things; and all in the interests of maintaining my own purity. I was poisoning the wells; I was denying and blinding myself to beauty; I was teaching myself a mean, pinched, ugly – and safe – vision of things. It was profoundly destructive. Why would we pretend that beauty is not in front of us, when it is? It was much more wicked than it would have been simply to admit to myself that I had a harmless crush on some poor unsuspecting kid whom I kept passing on the way to my next lesson.

Maybe, even, it was more wicked to blind myself like that, than it would have been to act on the crush, if I'd ever got the chance. Maybe it was worse to darken my own vision of the world, in the interests of my own moral purity, than it would have been to spend a term or two joking, and tickle-wrestling, and making daisy chains in the summer hay, and singing like birds in the cage, and laughing at gilded butterflies, with some beautiful boy who felt for me – at least for a while – the same infatuation that I felt for him.

If there ever had been a boy who reciprocated like that. And these things are not as impossible as I then thought they were. Even in a determinedly boorish and homophobic school in Seventies-to-Eighties Lancashire, there could have been. And if there had been, what a lot we could have learned about life while we were together – however long that might have lasted.

But as a matter of fact, unfortunately there wasn't.

1.38: Fight the good fight

Being transgender, then – to sum up the narrative that I've been telling since 1.33 – is not just a confused version of being gay. No more, despite what the authorities seem to think in Iran, than being gay is a confused version of being transgender. The two things are different; nonetheless, there is such a thing as a distinctive trans woman's sexuality. Or at least, there is in my case. And why shouldn't there be? You might find it all a bit strange; and maybe it is all a bit strange. But I don't see why you should find it repellent, unless you just find trans people repellent.

And if I had had better information and self-understanding; and if I hadn't been exposed to so much hostile, trans-exclusionary, and, indeed, homophobic gender ideology, this is what I would have understood a long time ago.

But how was I ever going to admit any of this? I was in a civil war. And, O Jesus, I had promised. Promised to *fight*.

O let me feel Thee near me:
The world is ever near;
I see the sights that dazzle,
The tempting sounds I hear;
My foes are ever near me,
Around me and within;
But, Jesus, draw Thou nearer,
And shield my soul from sin.

Don't dream it, be it, said the song at the end of *The Rocky Horror Show* – a film that, psychologically, I blocked my ears and ran away from, to avoid hearing what it was saying to me. Don't dream it, be it. But I was busy doing best not even to dream it. If my surroundings were harsh and discouraging about what I really was, I took that harshness and discouragement into myself. Maybe, if life 'out there' was giving me a wire brush soaked in disinfectant, I needed to take the same approach to life 'in here'. Maybe the savage process of excoriation of who I was, that others seemed to want to impose on me, needed to be combined with a savage process of self-excoriation.

Another hymn that mattered deeply to me, and still does, was the Easter hymn 'Thine Be the Glory'. The promise of resurrection; of leaving all this behind and becoming completely shining-white new; of *just stopping being so bloody complicated and difficult.* Every year when Easter came around I would turn away from the manifold failures of Lent to the hope of suddenly becoming pure, just like that; of looking the Lord in the eye at last, and just being *sorted out for good.*

> No more we doubt thee, glorious prince of life;
> Life is naught without thee; aid us in our strife.
> Make us more than conquerors through thy deathless love;
> Bring us safe through Jordan to thy home above.

And there were (and there are) moments of glory, moments of new life, moments where it felt – though often only briefly – like something transformative and transfiguring really had happened to me.

I think that was real; and is real. But it has never involved my character being wiped clean like a computer disk. Even after Easter I was *still me.*

It's taken me much longer than it should have done to realise that this is how it's meant to be, because this is how *I* am meant to be.

1.39: The best days of your life

As the internet sometimes asks: 'What was your happiest day at school?' No-brainer. The day I left, of course. What else would it be? After all, leaving school meant no more school. It also meant going to Magdalen College, Oxford, which felt like I'd been lifted out of the ordinary world and ascended directly from hell to heaven. (Philip Larkin: 'When I was a child, I thought I hated everybody. When I grew up, I realised I just hated children.')

But in one respect at least when I left school, there was a side of me that was stuck in hell and wasn't getting out of there any time soon. By that time, I had got entirely used to denial: it had been true for years by then that there were whole sides to my being that I had done everything in my power to crush, extirpate, erase – and mostly successfully, give or take the odd moment of mad giving-myself-away in a stairwell. Yet still I was like a person who is being pulled about by a powerful dog on a lead.

The things that pulled me were obvious, unsurprising, but to me deeply shameful. Most men are drawn to women's beautiful looks, beautiful clothes, beautiful hair, beautiful movements, to all kinds of feminine beauty. I was drawn too, but not in the same way. It wasn't (or not just) about how I wanted my hypothetical Dream Girl to be. It was about how I wanted my actual me to be. I wanted to be the Dream Girl – and be swept off my feet by a Dream Boy.

The magnetic force of all this was overwhelming at times; but I spent those harsh school years training myself not to respond. I couldn't get it to go away, but by a massive and prolonged effort of will I had managed, by the time I was twenty, to make the powerful dog invisible, even to me. Still there, but unseen, unacknowledged, unrecognised, unallowed. Still tugging away and knocking me off balance at times, but, it seemed, less and less – I even thought I was 'growing out of it' at times. I would not talk to it, I would not try to understand it, I would not make my peace with it. I just wanted to cut my link with it and be free of it. But I never could be free of it, for a reason I could not admit: because it was not something evil outside me, it was me.

So I did my best to lock it away, then wondered why my life always seemed to be lacking something; why everything I ever experienced had a note of melancholy to it; why it was always like there was a whole dimension of happiness that I was simply missing.

1.40: The Manichee

As you'll have gathered by this point: I'm a Christian, and always have been. And I took it that the forces of good and evil were at war not only, self-evidently, around me, but also within.

By the time I left school I wasn't praying with all my heart, last thing at night, that I would wake up the next morning and find I'd been turned into a girl. I was praying with all my heart, last thing at night, that I would wake up the next morning and find that the side of me that wanted to be a girl had just disappeared. I was a city divided against myself, and in the civil war within me, a lot of the time, I didn't even know which side I was on, or which side of myself loathed the other more.

As above, it wasn't only for religious reasons that I thought it was bad to be transgender. Everything I knew seemed to enforce that message for every other kind of reason too. I wanted a family, for instance, I wanted children, I wanted a wife (and even after she had definitively jilted me, I still hoped sometimes that it might be the Dream Girl); so how, logically, could I also want boys? Or want to be a woman myself? And alongside hopes and desires that simply went in contradictory directions to my transgender hopes and desires, and guilt whether religious or cultural, the self-loathing I've just talked about was always within easy reach.

But I did naturally see the turmoil within me – rather grandiosely, to be sure – as one small part of a universal Manichaean cosmological conflict. This was my bit-to-do in the wider battle in the cosmic war. This was my cross to bear, the self I had to crucify or deny or die to, the thorn in my side. The thing of darkness that I'd do anything not to acknowledge mine was – being transgender. It was a Horcrux, an evil alien implant, a Trojan virus within me that I just couldn't seem to delete, that I had to build firewalls and quarantines around.

I couldn't shake off that side of me. But I couldn't accept it either. I knew perfectly well that if I carried on trying to get rid of my longing to be female, I wouldn't succeed. But I also knew perfectly well that if I tried to give in to that longing, to go with it, to make whatever small secret accommodations were possible in that direction, then I wouldn't succeed either; I wouldn't manage to convince myself that it was all right to be like this.

I knew this because I did try, sometimes, to give in to that longing. And whenever I did, I was immediately overwhelmed with guilt and self-hatred. I was caught, in fact, in what twenty years later I learned was called a 'purging cycle'. I found that I had to stop as soon as I started. And I found that as soon as I stopped, I had to start again. It wasn't accidental that, when I came to write a PhD thesis between 1989 and 1992, I wrote it on freedom of action, and weakness of the will.

There was a time where I sat on the damp grass in humid, hazy English sunshine in a litter-strewn field in Bedfordshire, on the Sunday morning of the Greenbelt Festival in perhaps 1982; listening to a slow, mournful, pleading soul-blues singer as Communion bread and wine were shared among the ragged, sleepy crowd; feeling as broken and as empty and as far from God as the singer sounded. And wondering if I would always feel this broken. And wondering *why* I always felt so broken. And not knowing at all.

The only thing I did was wrong
Was stay in the wilderness too long
Keep your eyes on the prize
Hold on

Hold on. Behind and above the rainclouds of the singer's desolation I sensed a luminous warmth of mercy and forgiveness, somewhere up there, somewhere out there. And somehow it included me as well. And somehow it understood me better than I understood myself.

Yet shining down on me from such an infinite distance. And I was still broken; *that* hadn't changed.

Pillar to post; twisting in the wind; a sucking whirlpool of – well, yes – confusions; and no end in sight.

1.41: De profundis

As a teenager I found myself trapped in another cycle too: a weekly cycle, from school to the weekend to Evensong and back to school. Even now, the Anglican liturgy of Evensong has associations for me that I can barely stand. 'Lone and dreary, faint and weary, through the desert thou didst go.' The past week of failure, guilt, derision, self-reproach, self-loathing, futile longing, and confusion; the long grey damp miserable Sunday afternoon/ evening of dark and dismal Pennine rain; the cold mostly empty church and the doleful slow liturgy with all its talk of sin and darkness and inner desperation; the insupportable weight of repressed, redirected, curdled or soured emotions that it seemed to carry; my own awful dull dread of school again in the morning, and the start of another week just the same as the last; and the whole of my being crying out to God for rescue like a drifting ship lost and alone on a stormy dark sea in a night that is empty of landmarks.

How long wilt thou forget me, O LORD? for ever? how long wilt thou hide thy face from me?
How long shall I take counsel in my soul, having sorrow in my heart daily? how long shall mine enemy be exalted over me?

Like the antinomian ascetics of the Early Church, I got as far as indulging my obsession with being a girl in order to prove to myself that it was nothing to me, that it was all in the past now, that it was a temptation that I had conquered and overcome.

Like them, I proved the opposite.

You can't be transgender and not know that there is a crack in everything. Because what you experience every single day is that there's a crack in you.

And I tell you what: it's all so tiring. It's all just so, so, SO bloody tiring.

1.42: The box

My love met me within a darkened wood
where no light was: I knew her by her hand:
but my grip slipped, her presence vanished, and
till dripping dawn I waited where I stood.

I saw my love upon a city street,
amid a thousand others gave her chase:
I found her longed-for look in many a face,
ten-score half-echoes, but not one complete.

I woke and washed and worried at my error,
a looking-glass behind me and before me;
ninety-nine times repeated there I saw me –
and then her image, in the hundredth mirror.

But my quest and her trail alike turned cold.
I've put my memories of her in a box
to hide inside a drawerful of socks
and finger through when all grows stale and old,

and I have lost the living patterns of
her stance, her grace, her glance so once adored;
have settled for sure less not dubious more,
have lived as if I was not made for love.

When I began so filled with venturous fire
how comes my world to dust and grit and sweat?

Is real-but-paltry really all we get?
How can we live so wide of heart's desire?

1.43: *In dreams*

I would wake up in tears in the middle of the night, drenched in sweat, my heart pounding, screaming inside, sometimes screaming out loud as well. I would be trembling all over as if with cold even when it wasn't cold at all. There were vivid nightmares about textures: I had nightmares of touch, of something both grippy and slimy in my hands that I couldn't get off them. And of being crushed and smothered and closed in and trapped. And about exponential and self-reinforcing processes: the more they happened, the more they happened. Sometimes I was watching a red line soar up and up on a graph, sometimes a pendulum was swinging with a horrible, inhuman exactitude, louder and louder and louder. That was the nightmare, that I was trapped in some process that fed itself, that accelerated with ever more momentum towards some unknown but horrible end.

Or I would lie awake pleading to God for something, pleading for I didn't know what, desperate and tearful because there was something that I needed more deeply than I could say and I had no words left even to ask for it.

Then desolation and panic and utter aloneness.

But there were also nights where it seemed like I saw the Heavenly City, where I would dream marvellous music and light and harmony, a vision of majesty and peace and the light of love behind my eyelids. And the magic of the night would hang over the day that followed it; at school after such a dream I would want to keep perfectly still, and not say or do anything at all, to keep that sweet and serene feeling alive inside me as long as possible.

Utter darkness and dazzling light; dazzling light and utter darkness. And, for all my urgent endless prayers, it seemed like this life of searing contrasts would never change.

In some ways, it still never has changed.

Before an icon

How little changes. Delight is always there,

waiting for us to fit it to our grasp
as it awaited her. And suffering is unending;
the contours of old pain etched in her face
are new in ours.
Prayers of healing, implorings of release
cannot go out of date
so long as birth and death are our boundary-marks;
that long the Holy City,
the beautiful, the forsaken,
will still remain a ransacked ruin behind us,
will still remain a perfect dream ahead.

And the frightened soul like a sparrow
that flickers in mid-air suspense
over an infinite drop
under an infinite height.

1.44: *Eustace and Ged*

Among the stories that I found to tell in all those years, two stand out in particular: Eustace and Ged.

Eustace is from C.S. Lewis's Chronicles of Narnia; he's in *The Voyage of the Dawn Treader*. On a desert island in the middle of their voyage, Eustace sneaks away from his companions into the cave of a dragon. He falls asleep there, on top of the dragon's treasure, and then he wakes up:

He had turned into a dragon while he was asleep. Sleeping on a dragon's hoard with greedy, dragonish thoughts in his heart, he had become a dragon himself …

In spite of the pain, his first feeling was one of relief. There was nothing to be afraid of any more. He was a terror himself now and nothing in the world … would dare to attack him. He could get even with Caspian and Edmund now …

But the moment he thought this he realised he didn't want to. He wanted to be friends. He wanted to get back among humans and talk and laugh and share things. He realised that he was a monster cut off from the whole human race. An appalling loneliness came over him …

When he thought of this the poor dragon that had been Eustace lifted up his voice and wept.

Eustace is made into a monster, is alienated from all humanity, by his own wickedness – his own greed, malice, unkindness and treacherousness. I sometimes felt that way as well: that because of what I was – because I was both bisexual and transgender in a world that had no place at all, and hardly any words, for being either – I was a monster too, and equally isolated from others.

If Eustace's dragon condition is a painful one, so is the cure. As he himself tells the story afterwards:

[As if in a dream] I looked up and saw … a huge lion coming slowly towards me … it came close up to me and looked straight into my eyes. And I shut my eyes tight. But that wasn't any good because [without words] it told me to follow it … at last we came to the top of a mountain and on the top of this mountain there was a garden – trees and fruit and everything. In the middle of it there was a well … I thought if I could get in there and bathe it would ease the pain … But the lion told me I must undress first.

I was just going to say that I couldn't undress because I hadn't any clothes on when I suddenly thought that dragons are snaky sort of things and snakes can cast their skins. So I started scratching myself and … my whole skin started peeling off …

But just as I was going to put my feet into the water I looked down and saw that they were all hard and rough and wrinkled and scaly just as they had been before … So I scratched and tore again and this under-skin peeled off beautifully and out I stepped … [But] the same thing happened again. So I scratched away for the third time and got off a third skin … But as soon as I looked at myself in the water I knew it had been no good.

Then the lion said … 'You will have to let me undress you.' I was afraid of his claws, I can tell you, but I was pretty nearly desperate now. So I just lay flat down on my back to let him do it.

The very first tear he made was so deep that I thought it gone right into my heart. And when he began pulling the skin off, it hurt worse than anything I've ever felt. The only thing that made me able to bear it was just the pleasure of feeling the stuff peel off. You know – if you've ever picked the scab of a sore place …

Well, he peeled the beastly stuff right off – just as I thought I'd done it myself the other three times only they hadn't hurt – and there it was lying on the grass … And there was I as smooth and soft as a peeled switch and smaller than I had been. Then he caught hold of me … and threw me into the water. It smarted like anything but only for a moment. After that it became perfectly delicious and as soon as I started swimming and splashing … I saw why. I'd turned into a boy again.

For years, I took this, as Lewis certainly intended it, as a picture of how hard and how costly it is to be set free from our besetting sins. For years, I saw myself as in need of what Aslan does to Eustace: in need of a kind of psychological flaying, of radical spiritual curettage, of having the hideous horny carapace of wickedness and evil cut away from me until there was nothing left of me but the innocent, naked, skinless, raw, stinging essence that is, at any rate, ready for baptism. Yet it is worth that pain, to be 'a boy again' – isn't it? And the end of such a cutting-down process, for me, would be that I would end up *a boy* – wouldn't it?

Redemption is subtraction: everything that is bad in you will simply be taken away from you. Redemption is extirpation: everything that is bad in you will just be destroyed, snuffed out. We might almost say, with a whiff of Origen, that on this picture redemption is amputation: 'If your right hand offends you, cut it off.'

It was the same story of redemption as subtraction, extirpation, amputation that I found, a few years later in Jhelum in the Punjab, in Gerard Manley Hopkins's remarkable poem 'A Voice from the World', which he wrote in reply to Christina Rossetti's equally wonderful 'The Convent Threshold':

Who say that angels, in your ear
Are heard, that cry 'She does repent',
Let charity thus begin at home, –
Teach me the paces that you went.
I can send up an Esau's cry;
Tune it to words of good intent.
This ice, this lead, this steel, this stone,
This heart is warm to you alone;

Make it to God. I am not spent
So far but I have yet within
The penetrative element
That shall unglue the curst of sin.
Steel may be melted and rock rent.
Penance shall clothe me to the bone.
Teach me the way: I will repent.

The crust of sin, and how to unglue it – like Eustace says, pulling a scab off. The melting of steel, the splitting of rocks, an ascesis that goes as deep as the skeleton. And purity is all that matters; purity is non-negotiable; purity is supremely desirable, the pearl of great price. The cost of purity could be everything, and still worth paying.

Even now, I don't even disagree with this last bit. Only: what is purity? Is it just this kind of partial suicide, this deliberate self-immolation, self-cauterisation: this blocking and baulking of everything dark, deep, uncanny, unknowable, in ourselves?

A reason why Gerard Manley Hopkins's notion of self-extirpation hit me a whole lot harder than C.S. Lewis's was simply that what tempted Eustace was not really particularly appealing; I am no dragon, and I have never felt much of a lust for gold or jewels. Whereas what tempted Hopkins, the Hopkins of the poem, was spell-bindingly beautiful, and devastatingly seductive:

Once it was scarce perceivèd Lent
For orience of the daffodil;
Once, jostling thick, the bluebell sheaves
The peacock'd copse were known to fill;
Through other bars it used to thrill,
And carried me with ravishment,
Your signal, when apart we stood,
Though far or sick or heavy or still
Or thorn-engaged, impaled and pent
With just such sweet potential skill,
Late in the green weeks of April
Cuckoo calls cuckoo up the wood,
Five notes or seven, late and few;

From parts unlook'd for, alter'd, spent,
At last I hear the voice I knew.

These lines made me ask myself: 'If temptation is really this beautiful, how can heaven be any better?'

Though it was years before I was ready to understand it, I found a different kind of redemption myth in Ursula Le Guin's *A Wizard of Earthsea*: in her story of the over-ambitious young wizard Ged. By trying for a magic beyond his power, he sets free a violation, an evil from beyond the walls of the world; the demon pursues him relentlessly across the oceans of Earthsea, until at last he turns and begins to pursue it; and in the final showdown the wizard and the demon come face to face, and each speaks the secret word of power over the other, the other's true name. But then, the demon and the wizard have the same name; the demon and the wizard are just two sides of one and the same young boy.

This thing of darkness I acknowledge mine: the monster recognised and understood is the monster tamed and integrated; and purified too. And no longer, in fact, a thing of darkness at all, but transfigured into a power of piercing light.

'Man's first business in life is to set [disordered] love in order.'[48]

One old word for purity is holiness; which is historically the very same word as wholeness.

We shall not cease from exploration
and the end of all our exploring
will be to arrive where we started
and know the place for the first time.

---

[48] John Sinclair, *Dante: Purgatorio* (Oxford University Press, 1939), p. 139, quoting E.G. Gardner.

PART II

This Is Now

2.1: Patriarch Kirill on the Gay Pride Parade

'In the name of the Father, the Son, and the Holy Spirit!

'To all of you, my dear lords, fathers, brothers, and sisters, I heartily congratulate you on today's Sunday, Sunday of forgiveness, the last Sunday before the beginning of the journey of the Holy Quadragesima, the Great Lent!

'Many devotees call Great Lent a spiritual spring. It coincides with the spring of the physical and at the same time is perceived by the consciousness of the Church as a spiritual spring. And what is spring? Spring is the rebirth of life, it is renewal, it is new strength. We know that it is in the spring that powerful sap bursts forth ten, twenty, a hundred feet high, reviving the tree. It is indeed God's amazing miracle, the miracle of life. Spring is the rebirth of life, it is a certain and great symbol of life. And that is why it is no accident that the main spring holiday is the Easter of the Lord, which is also a sign, a sign, a symbol of eternal life. And we believe that this is so, and this means that the whole Christian faith, which we share with you, is a faith which affirms life, which is against death, against destruction, which affirms the necessity of following the Divine laws in order to live, in order not to perish either in this world or in the world to come. But we know that this spring is overshadowed by grave events related to the deterioration of the political situation in Donbass, almost the beginning of hostilities. I would like to say something on this topic.

'For eight years there have been attempts to destroy what exists in Donbas. And in Donbas there is a rejection, a fundamental rejection of the so-called values that are offered today by those who claim world power. Today there is a test of loyalty to this power, a certain pass to the "happy" world, the world of excessive consumption, the world of apparent "freedom". Do you know what this test is? The test is very simple and at the same time terrible: it is the Gay Pride Parade. The demand for many to have a gay pride parade is the test of loyalty to that very powerful world; and we know that if people or countries reject these demands, they are not part of that world, they become strangers to it.

'But we know what this sin is that is promoted through the so-called marches of dignity.[1] It is a sin that is condemned by the Word of God, both Old and New Testament. And God, in condemning sin, does not condemn the sinner. He only calls him to repentance, but in no way makes sin a standard of life, a variation of human behaviour that is respected and tolerated through the sinful person and his behaviour.

'If humanity accepts that sin is not a violation of God's law, if humanity accepts that sin is a variation of human behaviour, then human civilisation will end there. And gay pride parades are designed to demonstrate that sin is one variation of human behaviour. That's why in order to join the club of those countries, you have to have a gay pride parade. Not to make a political "we're with you" statement, not to sign any agreements, but to have a gay pride parade. And we know how people resist those demands and how that resistance is suppressed by force. So it's about enforcing by force the sin condemned by God's law, which means enforcing by force the denial of God and His truth on people.

'Therefore, what is happening today in the sphere of international relations is not just about politics. It is about something else and far more important than politics. It is about human salvation, about where humanity will be on the right or on the left side of God the Saviour, who comes into the world as the Judge and Creator of creation. Many today, out of weakness, stupidity, ignorance, and most often unwillingness to resist, go there, to the left side. And all that has to do with justifying the sin condemned in the Bible is the test today of our faithfulness to the Lord, of our ability to confess faith in our Saviour.

[1] Relatively uninformed Western-European readers, such as me till I looked it up, may miss that this is a (hostile) reference to the 2014 'Revolution of Dignity'. This was the popular uprising in Ukraine, also known as the Maidan uprising, that began in protests against the corrupt pro-Russian president Yanukovich's sudden decision to halt the popular momentum towards Ukraine's aligning itself with the West and the EU, and ended with the overthrow of Yanukovich and the restoration of Ukraine's 2004 Constitution. https://en.wikipedia.org/wiki/Revolution_of_Dignity.

'All that I say has more than just some theoretical meaning and more than just spiritual meaning. There is a real war going on around this topic today. Who attacks Ukraine today, after eight years of suppression and extermination of people in Donbass; eight years of suffering, and the whole world is silent – what does this mean? But we know that our brothers and sisters are really suffering; moreover, they may suffer for their loyalty to the Church. And so today, on Forgiveness Sunday, I, on the one hand, as your shepherd, call everyone to forgiveness of sins and offences, including where it is very difficult to do so, where people are at war with one another. But forgiveness without justice is surrender and weakness. For this reason, forgiveness must be accompanied by the indispensable right to stand on the side of light, on the side of God's truth, on the side of the divine commandments, on the side of what the light of Christ, His Word, His Gospel, His greatest covenants given to the human race, reveal to us.

'All told, we are engaged in a struggle that has metaphysical rather than physical significance. I know how, unfortunately, Orthodox people, believers, choosing in this war the path of least resistance, do not reflect on all that we are reflecting on today, but go obediently along the path that is indicated to them by the powers that be. We do not condemn anyone, we do not invite anyone to ascend to the cross, we simply say to ourselves: we will be true to God's word, we will be true to His law, we will be true to the law of love and justice, and if we see violations of this law, we will never put up with those who destroy this law, erasing the line between holiness and sin, and especially those who propagate sin as a model or one of the models of human behaviour.

'Today our brothers in the Donbass, Orthodox people, are undoubtedly suffering, and we cannot help but be with them – first and foremost in prayer. We must pray that the Lord will help them to preserve their Orthodox faith and not succumb to temptation after temptation. At the same time we must pray that peace will come as quickly as possible, that the blood of our brothers and sisters will cease to flow, and that the Lord will have mercy on the long-suffering land of Donbass, which for eight years has borne the grievous stamp of human sin and hatred.

'As we enter the season of Lent, let us try to forgive everyone. What is forgiveness? If you ask forgiveness of someone who has transgressed the law or done something unjust and evil to you, you are not justifying their behaviour, but you simply stop hating that person. He ceases to be your enemy, which means that by forgiving him you put him on trial before God. This is the real meaning of forgiving each other for our sins and mistakes. We forgive, we renounce hatred and vindictiveness, but we cannot cross out human wrongdoing there in heaven; therefore, by our forgiveness we deliver our wrongdoers into the hands of God so that both judgement and God's mercy may be upon them. That our Christian attitude toward human sins, wrongs, and offences may not be the cause of their ruin, but that the just judgement of God may be completed upon all, including those who take upon themselves the heaviest responsibility, widening the chasm between brethren, filling it with hatred, malice, and death.

'May the merciful Lord execute His righteous judgement upon us all. And lest as a result of that judgement we stand on the left side of the Saviour who came into the world, we must repent of our own sins. Approach our lives with a very deep and dispassionate analysis, asking ourselves what is right and what is wrong, and by no means excusing ourselves by saying, 'I had a fight with this or that because they were wrong'. That is a false argument, that is the wrong approach. We must always ask before God: Lord, what have I done wrong? And if the Lord helps us to realise our own wrongness, then repent of that wrongness.

'It is today, on Forgiveness Sunday, that we must accomplish this feat of self-denial from our own sins and our own unrighteousness, the feat of surrendering ourselves into God's hands and the most important feat – forgiveness of those who have wronged us.

'May the Lord help us all to pass the days of Holy Quadragesima in such a way that we may enter with dignity into the joy of Christ's Resurrection. And let us pray that all those who are fighting today, who are shedding blood, who are suffering, will also enter this joy of the Resurrection in peace and tranquillity. For what joy would there be if some were in peace and others in the power of evil and in the sorrow of internecine strife?

'May the Lord help us all to enter the journey of Holy Lent in such a way, and not otherwise, that we may save our souls and promote the multiplication of good in our sinful and often fearfully mistaken world, so that the truth of God may reign and rule and lead the human race. Amen.'

2.2: *Sunday Bloody Sunday*

Sometimes I cut and paste, and save on my laptop for further scrutiny, utterances that I think are not only mistaken but wildly mistaken: mistaken to the point of being outright barmy, positively evil, or both. And I cut and paste the whole of them. I know 2.1 goes on a bit, but to see what it is properly, you do need to see the whole of it. (There are times I can think of where I perhaps should have walked out of some awful bigoted philosophy-of-gender talk, but didn't walk out, for exactly this reason: I wanted to be in a position to think about the whole of the talk, not just the first 40 per cent of it.)

I cut and paste like this because I am, as any ethical philosopher must be, interested in moral disagreement. How is it possible for intelligent well-informed people – people who in some cases, including 2.1, apparently share my Christian faith – to reach such radically different conclusions from me? How does someone confronted with the same 'facts' as me, the same information, arrive at a position like the one enunciated in 2.1 – a position that, not to beat around the bush, strikes me as utterly deluded and ethically quite monstrous?

If you are an ethical philosopher, as I am, these are not merely rhetorical questions. It is your job to try and get somewhere with answering them. And so I read and study such wild words as these with deep attention. This is why, for instance, I have risen above my nausea (and my boredom) sufficiently to read *Mein Kampf* right through twice (at least twice, maybe more, it's a bit of a blur). It's a dirty job, but someone has to do it. 'I study hatred with great diligence.'

The words in 2.1 are the full text of the Sunday sermon given by the Patriarch Kirill of Moscow, the leader of the Russian Orthodox Church. This is what Kirill saw fit to preach in St Basil's Cathedral in Moscow on 6 March 2022, the last Sunday before the Russian Orthodox Lent, which, as Kirill observes, is known in the Orthodox tradition as 'Forgiveness Sunday'.

The 6th of March 2022 was also the eleventh day of the Putin regime's brutal and illegal war of conquest against the independent sovereign state bordering it to the south-west: Ukraine. On this 'Forgiveness Sunday', at the same time as Kirill was preaching his sermon, Vladimir Putin's soldiers were pursuing – with the Patriarch's evident approval – a brutal and vindictive war of revenge: they were shelling the Ukrainian cities of Kyiv, Kharkiv, Mykolaiv and Mariupol with bombardments, including thermobaric weapons and cluster munitions, that were not merely indiscriminate, but actively targeted civilians, and places crucial to civilian life and of no military value such as hospitals, schools, bread factories, theatres, and town halls. In particular, Putin's troops were shelling and mining a civilian safe evacuation route out of Mariupol that they themselves had just agreed to set up. As I write these words, they are still at it, and the situation in Mariupol is even more terrible than it was fifteen days ago.

I first encountered Kirill's sermon on the Facebook pages of my distinguished friend Eleonore Stump, where she too had reproduced some of what he says in order to study it with close attention. Reading the sermon through is a surreal experience; it gets more surreal every time I look at it. In some ways this homily looks like it has come straight out of Dostoevsky: doesn't Father Zosima say some decidedly similar things, for example the opening paean to the spring? In other ways it seems to me a breath-taking record of moral blindness. No doubt there has been suffering in the Donbas since pro-Russian separatists started their Putin-backed insurrection there in 2014; perhaps some of that suffering was even Ukraine's fault. Even if so, to concentrate one's attention solely on that, and simply ignore the bloody state terrorism being inflicted on Mariupol by Moscow that same Sunday morning, at the very hour that Kirill was speaking: that is a quite astonishing feat of mental perversity.

What seems most surreal of all about Kirill's sermon is his obsession with gay pride parades. It is tempting to go for the low blow here (and not necessarily an illegitimately low blow, given the absolute state of Kirill's discourse). It is tempting to wonder why exactly LGBTQ+ inclusiveness, all that 'being relaxed about blokes in frocks', might be such a red rag to – might provoke such rage and apparent envy in – someone who habitually appears in public in a great big dress.

Cheap and dirty (but cheerful) *ad hominems* aside, the obvious comment on Kirill's remarks is that they seem another instance of mental perversity: another case of getting things wildly and spectacularly out of their true proportion. Gay pride parades represent the sin of all sins? (There is a 'sin of all sins', a sin against the Holy Spirit – Matthew 12.31; but it isn't gay pride parades.) Gay pride parades are the way in which

Western societies express their freedom – and their decadence? Gay pride parades are the test for membership that liberal democracies impose on societies that want to be like them in some ways, such as Donbas? And compliance with this gay-pride-parade test is coerced in liberal democracies, by force? And on a day when terrified and unarmed civilians trying to escape a war zone are being shelled by an army that has just promised not to – gay pride parades are the clearest example of sin that Kirill can come up with?

2.3: The canary in the mine

So yes: it is extremely tempting simply to dismiss Patriarch Kirill's remarks as no more than mental perversity and a drastic failure of proportion. But actually, I think it would be a mistake to go this way. Actually, I think Kirill is on to something.

As his paymaster Vladimir Putin also understands, there really is something particularly crucial to liberal democracy about recognising and respecting LGBTQ rights. For any society that claims to be humane and to believe in individual freedom, it really is a test-case of fundamental importance whether that society is or isn't open to gay, queer, trans, bi and otherwise nonconforming people. Not because LGBTQ rights is the only issue that matters. Plenty of other things matter too – Ukraine keeping its freedom, for example. Nor yet because nothing matters more than LGBTQ rights. Plenty of other things matter more – reversing climate change, for example.

But LGBTQ rights are, as the saying is, a canary in the mine. If we are incapable of respecting and enforcing people's right to self-determination, their right to choose to live as they wish and as who they really are, in these fundamental aspects of their own lives, then that specific failure says very bad things about our ability to respect human rights in general. As with anti-Semitism, as with religious freedom, a society that begins to fail to respect these sorts of rights is heading down a dark and dangerous path, a path along which lie some extremely frightening threats to anybody's and everybody's freedom – and at the end of which is a prospect that actually does deserve the name that Kirill bestows on respect for LGBTQ rights: 'the end of human civilisation'.

Not only is there something particularly crucial to liberal democracy about recognising and respecting LGBTQ rights. There is also something particularly crucial to fascism about denying them. In Jason Stanley's words:

> Fascism is a cult of the leader, who promises national restoration in the face of supposed humiliation by ethnic or religious minorities, liberals, feminists, immigrants, and homosexuals. The fascist leader claims the nation has been humiliated and its masculinity threatened by these forces. It must regain its former glory (and often its former territory) with violence. He offers himself as the only one who can restore it.[2]

In that article in the *Guardian*, Jason Stanley was writing primarily about the place of Jews and anti-Semitism within the fascist menagerie of fear; but, as he says, gays and trans people have a place in that demonology too. Indeed 'men who turn into women' have a particularly vivid place in the fascist's catalogue of horrors. Fascism is all about threatened masculinity, and there could hardly be a more direct way for masculinity to be threatened than orchidectomy and vaginoplasty. (No surprise then that fascists find trans women scarier than trans men – if they even notice the latter category.)

Once we see that a fascism like Putin's is ideologically based on the atavistic fears of threatened masculinity, and on our supposed need for a 'strong man' to rescue us from that threat, all sorts of aspects of fascism quickly check out: the love of brute force, the anti-intellectualism, the terror of diversity and questioning and nonconformity, the vicious sexism, the rape culture and the violence against women, the strident ableism, the cult of heterosexual 'normality' and 'family values', the cult of 'purity' (whether racial or genetic or religious or bodily or sexual or even, as in the case of Hitler's vegetarianism, dietary). Also the weirdly constant fusion, hardly avoidable in so much fascist iconography, of extreme homophobia with blatant homoeroticism. All those man-worshipping-man energies go in to making fascism; yet once they

[2] https://www.theguardian.com/world/2022/feb/25/vladimir-putin-ukraine -attack-antisemitism-denazify.

are in fascism, they can never be allowed to appear as what they often actually are. They have to be sublimated.

Putin himself, when he makes a list of things that he hates most about the West, reaches immediately for 'oysters, foie gras, and so-called "gender freedoms"'.[3] Translated: the West is decadent and soft, and its openness to gay and transgender people is a key part of this decadence and softness; a key part for which Putin and his circle have a close to deranged hatred. (He has also described gender fluidity as 'a crime against humanity'. From a man whose hapless quest to make peace with his own ego has led to twenty years of his armies bombing primary schools and hospitals, kidnapping and brainwashing thousands of children, poisoning political opponents, booby-trapping the corpses of their victims, and flattening whole cities, this is, we might say, a fairly remarkable piece of chutzpah.)

Recall a bigoted claim that I noted in passing in Part I: the claim that trans people, or other queer people, simply don't exist – not, at least, as what they claim to be. This claim is a staple of contemporary fascism. Ramzan Kadyrov, the Putin stooge and war criminal who currently runs Chechnya, likes to claim that there simply are no homosexuals in his jurisdiction – though if there were, their families would already have murdered them.[4] In a milder form, Kadyrov's claim is echoed with surprising vividness – well, maybe not so surprising, actually – in one veteran actor's recent outbursts about the Jane Campion film *The Power of the Dog*. It seems that Sam Elliott can't bear to think that any cowboy at all might actually have been gay.[5] Or to take a third case: the horrendous 'Don't say gay' legislation recently enacted in Florida, Texas, Oklahoma, Louisiana, Mississippi, and other US states.[6] In all these cases alike, the

---

[3] https://twitter.com/b_judah/status/1504159492849680386.

[4] https://en.wikipedia.org/wiki/Ramzan_Kadyrov#Rounding_up,_torture _and_execution_of_gay_men.

[5] https://www.mercurynews.com/2022/03/07/benedict-cumberbatch -deconstructs-sam-elliotts-odd-homophobic-rant-about-power-of-the-dog/.

Update, 11/04/22: Sam Elliott has apologised for his remarks: https://www .theguardian.com/film/2022/apr/11/sam-elliott-apologises-for-the-power-of-the-dog -comments.

[6] https://www.bbc.co.uk/news/world-us-canada-60576847. https://www.open democracy.net/en/5050/texas-trans-parents-child-abuse/.

purity thinking is transparent: only 'degenerate' nations (or states) have gays or trans people in them; gays and trans people cannot be allowed to exist in our nation or state, because we are pure and strong; so they mustn't exist; or if we don't yet dare to push to erase them altogether, we want to make them invisible.[7] Does this really not remind us of the supposed feminists who have been claiming recently, for example in the conferences of 'the LGB Alliance', that trans people (or kids) don't exist? Or of their recent calls for 'the elimination of transgenderism'? The poison all comes out of the same bottle.

This book isn't investigative journalism; I'll leave it to others who are better at it to do the hard slog of the gumshoeing on that. But I do have a prediction for you: once the investigative journalism is in, it's going to turn out that a shockingly high proportion of the UK's and the US's current obsessive hating of trans people is in one way or another Putin-sourced, or Putin-influenced, or both.[8] There was, after all, relatively little of such transphobia in the US before Trump, or in the UK before Brexit; in the UK House of Commons, the fight for a gender-recognition act was led in 2014–15 by Theresa May and Maria Miller, both Conservative MPs. Thanks to the hard work and courage of Carole Cadwalladr and others, we know already how, especially since 2015 or thereabouts, Putin has used troll farms, money, the press,

---

[7] See also this heartrending open letter by the Texas philosophy professor Adam Briggle: https://eu.usatoday.com/story/opinion/voices/2022/02/25/texas-trans-order-betrays-transgender-child/6931588001/.

[8] That is, for comparison, clearly the case in the EU: 'Based on a systematic review of 11 countries' secret service reports, the Russian government is repeatedly identified as the main foreign actor when it comes to attempts "to influence European politics and decision-making most, and more so than China and other states." ... The Russian government's interference is motivated by a desire to ensure long-term regime security and the resurrection of its world-power status, which are contingent on a weakened EU and NATO ... The West and Europe is consequently targeted using a divide-and-rule approach, where identifying and exploiting divisive social issues is a core strategy. Equal rights for lesbian, gay, bisexual, transgender and intersex people (LGBTI+) appear to have been singled out as a particularly opportune topic to sow friction and disunity between EU Member States ... Targeting LGBTI+ people lies at the heart of the Russian government's self-identification as opposed to a decadent West.' https://www.europarl.europa.eu/RegData/etudes/BRIE/2021/653644/EXPO_BRI(2021)653644_EN.pdf, pp. 7, 14.

and a whole variety of disinformation tactics on the West, to spread confusion and ignorance and conspiracy theories, to debase and discredit democratic discussion, to push wedge issues, to promote tribalism and acts of violence of the kind sometimes called 'stochastic terrorism', and to induce Western democracies to make crazily stupid decisions like voting for Brexit and electing Donald Trump. Is it really so surprising, especially given the brief profile of fascist psychology laid out above, that one of Putin's favourite wedge issues to push in the West is transgender – to the extent that he will even declare himself a J.K. Rowling fan, since she looks like an ally to him?

Putin does all this partly because of the oil in the Black Sea just off Mariupol – yes, I'm afraid it's yet another oil war[9] – and also because he doesn't want liberal democracy in Russia. He invaded Ukraine for the same reason as he installed a puppet government in Belarus and has meddled in the politics of Hungary and Poland (and, both before and after 2014, in Ukraine too): because if Ukraine or Belarus or Poland or Hungary were to become a full-on Western liberal democracy, a danger is that Russia would follow. (To some extent, in fact, Russia already is turning liberal; that's why there is an opposition to the Ukraine war in Russia, for all Putin's brutal attempts to repress it.) LGBTQ rights are a canary-in-the-mine issue – or to change metaphors, a flagship issue – for Western liberal democracy. So it is no coincidence that Putin attacks LGBTQ rights. Nor is it any coincidence when they are attacked by Donald Trump's tribe in the US; or by Putin's top tame cleric, Patriarch Kirill of Moscow.

Will pointing out these clear and indubitable connections be enough to make trans-exclusionary people worry about who their allies are? Given their generally unedifying track record for shamelessness, I very much doubt it. But it should. The 'culture war' that they have been so busily waging on transgender, bisexual, non-binary, and other queer people is now, horrifyingly enough, a literal war: what Ukraine is fighting for is precisely the right to be an independent liberal democracy, with all that that entails, including LGBTQ rights, despite the fascist tyranny to their east. (So, despite a persistent Western leftist obsession with

9 https://www.forbes.com/sites/arielcohen/2019/02/28/as-russia-closes-in -on-crimeas-energy-resources-what-is-next-for-ukraine/.

'NATO expansion', their battle is much more about membership of the EU than of NATO.) To stand with Ukraine is to stand for liberal democracy against tyranny; for the humane and cosmopolitan values of the EU against the surly nationalist insularity of Brexit; and for LGBTQ rights against homophobic and transphobic bigotry.

It's our battle. It's everyone's battle. Make sure you pick the right side.

'But that's enough geopolitics, Sophie Grace', I hear you saying. 'How are you today?'

2.4: *The Boy Scout and the Blue Angel*

Me? I'm fine, thanks. Well, basically fine. Most basically of all: after three decades or so of living as described in Part I, I got there in the end. I've been living openly as a woman now since September 2014.

Is life better this way? Of course it is. I reached a stage, before I finally grasped the nettle and came out, where I was finding life almost unbearable; where I felt like I was being constantly suffocated or strangled, and where it seemed like I was deceiving pretty well everyone

around me about who I really was. One of the biggest things of all, for me, was the question 'Could people know what I'm really like, and still like me?' (Or even: love me?) I have my answer to that question now; and all in all, it's a pretty positive one.

Is life perfect this way? Of course it isn't. Not everyone I'd like to accept me, has accepted me. There are people close to me, people who should have known better, who have been far less accepting than I hoped for. In some cases their indifference or equivocality has turned into a kind of shouting-in-my-face insistence, which they won't abandon even when directly asked to, and which turns at times into something indistinguishable from full-on transphobia. This hurts. And it hurts too when people just *drop* me for being trans; no aggression, no insults, but a deathly silence of ghosting and erasure. But that isn't how most people have responded; and it is important to focus on the good things, not the bad.

Short of magic wands – which we have established are not available – every decision about how to live that a trans person can make is a compromise of some sort. Well, I compromise too; and some of the compromises are frustrating. And like most women of my age (I imagine), I would love to be twenty-five years younger than I am, and six times as good-looking.

But transitioning does enable you to focus on other things: to think about yourself a little less, and about others a little bit more. Being transgender becomes, in a way, almost less important to you, once it's no longer a secret. Or rather: while the thing is still the same size, it no longer dominates the scene like it used to. It becomes ordinary. And thereby it becomes possible to think about philosophy, or climbing, or tennis, or the gardening, or whatever, without that fact about yourself blocking the view. You become less self-absorbed (though in my case still, no doubt, nowhere near un-self-absorbed enough). You realise for how much of life it doesn't actually matter a bit whether or not you're transgender. And you discover that you have lots and lots of friends who don't mind a bit: it just doesn't make any difference to them. At least in relation to them, the whole turmoil inside you was over nothing. This is something that comes as a huge relief in most ways (and as a mild disappointment in some others; you don't unreservedly want being transgender to stop being a big deal).

What transitioning does, in brief, is set you free from a battle inside yourself. That release does not come easy, and in my case at least, as we shall see, it took something like an inspiration that came from outside: 'Where the Spirit of the Lord is, there is freedom' (2 Corinthians 3.17).

There was this silly Facebook meme of comparing pictures of yourself in 2009 and in 2019. Well, I transitioned in 2014. So, if I played the game, maybe 'Me in 2019' would be a Boy Scout… and 'Me in 2019' would be Marlene Dietrich as the Blue Angel.

From the hopelessly gauche to the outrageously louche, in one swell foop? From spotty rumpled-uniformed trainspotting Boy Scout to breathy-voiced vampish perfection – express, direct, and without any intermediate stops? From picky, reticent, bumbling adolescent to night-club goddess, just like that? From totally repressed to letting it all hang out, with no intermissions?

Well, you know. Yes and no. Probably not just like that, and there is more to say on both sides of the equation; I've already been saying some of it. It's not like I would actually appear in public as Marlene, except perhaps for a suitably outrageous Gay Pride Parade; underwear, after all, is for wearing *under*. But one thing that transition does give you – or at any rate it's given me this – is an ability to laugh at myself; and to do it more openly. Life is funny; the world is funny; humans are funny; and I in particular am exceedingly funny. It gives me a great deal of amusement to live a life that is, in some ways at least, suspended somewhere in between the Boy Scout and the Blue Angel. (And in other ways is nowhere near either; as I say above, there are parts of my life where it simply doesn't matter whether or not I'm transgender.) This is especially so given how much Boy Scout there really is in my constitution anyway, and how very little Marlene Dietrich. The first time in my entire life that anyone ever called me 'louche' was in New Zealand, in February 2020. I was delighted and touched; I was also enormously amused; and I did wonder whether the idea would even have occurred to them if they hadn't known I was a trans woman. 'Louche? Me?' I thought. 'I'm about as louche as a bus timetable.'

Maybe being transgender, and openly transgender, brings hidden potentialities out in all of us? I don't know about that; but I do know that being openly transgender is the most tremendous *fun*. I suspect it would be a very good thing for all of us, if more people 'on both sides' of the current arguments about transgender could laugh at themselves a little bit more; could show a greater capacity for fun; could be a touch more open to the possibilities of irony, self-mockery, send-up, and parody; could stop being furiously angry with everyone and everything for long enough to see the essential humour of everyone's human predicament, including their own. And to celebrate that predicament.

2.5: Lining up ten myths

In the rest of this part of the book, Part II, just as a way to sum up The Story So Far, I'm going to line up ten familiar charges and claims that we all keep hearing about transgender, alongside some bits of my own experience. After that, in Parts III, IV, and V, I will, as promised in 1.16, move on to something more like straight philosophical argumentation. Then Parts VI and VII offer other things again: an Open Letter, and a piece of sci-fi fantasy. (Here as elsewhere, another name for 'sci-fi fantasy' is 'imaginative thought experiment'.)

The charges and claims – the myths, as I shall unequivocally call them – may or may not be based on the rush to theorise, the will to system, that I attacked in 1.15; they might alternatively be based on simple prejudice. Either way, there are striking contrasts between these myths and the reality – at least as I have experienced it.

One thing these myths most certainly are based on – one thing that keeps them circulating and believed – is favourable press coverage. And perhaps we should address that briefly: the problem of the scabrously transphobic, bigoted, and nasty press? In the UK, this almost always means the right-wing press (either self-identified as right-wing, or effectively right-wing, given the alliances they form). And in a way, my feeling about this problem is simple bafflement: *how come anyone still takes them seriously?*

I mean this especially post-Brexit (the overlap between anti-trans and pro-Brexit journalism is almost complete). Now that it is crystal clear that Brexit was a scam and is an unfolding economic and social disaster, this would be a very good time for the UK to sit down and have a word with itself, and ask itself some rather probing questions. Why did we allow ourselves to be so comprehensively deceived about what Brexit involves, by unscrupulous liars in the press and in Parliament? Why are we not holding those liars properly to account for the catastrophic damage that they have done to us all, and the billions of pounds that they individually have made out of our society's collective losses? Why are so many of the main miscreants still in office? Why are they and the lying press that they overlap with not as irreversibly discredited as they deserve to be? Given how diametrically mistaken the *Daily Mail*, the *Daily Telegraph*, and the *Daily Express* were and are about Brexit, why does anyone still pay any of those 'news outlets' the slightest attention – not only on Brexit, but on any subject at all? If they lied so badly and so shamelessly about Brexit, why assume that they are in the least reliable about any other topic whatsoever: about climate change, for example, or again, about transgender? More about the iniquities of the press in due course. For now, here's the list of myths.

Of course, here as elsewhere, I'm not necessarily disproving the myths that I'll list by saying that they don't fit my experience. Maybe they're generally true, and I'm just atypical. But they don't look true to me, in the light of my experience; and I don't actually know of anyone in the light of whose experience they do look true. So my argument ought to have at least an undermining tendency relative to these ten myths, most of which seem to me to be the propositional equivalent of celebrities: celebrities are only famous for being famous, and these claims are only thought true (at least in some circles) because they're thought true (in those circles). With the help of all the autobiographical evidence that I've assembled in Part I, and as a way of summarising what I think that evidence tells us, I want to make at least a start here on debunking these ten myths.

So here we go.

2.6: Myth one: 'Trans is a fad, a recent fashion' (1)

Nope. It's not transgender that is the recent fashion or fad. It's transphobia.

In the UK from about 2000 till about 2015, there was a wide cross-party consensus in politics and the media that trans people were a vulnerable minority who needed and deserved protection; as I noted above, it was two Conservative women MPs who introduced the first gender-recognition bill at Westminster. The weaponisation of ignorance and fear and prejudice against transgender people is a very recent thing, both here and in the US.

Yet to read nearly all of the mainstream media in the UK today, you'd think that transgender is a scary dangerous moral-panicky thing, invented in about 2010 by shadowy cultural Marxist villains. (Whatever a 'cultural Marxist' is. As with 'critical race theory', the more people use the phrase, the less clear they seem what they mean by it. The anti-Semitic overtones of the first cliché are as well documented as the racist overtones of the second.)

This trope of 'trans as the latest fashion' is very obviously both cruel and superficial, given how difficult and how very non-whimsical decisions to be open about being transgender typically are. It is also an extraordinarily uninformed – or just downright dishonest – trope.[10] Everyone knows that there was a Hirschfeld Institute in Berlin from 1919 to 1933[11] – where patients included 'the Danish girl', Lili Elbe.[12] And long before that there is the well documented existence in European history, both of people who were 'born male' and chose to live as women, such

---

[10] There is a distressing tendency at present for people who are eager to sneer at trans people online, for example on Twitter, to respond to random reports of atrocities like rape with words like these: 'Horrendous – these poor girls could not identify out of their biology!' (That is a direct quotation; never mind from whom.)

Such sneers simultaneously trivialise both rape and being transgender. And there are, to put it mildly, some odd assumptions going on. For a start: for all that commenter knows, some of the very rape victims she was sneering at were in fact transgender.

The underlying thought, if we can dignify it with that name, is apparently that somehow being trans 'isn't serious' (is a fad?) and therefore disappears in wartime. But to state the obvious, trans people get raped and murdered too, and not only during wars. Often, in fact, they are targeted by rapists and murderers precisely because they're transgender; there aren't many wartime situations where it helps to be visibly different, and the 'clearing' of a town by trigger-happy assault troops is certainly not one of them. Truth to tell, in any war, especially one with the underlying fascist ideology of Putin's illegal and brutal invasion of Ukraine, being (visibly) transgender must be unimaginably terrifying.

People should think a bit more before they sneer, and try to relocate their apparently lost humanity.

[11] https://en.wikipedia.org/wiki/Institut_f%C3%BCr_Sexualwissenschaft.

[12] https://en.wikipedia.org/wiki/Lili_Elbe. https://www.scientificamerican.com /article/the-forgotten-history-of-the-worlds-first-trans-clinic/.

as – among many other examples – Eleanor Rykener (alive in 1394)[13] and Lucy Hicks Anderson (1886–1954),[14] and of people who were 'born female' and chose to live as men, such as Hannah Snell (1723–92),[15] James Barry (1789–1865),[16] the Chevalier d'Éon (1728–1810),[17] and Alan Hart (1890–1962).[18]

I am happy to defend the claim that 'There have always been transgender people'.[19] But before I say any more to defend it, there is a technical-philosophical caveat to the claim that I ought to observe. I mention it not just as a matter of pedantry or tidiness or book-keeping, but rather, because the caveat has interesting consequences. The caveat is that 'transgender' is what philosophers call a thick concept; and thick concepts, by definition, have histories.[20]

That is to say: what counts as being transgender is historically and socially conditioned. Like marriage and the concept of law, transgender is a cultural formation – a social construct, if you like. (If you think being a social construct implies being unreal, reflect on the fact that money and court convictions and Nobel prizes and ambitions and parliaments are social constructs.) Our concepts don't always reach all the way into the social and conceptual space of other societies, just as their concepts don't always reach all the way into ours. Hospitality is a concept, and a social construct, that we have in our society. And something like that concept is there in almost all human societies; they'd barely be societies if it wasn't. But what hospitality comes to in different societies, and in different times, is famously variable.[21] Some other examples of thick concepts (and social constructs) are not just variously realised in different societies, but

---

[13] https://en.wikipedia.org/wiki/John/Eleanor_Rykener.
[14] https://www.blackpast.org/african-american-history/anderson-lucy-hicks-1886-1954/.
[15] https://en.wikipedia.org/wiki/Hannah_Snell.
[16] https://en.wikipedia.org/wiki/James_Barry_(surgeon).
[17] https://en.wikipedia.org/wiki/Chevalier_d%27%C3%89on.
[18] https://en.wikipedia.org/wiki/Alan_L._Hart.
[19] https://en.wikipedia.org/wiki/Enaree.
[20] For more from me on thick concepts see T. Chappell, 'There are no thin concepts', in S. Kirchin, ed., *Thick Concepts* (Oxford University Press, 2013).
[21] For a fascinating and accessible book-length study of this variability, see Will Buckingham, *Hello Stranger* (Granta, 2021).

completely absent in some. In the UK today, nothing counts as being a geisha or a samurai, or a knight of chivalry or a troubadour; in ancient Japan, and in mediaeval Europe, nothing counted as being a Premier League footballer or a consultant physician or a postie.

Again, from the fact that various sorts of sexual activity certainly happened between men in at least some parts of classical Greece, it clearly does not follow that those Greeks had exactly our concept of homosexuality. Very plainly they did not (when you think about it, how could they have done?); but they did have something similar to it in some ways, and unlike it in others.[22]

Likewise with transgender, and for the same kind of reasons. We should not expect historically or geographically distant societies from us to have exactly the same notion as us of what it is to be transgender, and of what expectations and freedoms are involved in being transgender.

My point is not that these historical and geographical differences lead us to a paralysing relativism, so that we can't even say whether or not anyone in some other time or place is or is not transgender, because we can't decide 'which concept of transgender to use', because we don't know 'which of them is the correct concept'. Obviously enough, the right question about any thick concept is not whether it is (on/off) 'the correct one', but whether it is illuminating and coherent; and obviously enough, we should at least start from our own concept of transgender – deployed with an ear for historical and geographical variation.

This is worth doing, not out of mere academic pedantry, but because the variations are interesting and instructive. Touring around the possible inflections of what does or might count as being hospitable, or a geisha, or gay, or transgender, is an exercise of the imagination. And it opens us up to possible ways of improving our own concepts, of making them more illuminating and coherent: as philosophers now say, of 'conceptually engineering' them. I shall say more about conceptual engineering, with particular respect to the gender concepts 'man' and 'woman', in Part V; and in Part VII, I shall present a full-blown (if slightly tongue-in-cheek) attempt to describe a radically different account of the gender concepts,

---

[22] The classic study is K.J. Dover, *Greek Homosexuality* (Harvard University Press, 1978).

in the context of the very different society that radically different gender concepts would of course imply.

Having marked that caveat about the thickness of the concept of transgender, I turn back to our transgender history. I won't rehearse the manifold and familiar evidence for this history (both in Europe and, even more abundantly, in other traditions in other parts of the world): it's been pointed out plenty of times elsewhere. It's all on Wikipedia, for a start;[23] or, for some of the history of trans men in particular, see Jen Manion's *Female Husbands*.[24] What is striking here is not just the abundance of the evidence that transgender people are no new phenomenon in European culture; it is the persistence of the will in our society today to ignore that abundant evidence.

It is certainly clear that, in the West, attitudes to (what we now call) trans men and trans women have often been sharply contrasted. For the most part in European history where anything like either category has been recognised – which is not always – the tendency has been, roughly speaking, to see trans men as unfathomable but harmless eccentrics, and trans women as scary and/or ridiculous perverts. Masculinity is seen, in the usual Aristotelian-gender-unary way, as the norm, and femininity as a kind of aberration or falling-off from that norm. (This is associated with the recurring error of treating transgender as if it were just a side-aspect of homosexuality: see Edward Carpenter's *The Intermediate Sex*.[25]) So 'women who live as men' are treated as idiosyncratic honorary males, on the understanding that they want to 'cheat' their way upwards into the more privileged gender. Whereas with 'men who live as women', there is little understanding of why anyone might want to live that lifestyle, moving downwards in the gender hierarchy. So because they can't understand it any other way, and haven't gone to the trouble of listening to trans women's own accounts of why they do it, people conclude that trans women do this because they 'get a sexual kick out of it'. Unsurprisingly, then, trans women often show up in European

[23] https://en.wikipedia.org/wiki/Transgender_history.

[24] Jen Manion, *Female Husbands: A Trans History* (Cambridge University Press, 2020).

[25] Edward Carpenter, *The Intermediate Sex: A Study of Some Transitional Types of Men and Women* (1928). https://www.gutenberg.org/ebooks/53763.

history either as socially marginal and precarious figures like sex-workers; or don't show up at all, because they are marginal and disreputable.

It isn't true that transgender is a fad or a fashion; but what is true is that we now have a much better stock of names and concepts for these ways we are. Trans people have spent centuries labouring under all sorts of epistemic injustice;[26] one is the 'hermeneutic injustice' of having no words or concepts to describe how the world is for us, and how we feel in our own skins. Take me, for example: like I said in 1.2, I didn't even know the word 'transgender' till I was thirty-three or thirty-four.

Sometimes I wonder how things might have gone for me if I had lived in George Herbert's time, or Gerard Manley Hopkins's – two people who seem to me to have had, in their different ways, what we might well call (with the usual caveats and reservations) an extraordinarily 'feminine sensibility'. This is Friedrich Nietzsche's scornful phrase for Christianity – that it is a 'womanish' spirituality (see in particular *The Antichrist* and *The Genealogy of Morals*). Subtract Nietzsche's characteristic scorn, spleen, and hyperbole, and I actually think he's on to something. It seems to me entirely likely that many transgender people in the past simply sublimated, spiritualised, their transness. It turned up in them as something else, for example as a conception of their relatedness to God as bride to bridegroom; in a motif that is not unfamiliar from my own experience, they conceived of Christ as the lover, and themselves as the beloved. (In other traditions, we can see something strikingly similar in the Bengali mystic Tagore, or in the Persian Sufi Jalal ud-Din Rumi.[27])

---

[26] Miranda Fricker, *Epistemic Injustice: Power and the Ethics of Knowing* (Oxford University Press, 2007). When, in her vitally important book, Fricker names the oppressive phenomenon of being unable to name the oppressive phenomena, that is itself, with a pleasing reflexivity, a liberatory act. Just to be given the concept of hermeneutic injustice is itself to receive the righting of a key hermeneutic injustice.
[27] To be clear, I am not saying, or even speculating, that Tagore, or Jalal ud-Din Rumi, or Gerard Manley Hopkins, or George Herbert, or anyone else I might have put in this list, *was* transgender. We can't know that one way or the other; but we can suggest, as I do, that trans women with a mystical streak are quite likely to end up with a spirituality rather like these mystics. (As usual, I speak from experience here.)

Maybe, too, there were secretly transgender Christians in history to whom it was important that the Christian tradition has always had a central place for the notion of the resurrection of the body. 'It does not yet appear what we shall be' (1 John 3.2); 'For our conversation is in heaven; from whence also we look for the Saviour, the Lord Jesus Christ: who shall change our vile body, that it may be fashioned like unto his glorious body, according to the working whereby he is able even to subdue all things unto himself' (Philippians 3.20–21); 'And we shall be changed' (1 Corinthians 15.53); 'So that He might present to Himself the church in glory, not having spot or wrinkle or any such thing, but that it would be holy and blameless' (Ephesians 5.27); 'For now we see through a glass, darkly; but then face to face: now I know in part; but then shall I know even as also I am known' (1 Corinthians 13.12); 'And the angel said to me, 'Write this: Blessed are those who are invited to the marriage supper of the Lamb' (Revelation 19.6). Perhaps many a Christian in the past who would, today, be seeking gender-affirmation surgery, read words like these in their particular centuries, and concluded: 'This is all real, for sure, but the physical fulfilment of it all must wait until I am resurrected.'

I am not entirely sure that I even disagree with that conclusion. This is a matter partly of my own faith as a Christian, and partly of the solidarity with the past that I mentioned in 1.23, a solidarity that we might also call by a more theological name, 'the communion of the saints'. It is certainly the truth about me that I have always had that kind of being-in-love relationship with the Divine, as I conceive of Him. (As the Risen Christ, basically.)

Long before I arrived at a clear adult understanding of myself as transgender, a clear, strong, radiant, sometimes overwhelming sense of being loved by God was always part of my own religious experience. The Bible's mystical imagery of bridegroom to bride fits the experience exactly; Rabbi Akiva's description of the Hebrew Bible's strangest and most passionate book, *The Song of Songs*, as 'the holy of holies' fits exactly too. It has always been like this with me, and it still is. But until, in May 1998, I underwent nearly a month of deep and intense 'shewings', it never occurred to me that there might be a connection of some kind between that aspect of my spirituality and the fact that I was transgender: between, as I saw it then, the very best thing in my nature, and the very worst. To see the connection – or more exactly, I believe, to have it shown to me – was an epiphany, a life-changing revelation; it turned everything upside down. Or rather: it turned everything that *was* upside down the right way up.

> You give me your spectrum-white:
> You kaleidoscope all my colours
> To one simple vision of light
> In your prism-, your spectrum-white.

Alongside the history of spirituality, another place we might look to find (perhaps concealed or veiled or sublimated) transgender sensibilities is in the history of art. And here the myths are deep, potent, and recurring. There is the androgynous Teiresias,[28] and there is Achilles on Skyros.[29] There is the horrifying transformation that Pentheus undergoes in Euripides' *Bacchae*. There is the perplexing and uncanny tale of Hermaphroditus in Ovid's *Metamorphoses* (4.104ff.), and Catullus' Attis poem, number 63.[30] There are the boys playing girls playing boys that so delighted Shakespeare and his audiences (and no doubt infuriated contemporary Puritans). And there is the 'master-mistress of his passion' in Shakespeare's Sonnet 20:

> A woman's face with nature's own hand painted
> Hast thou, the master-mistress of my passion;
> A woman's gentle heart, but not acquainted
> With shifting change as is false women's fashion;
> An eye more bright than theirs, less false in rolling,

---

[28] See Ovid, *Metamorphoses* 3.314–337, and https://en.wikipedia.org/wiki/Tiresias#:~:text=In%20Greek%20mythology%2C%20Tiresias%20(%2F,Everes%20and%20the%20nymph%20Chariclo.

[29] See Statius, *Achilleid*, Book 1, and a host of further references collected e.g. at https://en.wikipedia.org/wiki/Achilles_on_Skyros#Literature. As with Cherubino, Achilles-as-a-girl has caught many people's imagination; as with Cherubino, it is tempting to speculate about why exactly that might be. In Part VII, I play with the theme of Achilles on Skyros myself.

[30] http://www.perseus.tufts.edu/hopper/text?doc=Perseus%3Atext%3A1999.02.0003%3Apoem%3D63.

Gilding the object whereupon it gazeth;
A man in hue, all hues in his controlling,
Which steals men's eyes and women's souls amazeth.
And for a woman wert thou first created,
Till nature as she wrought thee fell a-doting,
And by addition me of thee defeated
By adding one thing to my purpose nothing.
But since she pricked thee out for women's pleasure,
Mine be thy love and thy love's use their treasure.[31]

Or, to take another blindingly obvious example, what on earth do people think is going on with Cherubino, if not something transy? 'Forced feminisation' – being coerced into dressing as a girl – is one the most familiar gender-bending fantasies of all. (You are being forced into a particular gender-presentation, but – finally – it's the one you want; you are doing what you most want to do and feel most horribly guilty about doing, but your sense of guilt is powerless to stop what's happening, because you're being *made* to do it.) Just this is what happens to the youthful Achilles in what seems to be an extremely old myth, when he is compelled to dress as a girl by his mother Thetis, and hidden away from the recruiting sergeants for the Trojan war on the island of Skyros (Ovid, Metamorphoses 13.162ff.). And it is exactly what happens to Cherubino at the hands of Susanna in Act Two of *Figaro*.

This is eroticised and sentimentalised material, no doubt. But it is also, pretty obviously, a kind of transgender sensibility, hiding in plain sight, right smack in the middle of one of the most canonical works in the history of European civilisation. And did *Figaro* cause a scandal? Was it rejected by its audiences with disgust and condemnation? On the contrary, if *The Marriage of Figaro* struggled to get past the censors, it was not for this reason; and once past them, *Figaro* – transy bits and

[31] The rude pun in line 13 is obvious. There are at least two more rude puns in the sonnet that are less obvious, in lines 11 and 12. 'By addition me of thee' is ambiguous, but one thing it means is 'by adding me to you', i.e. 'by adding will(y) to you'. And in 'by adding one thing to my purpose nothing', the word 'nothing' puns on 'an O thing', which in the slang of Shakespeare's time means 'a vagina'; the same pun is there in quite a few other places in Shakespeare, for example in the play title *Much Ado About Nothing*.

all – was acclaimed as a masterpiece from the very beginning, and still is, and deservedly so.[32]

Another case again is familiar to every reader of Roland Barthes's *S/Z*, in which the author subjects a minor classic of French literature to a rather lumbering and mechanical kind of structuralist analysis (another case of overdependence on systematic theory, it seems to me: see 1.15 above). The work in question is Balzac's heavily perfumed, almost soft-porn, 1830 novella *Sarrasine*. As Wikipedia summarises the plot:

> Around midnight during a ball the narrator is sitting at a window, out of sight, admiring the garden. He overhears the conversations of passers-by regarding the origins of the wealth of the mansion's owner, Monsieur de Lanty. There is also the presence of an unknown old man around the house, to whom the family was oddly devoted, and who frightened and intrigued the partygoers. When the man sits next to the narrator's guest, Beatrix de Rochefide, she touches him, and the narrator rushes her out of the room. The narrator says he knows who the man is and says he will tell her his story the next evening.
>
> The next evening, the narrator tells Mme de Rochefide about Ernest-Jean Sarrasine, a passionate, artistic boy, who after having trouble in school became a protégé of the sculptor Bouchardon. After one of Sarrasine's sculptures wins a competition, he heads to Rome where he sees a theatre performance featuring Zambinella. He falls in love with her, going to all of her performances and creating a clay mould of her. After spending time together at a party, Sarrasine attempts to seduce Zambinella. She is reticent, suggesting some hidden secret or danger of their partnership. Sarrasine becomes increasingly convinced that Zambinella is the ideal woman. Sarrasine develops a plan to abduct her from a party at the French embassy. When Sarrasine arrives, Zambinella is dressed as a man. Sarrasine speaks to a cardinal, who is Zambinella's patron, and is told that Zambinella is a castrato. Sarrasine refuses to believe it and leaves the party, seizing Zambinella. Once they are at his studio, Zambinella confirms

---

[32] There is plenty more to say about *Figaro*, including some comments on the unpleasant misogyny that it also contains in places, for example in Figaro's own aria 'Aprite un po' quegli occhi'. Not that *Figaro* is the worst work in Mozart for misogyny; *Cosi Fan Tutte* and *The Magic Flute* and, in particular, *Don Giovanni* are all worrying in that respect too ('Batti, batti, O bel Masetto…'). But I had better not get started on this, or I will never stop.

that she is a castrato. Sarrasine is about to kill him as a group of the cardinal's men barge in and stab Sarrasine.

The narrator then reveals that the old man around the household is Zambinella, Marianina's maternal great uncle. The story ends with Mme de Rochefide's expressing her distress about the story she has just been told.[33]

It seems fairly clear that Balzac's story about a castrato is (also) a story about someone whom we would describe as a trans woman. What is unfortunately striking about his novella is the way that its story casts the beautiful Zambinella as the villain of the piece, simply because she is not what she seems. Sarrasine falls in love with her and (despite her foresighted attempts to dissuade him) tries to seduce her. But we are evidently supposed to believe that she is cheating him, and cheating in a way that entirely justifies Sarrasine's threatening and violent behaviour towards her. When the wicked cardinal's men murder Sarrasine to protect Zambinella from his assaults, we are apparently supposed to see them as striking a blow against the (cis, hetero) 'normality' that he represents, and in favour the kind of twisted deviance represented by Zambinella. This gender-deviance she can no longer sustain in her wrinkly old age, when her looks are gone and she is reduced to loitering around Marianina's house in the gnome-like guise of her birth gender. And, we are perhaps supposed to conclude, that serves her right.

Perhaps all this is the intended reader response. There again, of course one reason why Barthes chose this strange and lurid tale is precisely because of its obviously double-edged nature. It would be naive just to take the novella 'straight', as an anti-clerical denunciation of the wicked sexual perversions of the cunning Catholic priestly caste, without considering how its lugubrious sensuality might be intended to subvert that 'official response'. Still, the novella is full of tropes that are, on the face of it, (what we call) transphobic, about the trans woman as a sexual deceiver and a cheat, and about the legitimacy of anti-trans violence as a response to that deception. These tropes are as sadly familiar as Statius' idea that Achilles among the girls was like a fox in a hen-coop – that was how he ended up seducing Deidamia the princess of Skyros, and fathering Pyrrhus on her; and indeed the frequent insistence in da Ponte's libretto

[33] https://en.wikipedia.org/wiki/Sarrasine.

for *Figaro* that Cherubino too exploits his disguise as a woman for the purpose of seducing women. In all these ways, it is almost as if trans women can only ever be conceived by their socially licensed depicters either as deceivers or as rapists. *Plus ça change…*

It is nothing new for trans women (or something like them) to be presented as deceptive and predatory. But that does at least show that it is nothing new for trans women or trans themes (or something like them) to be presented. It simply won't wash to pretend it's all been made up in the last twenty years. This stuff is not new; it's been there all along. You can't get the trans out of the canon.

2.7: Myth one: 'Trans is a fad, a recent fashion' (2)

And, to come back to my own case, you can't get the trans out of me. As we've already seen in Part I, being transgender was never a fad or a fashion in me either. Like I've explained, I grew up in a rather down-to-earth, decidedly gritty and macho Lancashire mill-town in the 1960s to '80s. In the relentlessly thought-policed and deeply unkind, conformist and intolerant society that was my school, *poof* and *cissy* and *bender* and *big girl's blouse* and *fairy* and *nancy-boy* and *pansy* and *queer* and *gay-boy* and, indeed, just *woman* were all standard forms of abuse, applied indiscriminately to people who were transgender, such as me, and to people who were homosexual or bisexual, such as me, and to people who merely looked (long-term or short-term) as if they might be transgender or homosexual or bisexual, such as me, and such as many of my friends, and actually, such as pretty well all of us. No discrimination in that school: everyone got shit, tons of shit, all the time, from everybody; often this was because adolescent males are incapable of thinking of any way except the violent way of touching each other. (After all, if I am right that transgender and gayness in European history has often been disguised as something else, transphobes and homophobes need to be vigilant to spot it turning up in one or another sublimated form.)

So no one brainwashed me to be transgender. On the contrary, as detailed in Part I, my parents and my peers and everyone around me did everything they could to push me the other way, to be not trans. The pressure was all to be a gender conformist, a Boy Scout. The idea of being a gender rebel, or even perhaps a Blue Angel, was not so much disapproved of as disappeared: it wasn't even on the radar. Certainly nothing could have been more unfashionable, more profoundly not a fad, at that time and that place, than to be what I was, a boy who wanted to be a girl. Being that in Bury or Bolton in 1970 was not a coolness marker, as it's sometimes said to be for kids today. (The lucky little sods, if it's true. Though to judge by the self-harm rates among gay and trans young people, I doubt it's always true.[34]) Being a boy who wanted to be a girl was not so much a way of 'getting (positive) attention'; more like a way of getting stoned to death. But that was what I was, from the very beginning, and I knew it.

So it wasn't learned behaviour, for me, to be transgender. What was learned behaviour was learning (in the interests of personal safety as much as anything) to suppress the fact that I was transgender. As we've seen, I didn't suppress it when I was really little: as soon as I was capable of putting clothes on myself, I spent as much time as I could get away with dressed as a girl. But I was very quickly and very forcibly taught that I couldn't get away with it even for five minutes, and that it was very, very bad of me to behave and to be that way. So I learned to hide it, and not only to hide it but to see it myself as something very, very bad that was hidden inside me. I had already learned this by the time I went to school. I'm still unlearning it.

And I fought it so hard, for so long, so dutifully. I was a very good Boy Scout; a very brave little soldier.

I can't tell you how awful it is to be like that: to know that you are wired completely differently from everyone around you, and in a way that you are profoundly ashamed of: to feel an utterly desperate urge to be and look a certain way that (it feels to you) no one else in the whole world has ever felt and no one finds anything but ridiculous and repulsive. These things take you right to the bottom, to the abyss of the abyss; you just keep feeling worse and worse and it seems like there's no endpoint to it, 'no worst', no way of getting away from the hopeless hunger that you feel to be a girl, and the despairing anger and shame that you feel with yourself for feeling that hunger. How wonderful by

---

[34] A thoughtful and balanced account of a very positive experience of being a trans boy at school: https://inews.co.uk/opinion/what-its-really-like-being -transgender-in-school-1547865?utm_source=Sailthru.

contrast it is when you finally stop fighting the forbidden side of yourself and allow your 'inner girl' to exist and express herself, instead of crushing her and stamping her down. When that finally happens – and it took me so long, thirty-three years, before I let it – you feel like you can't breathe, you feel like you're floating away, you wonder if you're going to faint or just burst into tears of happiness.

One day not so long ago I went back to all those words that were used as sticks to beat you with if you were different, and that I used to use as sticks to beat myself with, come to that. I did what is sometimes called reclaiming them. I stood in front of the mirror and I said them all at myself. Then I said: 'Yes. That's what I am and who I am and it's not just OK, it's great, and I should worry less and live it more.' So I do.

And another thing that happened not so long ago: I got one of those routine Old Boys' letters from the headmaster of my school about how wonderful it is to be a pupil there, and something snapped in me, and I wrote him a really furious letter about how very un-wonderful I found it to be a pupil there.

I still have my letter to him on file. It's eye-wateringly, paint-blisteringly, incredibly rude. I am most certainly not reproducing it here; it's quite bad enough that I lost my rag like that in a private letter. I expected no answer to this letter-bomb whatsoever. But the headmaster, bless him, not only replied, with an extraordinarily kind and gentle response; he actually invited me to come and give a talk about transgender at the school. So I did. It was a good experience, but an utterly surreal one. I was back in the very belly of the Beast. Except now it wasn't a beast any more at all. I was back in my old school's Great Hall, giving a talk... as a woman; and all the old nightmares had changed into something I would never have dreamed of predicting – or dared to predict.

No amount of telling transgender people that trans is a fad or a fashion is going to make them cisgender. You will never succeed in doing that. Though you might succeed in making them miserable.

For example, one thing that the current bombardment of public transphobia in the UK has sometimes done to my own psyche, especially during the pandemic, is to make it harder for me to go out. At the moment I sometimes find it difficult to leave the house, because I don't know what will be out there, and so much of what I read about seems profoundly and perhaps dangerously hostile. (I have occasionally faced direct physical aggression on the street; it is an unsettling experience.) And I find I have a general paranoia about my own appearance. Like any other woman (only more so, perhaps), there is only so much I can do about it. And there are plenty of people – especially online – who are ready to jeer and to mock. When my self-confidence is as low as it often is, today for instance, even kindly meant criticism can be hard to take.

Another thing that the current state of the UK is doing to my mind is giving me anxiety dreams. Like this one:

> I am in a taxi, on my way to give a paper at College X in Oxford. We are running very late. Suddenly I realise – I don't know why I hadn't before – that I am in a state of undress. Not naked, but if I try to give the paper looking like this there will be overwhelming derision.
>
> My clothes are back at College Y where I stayed last night. I have to plead with the taxi driver, because he's very unwilling, to turn around so I can get into my clothes back at Y. We get stuck in traffic. We are getting closer and closer to the start-time of my paper. I am so anxious that – counterintuitively, and inside my dream – I fall asleep in the taxi. I wake up under the arch by College Y Lodge, still in the taxi. The driver is nowhere to be seen. The taxi is illegally parked. I can't find the key to my room. And anyway I am locked inside the taxi, and I can't get out or hide, and people as they walk through the archway are peering in and seeing me trapped in there in an unpresentable state, and laughing at me.

I've had this dream or similar more than once. The worse public hostility to trans people gets in the UK, the more frequently I get it.

2.8: Myth two: 'Society is being brainwashed by trans ideology, and anyone who resists is cancelled'

To reuse a phrase from 1.15: Come off it. Our society is *overwhelmingly* cis. And as I pointed out in 1.13, it is absolutely saturated with gender ideology – but not trans gender ideology. In the UK, especially on the right wing, the mainstream media is utterly dominated by trans-exclusionary voices; even on the left wing there is only the *Guardian*, and that has been, to put it mildly, a decidedly shaky and inconsistent ally to trans people. It is absolutely commonplace for prestigious research and policy institutes to investigate ethical issues about transgender people's lives without making any space for transgender people's voices to be heard or taken seriously. (After all – and people say this, astoundingly enough, in all seriousness – the trans voices might be biased.) It is entirely usual for trans voices to be simply ignored, or at best treated as 'just one side of a debate'.

In 2020–1 in the UK, there was a whole slew of debates about transgender people and those who are critical of them and their allies. Given that I am (or was then) the only transgender philosophy professor in the UK, you might have supposed that the UK press would have been after me immediately to hear what I thought about these issues. Er, no. Actually, and very much to my astonishment, I was hardly ever contacted by the media throughout the whole moral panic; and I am still decidedly rare in my appearances. Of course, I wouldn't necessarily have welcomed the attentions of the press, and of course whether I get a word in edgeways is hardly the most important point about these debates; but I do find it quite extraordinary that the UK media are, in general, so very uninterested in the views of trans people in controversial debates about trans people.

This general uninterest in hearing trans voices is pervasive in the UK media; and, to be perfectly honest, more than a little irritating, given how frequently it comes in close conjunction with baseless alarmism about 'trans activists taking over everything'. (If only we were; in a whole range of areas, we could hardly do worse.) On the contrary, and speaking from my own experience: as a rule the microphone is very carefully and very ingeniously kept away from us. If anyone is being cancelled here, it's not the parade of 'gender-critical martyrs' who are endlessly interviewed and profiled in the newspapers (very often, with a crashingly unsubtle irony that surely not even the martyrs themselves can miss, about how cancelled they are). It's us, the transgender people who are so frequently the polemical target of those same 'martyrs', and of the papers that expend so much ink and paper on platforming them – and are almost never given even the smallest platform in the media.

In part this is certainly an intergenerational conflict. Trans-exclusionary attitudes are very clearly correlated with age, and young people almost never find trans people 'problematic'. (Not for nothing is one of the trans-exclusionaries' own symbols a dinosaur.) It is tempting to read the virulent transphobia of the UK press as the panicky rage of a bigoted social hegemony that knows it is losing its grip. We'll have to see, of course; but I very much hope that reading is not only tempting, but correct.

2.9: Myth three: 'Trans women are deluded, mentally ill'

Really? So what is our delusion? What is the falsehood that we irrationally believe? I don't believe falsely that I was born with a typically female-shaped body, or that I have one now; I am perfectly well aware that, alas, I wasn't, and alas, I don't. That's the whole point about being transgender, at least as I experience it: it's a longing to be a certain way that essentially depends for its force and tone on your own awareness that at any rate anatomically you aren't that way, and (/or) weren't born that way.

Certainly it's all rather strange. Trans women are not like most people, and the way they are can seem both peculiar and unfortunate to people who aren't trans. In particular, it can seem odd, and a rather cruel stroke of luck – it's one I've been thinking about for half a century now – that trans women characteristically long desperately for what natural-born women have and take for granted, while trans men characteristically long desperately for what natural-born men have and take for granted.

Apart from dressing up as a girl whenever I could, another thing I did as a small child was go round waking up moths during the daytime. After all, I reasoned, they were attracted by light. So why would they go to sleep whenever the sun came up – when what they want is light, and the sun is the biggest light there is? Their behaviour seemed odd and kind of perverse to me. So might the wishes of trans people: always to be something other than they are.

When I get on to the last myth, I'm going to be saying that God made me transgender and loves me that way. But there's an obvious theological question about that that I might as well tackle in advance, since we are close to it here. When 'conservative Christian'[35] trans-excluders claim the backing of the Bible for their half-baked hogwash, part of my

---

[35] Scare quotes because they're neither. Conservatives seek to preserve what is best about the past; but on the whole, moral panics against trans people are not something from the past at all. And such moral panics are profoundly un-Christian.

answer is that God made me a trans woman. But to put it as I just have, that means someone who 'characteristically longs desperately for what natural-born women have and take for granted'. Well, then: why didn't God cut out the middle-man (ha, ha) and just make me a natural-born woman in the first place?

I did ask God this question once, and I think he answered it. No choirs of angels or flashing lights, but I think I heard him reply: 'To thicken the plot.' Whether or not I heard right – it certainly does that.

Maybe being transgender is not a mistake or an illness or a delusion? Maybe it is, in itself, a gift?

An *odd* gift, sure. Yes. But what does that prove? It certainly doesn't prove delusion. In fact, it might prove the opposite. Because I am a trans woman, there are lots of aspects of living as a woman that I absolutely delight in (being called 'Darlin'' on Dundee buses for instance, and having people assume – correctly in my case – that I'm totally, hopelessly, jaw-droppingly rubbish at DIY) and that, so far as I know, give natural-born women no particular pleasure at all, and perhaps just rather annoy them. Maybe they're missing something. Maybe it is delightful to live as a woman, and I register it while they miss it. Likewise, maybe there are delights in living as a man. And perhaps not all of them were lost, when I lived that way, even on me.

Here we meet up with another thing you often hear.

2.10: Myth four: 'Trans women are men really'

What should we say about that one (besides what I've already said about it in 1.18, and what I'm going to say about it in Parts IV and V)? Some trans women want to double down, as it's now called, on the insistence that they're women; some people unsympathetic to or uncomprehending of trans women want to double down on the insistence that they're men. Here, I think, not only doth the (wannabe?) lady protest too much; so doth the transphobe. Why insist on the extremes? Why not take a softer and more accommodating line? What if this is what Derek Parfit calls an 'empty question', a question where what matters is to know all the facts in virtue of which people say the one thing or the other, and then, which way you go is actually less important – or perhaps both hardline answers are clearly shown up as unjustified?

Here's what I think we should say: what Aristotle so often, and usually so wisely, says: *pros ti men, pros alla d'ou* – 'Yes in some respects; but not in others.' Or as he might also say, 'men' (the English word, not the Greek one) is 'said numerous ways' – is ambiguous. Remember the point from 1.18 that 'female' is a cluster concept: so 'male' is a cluster concept too. If by 'men' you mean humans with masculine anatomy, hormones, and chromosomes, then certainly some trans women are males – though the ones who've had gender-reassignment surgery aren't males in two of these senses: they have feminine anatomy and hormones. But if by 'men' you mean what Sally Haslanger means, namely humans who are socialised into our society's masculine gender role, then it depends how trans women live. The more time a trans woman spends living in our society as a woman, the more she will be socialised as a woman, not as a man – at any rate, that's what will happen if she 'passes', i.e. if she looks enough like a natural-born woman to be unquestioningly identified as a woman by the society around her.

Of course, society might also identify her, not as a woman, nor yet as a man, but as a member of a third category: as a trans woman. That I think is what mostly happens to me; I'd love to pass, but I very rarely do. The solution to this, in my view, is just to accept it, and live in society in the gender role of trans woman. I think that's pretty much how I live. And given that this isn't Saudi Arabia, it's fine – so far.

The point about the social and gender role of trans woman, in this third-category sense, is that it isn't the same as either cis social or gender role: and so far as I can see, it doesn't inherently involve oppression. Anyway, the development of a trans woman gender role might even be a way of pointing forward to a state of things where we have gender roles, but none of them is oppressive (or: they have all become social roles?). And to have something like such roles but without oppression, if that were possible: that would be a very good thing. (For a sketch of what society might be like in that case, see Part VII.)

So one thing I want to say round about here is that, apart from anything else, there's something rude and unkind in 'Trans women are men really'. It's rude and unkind in the way that it's rude and unkind to say 'An adoptive parent isn't a parent really' – or even more obviously in the second person: 'You, adoptive "parent", are not really a parent.' (More about adoption in Part IV.)

In one way, the genetic sense, the truth of 'adoptive parents aren't real parents' is of course undeniable. But in another way, the social and legal sense, the statement is false: and not just by-your-leave false or metaphorically false, but literally false. So when someone insists on stating the genetic truth that 'Adoptive parents aren't parents really' in a wide variety of social contexts, the question of why they are insisting on it is going to arise pretty fast. And an urge to hurt and exclude is quite likely to be the answer to that question. I think exactly parallel considerations apply with 'Trans women are men really'.

One last thing that people can mean by 'Trans women are men really': they can mean that trans women are disguised men, men pretending to be women. The charge of sexual predatoriness is not far away here (see below). Also close to hand is a reaction to trans women that frequently leads to violence against them. Some men find it threatening that trans women are people who present as female but have, or often have, male anatomy. Why so? Possibly because those men, rather in the Russian-fascist way described in 2.3, are insecure in their own masculinity: either they're afraid that if they don't react violently to trans women, they'll find that they want to dress up as girls themselves; or they're worried by the fact that they are sexually attracted to trans women (after all, 'only a poof would feel that'). Or they take exception to what they see as an attempt to deceive them – the thinking is that trans women want their sexual attentions, and are trying to con them into bestowing them. I don't need to say anything to bring out what Neolithic responses these all are. Still, it is worth taking a little time to try and understand these reactions, given that they regularly result in trans women's deaths.

2.11: Myth five: 'What trans women really need is not "the affirmation model" but aversion therapy or talking out of being transgender'

I've said a bit already about 'the affirmation model', i.e. the not-gaslighting-people-senseless model, in 1.25 above. If I have made anything clear in this book so far, I hope it is this: I know from my own experience that trying to talk people out of being transgender simply doesn't work. If it worked, it would have worked on me, because I wanted it to work, and indeed tried to make it work; I tried to talk *myself* out of being transgender. I tried incredibly hard, with the whole force of my psyche, with aversion and avoidance and with prayer and fasting (literally), not to be transgender, for decades on end. Well, as you see, it didn't work. There was no way of changing or denying the deep truth about who I am. It is far better to work with it than to work against it.

I take the next two accusations against trans women together, because they're a kind of enfilade – opposite political charges, from the opposite ends of the political spectrum. The right say the first, and the left say the second:

2.12: Myths six and seven: 'Trans women are cultural Marxists, part of a cunning ideological plan to overthrow the traditional family'; but also: 'Trans women are subverting feminism by reinforcing the ideology of the patriarchy'

I reject both these myths. I don't want to overthrow the traditional family. I live in a traditional family, or at any rate a fairly traditional one, and I like it very much. I can, if I try, imagine possible set-ups (see Part VII for one possibility); but I am quite happy with this one. And within this set-up, I just want to get on with my life. Which happens to involve my being married to the most wonderful woman in the entire world; and the most patient.[36]

On subverting feminism, see above. I think trans women can only plausibly be seen as reinforcing the patriarchy if we think that what they're after is the woman's gender role. But I don't think that is what most trans women are after; it's certainly not what I'm after. What it's about for me, like I keep saying, is having a body of the male shape, and wishing I had a body of the female shape, and trying to work out how to live with that mismatch between desire and reality. Unless there is

[36] One criticism I have sometimes encountered for the way I talk about my private life is this: 'Sophie Grace has a wife and children, yet *she never talks about them. The biological women* in her life have no place in her self-presentation! She *silences* them! She *erases* them!'

Apparently, these critics take it for granted that whether or not the 'biological women in my life' appear in my public discussions is something that is entirely up to me. That doesn't sound to me like a terribly feminist assumption. It certainly wouldn't pass muster with my wife and children.

something patriarchal about the anatomical differences between males and females – and how could there be? – there's nothing in this want that is necessarily a reinforcement of patriarchy at all. Quite the reverse, I'd suggest: the whole business of being transgender subverts patriarchy. About that at any rate, the right-wing headbanger transphobes are correct. The UKIPer in the Welsh Senedd who stated, with an echo of Patriarch Kirill, that tolerating transgender in Wales would mean 'the collapse of civilisation' was absolutely right. Tolerating transgender in Wales will indeed hasten the end of the kind of society that he values. Well, you know what? I grew up in a society exactly like that, and the sooner such societies all collapse, the better for everyone, transgender and cisgender alike.

On to another pair of charges that often come together:

2.13: Myths eight and nine: 'Trans women are really sissies, softies as the Beano used to call them (malakoi, 1 Corinthians 6.9), effeminate, weak, limp-wristed'; but also: 'Trans women are sexual predators'

As the biblical reference shows, the softy charge is an old, old charge. Women are weak, men are strong. So men who want to be like women must be weak too – unmanly, indeed, and effeminate. (Remember the cult of strength in fascism discussed in 2.3?) It's a charge I often think about while I stand for an hour or two (like I do most winters) on an icy belay-ledge 400 feet above the deck in a godforsaken Scottish glen five miles from the road, often in minus 20°C, a whiteout, and a force nine gale, halfway up some ultra-technical winter-climbing grade VII sick-fest that no one has ever climbed before. I mean there must be some truth to the charge, right? Because it's certainly true that I don't usually lead such routes, and Simon Richardson, my perfectly straight and cis partner, does all the really difficult stuff while I belay him. Still, I just wish the self-described real men who want to make this charge would come and find soft, sissy, limp-wristed, effeminate, pansy, big-girl's-blouse, mincing-nancy me while I am on that belay-ledge, and explain it to me a bit better.

As a matter of fact, though, I do think there's this much truth in the charge of effeminacy or unmanliness: judging by myself and the other

trans women I know, it seems to be roughly true in erotic matters. I've said something about this already, in 1.33. The thing is this: trans women are not usually – how can I put this? – very go-getting sexually speaking. Picky and reticent. They tend to respond rather than to initiate; they tend to be, and to want to be, passive in sexual and romantic encounters, rather than active. They don't want to sweep up someone in their arms and carry that person away on a white charger; they want to be swept away by some beautiful charming prince. Erotically speaking, if you'll forgive my directness, the fantasy for me is not conquering; it's being conquered.

Still less, for me, does the fantasy involve trolling lesbians on Twitter, and telling them that they're transphobic if they don't want to have sex with pre-op/non-op trans women. I am pretty horrified that anyone does that, and it strikes me as, well, a profoundly un-trans-woman-ish thing to do, precisely because it's so aggressive, and so obviously a violation of the most basic rules of decent interaction between civilised grown-ups. Being a trans woman for me is all about being the very opposite of aggressive, certainly in bed, and perhaps elsewhere too.

Or at any rate that's what I'm like, and lots of other trans women too apparently. And it has this consequence: I am the last person in the world who would be any good at all at being a sexual predator. That's why, when I hear trans women described as a sexual threat to other women, I tend to think 'Who, me? I wouldn't even know how to.'

Anyway, on to the final myth in my catalogue.

2.14: Myth ten: 'Transgender is unbiblical and sinful'

'The Bible tells us' (people frequently say) 'that all people are by nature either men or women, so it is sinful for anyone to be one and want to be the other.' They refer us to 'Male and female created he them' in Genesis 1.27 and 5.2. And we're supposed to see at once that this piece of narrative about what God did at the creation, in two ancient versions of the creation story, is a command about how we should act today.

So what about all the other things that God does in that story, such as separating the 'waters above' from the 'waters below' (Genesis 1.7)? Is that piece of narrative somehow a command as well? If it is, what does it command us to do?

We're not supposed to raise awkward questions about bracketing, either. Maybe God didn't create them {male} and {female}; maybe he created them {male and female}. That is, maybe what the text tells us is not just about an absolute division; maybe it's about a division between two polarities, both of which are present in each of us, but to different degrees. Read this way, the text is the very opposite of support for a trans-exclusive position.[37]

---

[37] I say maybe. But as a matter of fact, I now learn from a friend on Twitter, Rabbi Daniel Bogard, that there is venerable Rabbinical authority for *exactly this* reading of Genesis 1.27: 'Adam was "made in God's image", which according to Bereshit Rabbah 8:1 means: "At the moment when the Holy Blessed One created the first

No doubt Genesis 1.27 is pushed into prominence by the fact that Jesus cites it in Mark 10.6. But Jesus isn't condemning transgender there; he is condemning his contemporaries' casual misogyny. They get rid of the wives they don't want any more, perhaps out of mere inclination, or perhaps because they have in mind some other more politically or financially advantageous marriage. In so doing, they prove themselves profoundly selfish, oppressive, and unjust, and (given the sociological background, in which women simply cannot live alone) they force their abandoned wives to find some other man's protection, which involves those wives (and those new husbands) also in taking a far too instrumental approach to marriage. That is what Jesus is saying at Mark 10.6. So if the citation of Genesis 1.27 in this context tells us anything, it is that Jesus wants his hearers to understand that God cares about the women he created just as much as he cares about the men he created. Despite its frequent deployment to underwrite a legalistic opposition to divorce, the passage doesn't even do that. A fortiori, it has nothing to do with transgender.

The trans-exclusive position seems confused anyway: it tells us, apparently, both (1) that people are by nature either male or female and nothing in between, and therefore (2) that people go wrong if they allow themselves to be anything in between. But (1) is false: some of us are something in between, and the back-up argument, 'Well, but that's because you're sinful', entirely fails to put its finger on any non-circular way in which being transgender is sinful. And (2) not only doesn't follow from (1); it seems actually inconsistent with (1). If people are by nature either male or female, then how can it even be possible for anyone to

---

adam, God created them as an androginos, as it is written: "male and female God created them"' (https://twitter.com/RavBogard/status/1518611679587844098). Rabbi Bogard also points out, in the same thread, that there is Rabbinical authority for seeing Abraham and Sarah as what we would call non-binary: 'The rabbis of the Talmud even get into an argument as to which category of (the very much non-binary) sex/gender spectrum Abraham and Sarah fall into! Don't believe me that ancient Jews didn't see gender as a binary? Check out the 2000yo sacred Mishnah Bikurim 4:1–4' (https://twitter.com/RavBogard/status/1518610030588792834). For further references, Rabbi Bogard points us to Noam Sienna, *A Rainbow Thread: An Anthology of Queer Jewish Texts from the First Century to 1969* (Printocraft Press, 2019).

go wrong in this way? There is no fault of even integers tending to be *a bit* odd, to veer towards oddness. Integers are even, or they're odd, and nothing in between, and that's all there is to it. If human beings are male, or they're female, and nothing in between, then how can there be any more to this, either?

A broader and deeper question lying behind such ruminations – and how often over the years I've ruminated on them – is the simple question: what is it for the Bible to tell us anything? As I say, there is a particular problem about this when people try to extract a command, something in the imperative mood, from what is on the face of it a narrative, something in the indicative mood. But even when the Old Testament is written in the imperative mood – see Deuteronomy 22.5 for what looks like a fairly clear Mosaic condemnation of cross-dressing – awkward questions of all sorts arise. This is because no end of things are condemned in the Old Testament that we (unless we're Hasidim) have absolutely no moral problem with whatsoever today. We recognise, and reject, those condemnations for what they are, which I think is, if the Hasidim will forgive my bluntness, no more than primitive and now-pointless taboos. (See the brilliant website godhatesshrimp.com for a bravura development of this point.)

The more you look at it, the more you get the impression that trans-exclusive readers of the Bible are a bit desperate really. They're absolutely sure that being transgender must be wrong; they just need to find a text that says so. And, poor dears, they really struggle with this effort to close the gap between their antecedent prejudice and what the Bible actually says (and doesn't say). I know the struggle from the inside, because I did precisely this myself for many years; I too wanted to be sure that being transgender was wrong, and combed the Bible for evidence that it was wrong, and was decidedly baffled by the lack of anything clear at all on the subject. I'm also bisexual, and I was fighting that too, so it used to worry me deeply that I couldn't even find any very clear condemnation of homosexuality in the Bible – never mind of transgender. The Bible goes on and on and on about the wickedness of accumulating money, and plenty of rich evangelicals are very smooth and slick about talking their way round that mountain of evidence that condemns their monstrous and idolatrous greed. At the same time, they want to condemn me for being a trans woman on the basis of, essentially, no biblical evidence whatsoever. It just doesn't stack up.

But it's not merely that the trans-exclusive reading of the biblical evidence doesn't stack up in *au pied de la lettre* exegetical terms. Even less does it stack up if we move from the letter of the scriptures to the spirit of the scriptures. What is Christianity's holy book really about, taken as a whole? The New Testament and the Old Testament alike are, fundamentally, about human liberation: about setting us free from the taboos and mind-traps that enslave us. And they are about human redemption: about God taking what we are, however little we ourselves may feel able to accept what we are, and finding a place for everything that we are in the fulfilment of his good purposes. Why shouldn't it be possible for my transgender nature to be part of what God redeems? How, indeed, is it even possible that it wouldn't be?

There is a wonderful story in my favourite poet Gerard Manley Hopkins's journals of his travels, as a young man, in Switzerland. Hopkins was a deeply devout Catholic for many reasons. One of his less sensible reasons – and 'it takes one to know one', I know this psychology immediately when I see it, from my own case – was to enlist God's forces in his own internal civil war, his own struggles with a side of himself that he simply couldn't accept, his own homosexuality. There seems no doubt that some of the fiercest homophobia of all comes from those who are externalising an inner battle; once upon a time, as a keen young evangelical who was also a repressed bisexual, I did this myself. (And I think you have to have a parallel worry about the number of trans-exclusionary commentators who nowadays go around saying both 'It's terrible, this recent wave of young people identifying as trans and getting accepted for it!' and also 'If people had been so permissive about transgender when I was young maybe I would have identified as trans myself.')

So anyway – we get this, on Sunday, 19 July 1868 when Hopkins and his friend Edward Bond were on a walking tour in Switzerland, and when Hopkins was fasting, perhaps as a penance for having been unable to find a Mass to attend:

> We came up with a guide who reminded me of Father John. He took EB's rucksack and on finding the reason why I would not let him take mine said

Le bon Dieu n'est pas comme ça. The man probably was a rational Protestant; if a Catholic at least he rationalised gracefully, as they do in Switzerland.[38]

Oh, Gerard... the thing is, the guide was exactly right. And you don't have to be, horror of horrors, 'a rational Protestant', or any kind of 'rationaliser', to understand why. You just need to see that the real God accepted Gerard Manley Hopkins more completely and more graciously than Gerard Manley Hopkins ever managed to accept himself.

And that is exactly what I have found in my own life: that the way God sees me, as the trans woman Sophie Grace Chappell, is the way I really am; that the way he looks at me is with totally accepting grace, with freely given, liberating, undeserved love; and that the highest wisdom possible for me is to let myself be loved at least a tiny part of how much he actually wants to love me.

So ends Part II, and with it the main autobiographical narrative of this book. In Parts III–V, I present (much more briefly) something more like a conventional philosophical argument, a fairly continuous line that gets us from questions about the 'genderedness' of consciousness to issues about conceptual engineering. Then Parts VI and VII are something else again; two other somethings, in fact.

If this book has been your cup of tea up to this point, it may now begin to be less to your taste – and conversely. But of course, I hope my readers will enjoy both my narrative approach so far and my argumentative approach from here on in. When I rejected 'systematic theory' in 1.15, I was – as I was careful to say there – most certainly not rejecting straightforward argument in favour of narratively recounted 'experience' or of anything else. It never has to be one or the other; it always can, in the end, be both.

[38] W.H. Gardner, ed., *Gerard Manley Hopkins: Poems and Prose* (Penguin, 1967), p. 114.

PART III

Is Consciousness Gendered?[1]

3.1: The alleged inaccessibility of 'what-is-it-like?'

'What is it like', a man might ask, 'to be a woman?'

'Well, what is it like', a woman might retort, 'to be a man?'

What-is-it-like questions are always intriguing. And, some might add (perhaps the two in this dialogue), impossible to answer. For if a woman could say what it is like to be a man (or vice versa), that would have to mean that she could occupy his very viewpoint on the world. It would mean that his consciousness, his subjective viewpoint, could turn into her consciousness.

But how could that happen? My 'subjective viewpoint' is not a literal viewpoint, like the summit of Arthur's Seat, that I can occupy, or vacate to let you see the view from there. Nor is consciousness like a virtual-reality headset that anyone can wear. I can't just hand over to you the eye-goggles and the ear-phones of my experience, so that you can experience as directly as I do what it is like to be me.

But even if my consciousness was like a virtual-reality headset that you could just put on, what would you get by wearing it? You wouldn't get *my experience*. You'd get *your experience of* my experience. But when you asked 'what it was like to be me', that evidently wasn't what you were after.

'Come to our *musée folklorique* at Artisanal-en-Provence!', say the tourist brochures, 'Come and have an authentic experience of life as a French peasant!'. 'Hmm', says the philosopher (in her exasperating way). Whatever else a tourist may find to delight her in Artisanal-en-Provence, it seems a good bet that it won't be *that*. If things go well for her there, she will end up thinking, 'Wow, so this is what it is like to be

[1] Thanks for comments to Imogen Chappell, James Holden, Katherine Dormandy, and an audience at the University of Innsbruck in May 2023.

an authentic French peasant'. But by definition, this is a thought that would never even occur to an authentic French peasant. At least, not to an *authentic* authentic French peasant.

3.2: *The publicity of the mental*

Despite this line of objection, we should keep hold of an important truth that philosophy has often obscured. This is that, at least sometimes, others' consciousnesses, their mental lives, are known to us just by looking and seeing. Since at least Descartes's time, most philosophers have taken for granted 'the privacy of the mental'. But sometimes mental states are as public as anything else. When you hit your thumb with the hammer, I see, directly, that you are in pain. When the cabinet minister staggers out of Downing Street, I see, directly, that he is blind drunk. When the school bully humiliates the shy pupil in front of the whole class, her anguished embarrassment is not *private*, as most of her previous mental states were. Being shy, she is a specialist in hiding. But that is precisely her torment as she faces the bully's jeers: *this* mental state of hers is public, directly visible to everyone.

Connectedly, there is such a thing as vicarious proprioception. As I watch the climber reach for the crucial elusive hold, my finger muscles clench. When the pianist reaches the last few very testing bars of Chopin's Nocturne 9.2, I hold my breath in anticipation. When I see a toddler's parent step on a Lego brick lurking in a patterned carpet, I feel his pain – quite close to literally. In these and many other cases, the mental isn't private at all; at least not if 'private' means 'unobservable'. Despite Descartes, when we ask what-is-it-like questions, our questions needn't always be unanswerable; or even hard to answer.

3.3: *Bats and humans and men and women*

One classic modern source for what-it-is-like questions is Thomas Nagel's famous journal article 'What is it like to be a bat?'.[2] Nagel thinks that it is obviously true that there is *something* it is like to be a bat; there

[2] *Philosophical Review* 83.4 (October 1974): 435–450.

are *facts* about what it is like to be a bat; bats have consciousness, just as we do. But bats and humans have very different kinds of consciousness. So, for example, echolocation plays for bats roughly the function that sight plays for human beings. But even though they are functionally analogous, it seems obvious that there must be differences between the subjective experiences of seeing and echolocating. Or again (I would add; this isn't in Nagel), bats have a natural urge to take wing and fly through the night sky, scanning it for moths and midges to gobble up as they go. Humans have no such urge; or at least, none of the humans I've met have. (Perhaps humans who do feel that urge don't live long enough to be easy to meet; unless, alternatively, they are undead.) Conversely bats, as far as I know, display no natural urge to create works of art, or to fight wars.

These truths about perception (and, as I add, desire) make it a fact that bat consciousness is very different from human consciousness, just as it is a fact that bat bodies are very different from human bodies. How do the facts about consciousness relate to the facts about bodies? Nagel thinks that this is rather a deep philosophical mystery: a mystery that we might also call 'the mind-body problem'. On the one hand, we can't easily explain how, if at all, the two kinds of fact are connected. On the other hand, neither can we just deny the existence of either kind of fact. The mind-body problem leaves us scratching our heads. Perhaps it even *should* leave us that way. Alongside 'What is it like to be a bat?', we might equally ask the two questions I began with: 'What is it like to be a man?' and 'What is it like to be a woman?'. Is there anything that it is *distinctively* like to be a man or a woman, as there is something that it is *distinctively* like to be a bat, or a human (or a dog, or a llama, etc.)? At the level of our consciousness, is there 'a man's world' and 'a woman's world'? Are there two separate realms of consciousness here, each with its own particular flavour?

Sex is distinct from gender; I'll say how in a moment. So this question also can be divided in two. We can ask whether there is anything it is distinctively like to be female or male (a question about sex). And we can ask whether there is anything it is distinctively like to be feminine or masculine (a question about gender).

I think the answer to both these questions is 'Obviously yes'. Why yes? And why obviously?

3.4: Bodiliness

There is something it is distinctively like to be male or female because a crucial – and overwhelmingly obvious – aspect of what it is like to be human is bodiliness.[3] Our consciousness of our own bodies is fundamental to nearly all the rest of our consciousness. (There are 'out of body experiences', apparently; but they are exceptional.) The form of our bodies, and our awareness of our bodies from 'inside them', is an essential condition of the form of our phenomenology: *what it is like to be human* is, in key part, *what it is like to have a human body*. (Notice how this point can help us with Nagel's initial question 'What is it like to be a bat?', and also with Nagel's further question concerning how facts about bodies relate to facts about consciousness. Notice too how it *can't* help us with those two questions.)

But male and female bodies differ, and in distinctive ways. As male and female, they are typically differently shaped, e.g. in genitalia, in having or lacking breasts, in distribution of body fat and body hair, in size and in musculature. They are subject to different sensibilities: females feel the cold more, males are less good at coping with sleep-deprivation. They are affected by different hormonal secretions, and on different timescales, and these different hormones have different effects on their moods and their inclinations. Very crudely, females (or most of them within a certain age range) experience the menstrual cycle, while males (same caveat) experience ... testosterone. Male and female bodies even smell different (I gather this is related to the hormonal differences).

In the case of the sex distinction, male/female, what matters is the physical; in the case of the gender distinction, masculine/feminine, what matters is the political. *Male and female* consciousnesses differ because male and female bodies differ; *masculine and feminine* consciousnesses differ because male and female political roles have differed. So there is something it is distinctively like to be masculine or feminine, because a crucial – and overwhelmingly obvious – aspect of what it is like to be human is political life.

---

[3] On this aspect of what it is like to be human, see my *Epiphanies*, 4.4–4.5; on what it is like to human in general, see the whole of Chapter 4 in *Epiphanies*.

I mean this in a broad sense of 'political'. Wherever there are humans, there are power relations. One foundation of these power relations is the management of expectation. The task of predicting the behaviour of other humans (whether groups or individuals) is intractably huge. We reduce this task to manageable proportions via conventions and taboos, expectations and reliances, contracts and understandings, traditions and rules. From these, over time, grows ideology.

Central to many of these conventions, etc., is the profiling of other humans. One obvious way to profile them is by their biological sex (actual or perceived). From this, over time, grows the ideology of gender: we build up a story about what kind of social and communal role follows from membership of either biological sex. Our concepts of 'masculine' and 'feminine' are, precisely, stories of this kind. That such stories can and do encode not only power relations but also oppression, and that this has been their function throughout history, is obvious from the beginning of our culture.

3.5: Raising consciousness

'But hang on', some people might object at this point, 'consciousness is just subjective awareness of the world! What does *politics* have to do with whether *consciousness is gendered*?'. This objection attributes a false – and ideologically driven – unworldly purity to consciousness. The philosophy of mind is not, *pace* so many of its contemporary exponents, an ethically neutral or ideologically innocent study. The philosophy of mind is a part of 'human science'; politics has *everything* to do with it. When Karl Marx popularised the phrase 'class consciousness' (*Klassenbewusstsein*), his use of 'consciousness' was not a mere homophony. We humans are both physical and political beings: our political condition shapes our awareness of the world as surely as our physical condition.

Here is George Orwell on anarchist Barcelona in 1936:

When one came straight from England the aspect of Barcelona was something startling and overwhelming. It was the first time that I had ever been in a town where the working class was in the saddle. Practically every building of any size had been seized by the workers and was draped with red flags or with the red and black flag of the Anarchists … Every shop and café had an inscription saying that it had been collectivized; even the bootblacks had been collectivized and their boxes painted red and black. Waiters and shop-walkers looked you in the face and treated you as an equal. Servile and even ceremonial forms of speech had temporarily disappeared. Nobody said 'Señor' or 'Don' or even 'Usted'; everyone called everyone else 'Comrade' and 'Thou', and said 'Salud!' instead of 'Buenos días'. Tipping was forbidden by law since the time of Primo de Rivera; almost my first experience was receiving a lecture from a hotel manager for trying to tip a lift-boy. There were no private motor-cars, they had all been commandeered, and all the trams and taxis and much of the other transport were painted red and black. The revolutionary posters were everywhere, flaming from the walls in clean reds and blues that made the few remaining advertisements look like daubs of mud. Down the Ramblas, the wide central artery of the town where crowds of people streamed constantly to and fro, the loudspeakers were bellowing revolutionary songs all day and far into the night.[4]

I remember having a rather similar experience to Orwell's when I visited Bulgaria in the Soviet era and was forcibly struck by the difference in Bulgarian people's body language from how people held themselves in England: the bowed shoulders, the refusal to meet each other's eyes, the way even a walk across a railway-station concourse was a kind of furtive sidle, the constant sideways and backwards vigilance for the police – whose body language was completely different from everyone else's: it was the strutting, shameless, crotch-first body language of the cock of the walk, the school bully again. It sounds clichéd to say that when you live under a tyranny you are constantly watching your back; but it is the literal truth. The reality of ubiquitous surveillance charges your whole experience with a sense of vulnerability, exposure, *nakedness*. During my short time passing through communist Sofia, I not only not noticed how everyone else was, literally, watching their backs; I found myself doing it too.

Consciousness is not a mere bloodless abstraction: it is, among other things, politically charged. Nor is oppression a mere abstraction: for the oppressed, it shapes every aspect of how they see their environment, the obstacles and the affordances, the threats and the opportunities, in their

[4] G. Orwell, *Homage to Catalonia* (Secker and Warburg, 1938), Ch. 1.

way. To transpose a remark of Wittgenstein's, the world of the oppressed person *is a different world* from the world of the free person.[5]

3.6: A brief history of gender oppression

All of this applies as much to oppression via the category of gender as it does to class oppression. Consider Homer, *Iliad* 1.431–450 (my translation):

> Odysseus came to Chryse with his sacrifice.
> Once they were in the deep harbour, then his sailors
> took down the sail and stowed it within the black ship ...
> then disembarked and walked ashore through the surf,
> bringing the oxen to be offered to Apollo;
> and out of the ship there also stepped Chryseis.
> Led to the altar by Odysseus of the wiles,
> back in her father's hands, she heard him speak:
> 'Agamemnon lord of men has sent me, Chryses,
> to give you back your child, and to sacrifice
> a hundred oxen to appease Apollo,
> to stop the wide-wept woes he's brought the Greeks.'
> He spoke and gave her up, and Chryses had back
> his daughter, his delight. Swift then for sacrifice
> they placed the beasts about the firm-built altar,
> with pure hands took the sacred barley up.
> And Chryses raised his arms in prayer for them ...

Chryseis was captured in war by the Greek field-marshal Agamemnon, and became his slave-girl. Her father, the priest Chryses, begged Agamemnon to return her to him. Agamemnon rudely dismissed Chryses' request; the god Apollo disapproved and sent a plague on the Greek army. So now, to appease Apollo and end the plague, Agamemnon sends Odysseus as his envoy to return Chryseis to her father.

The transaction that is going on in the present passage is essentially one between the warlords Agamemnon and Achilles, neither of whom

---

[5] *Tractatus* 6.43.

is even present. The transaction is about Chryseis, but she herself is just a piece of property; she has no more standing to speak in this transaction than do the oxen that are brought along with her. (We can do the ideology of the 'human'/'animal' distinction another time.) In Homer's text, she does not even have her own name, any more than do the cattle that she travels with: 'Chryseis' is a patronymic not a proper name, meaning no more than 'daughter of Chryses' (which in turn apparently just means 'man of Chryse (the place)'). It takes a scholiast on Homer (a scholar annotating the margins of the manuscript) to tell us that she even had a name of her own, a name that wasn't just a derivative of her father's name, and that her own name was Astynome.[6]

Before the events described in the quotation, Chryseis (/Astynome) has watched one man, Agamemnon, kill her family and neighbours, burn her city down, rape, enslave, and imprison herself. Now she watches another man, Odysseus, hand her back to a third man, her own father. And through all of this she herself *never says a word*. She does indeed keep what Pat Barker, in the title of a wonderful novel about just these Homeric transactions, calls *The Silence of the Girls*.

This is a world where, on the basis of the masculine/feminine gender distinction, half the human species is treated as subservient to the other half. It is a world where the reality of women as human people, and as conscious experiencers, is close to completely erased. It is a world of war and violence; a world of religiously sanctioned pillage and rape, and the fetishisation of possession and status. It is a world (as Simone Weil so well sees in her famous essay 'The *Iliad* as poem of force') that is built upon the possibilities for violence that are present in the human body. And I agree with Weil, against Nietzsche, that this vision of the world as a terrible place of violence and oppression, a place where force turns its victim into a thing, is a vision which is to be wept over, not (as Nietzsche thought) celebrated.

[U]ne telle accumulation de violences serait froide sans un accent d'inguérissable amertume qui se fait continuellement sentir, bien qu'indiqué

---

[6] Latinised as Cressida, Chryseis' name was transferred to a quite different character in the Middle Ages: Shakespeare's Cressida is drawn, via Chaucer and Boccaccio, from Benoît de Sainte-Maure's twelfth-century *Roman de Troie*, and has little or nothing to do with Homer's Chryseis.

souvent par un seul mot, souvent même par une coupe de vers, par un rejet. C'est par là que l'*Iliade* est une chose unique, par cette amertume qui procède de la tendresse, et qui s'étend sur tous les humains, égale comme la clarté du soleil.[7]

The *Iliad*'s world is the world of the patriarchy. (Or *a* world of the patriarchy, one version of that world.) There is simply no possibility, in such a world, that masculine and feminine consciousnesses, men's and women's subjective experiences of that world, could be *anything but* different.

Consciousness is gendered, and obviously gendered, because the political realities of what it is like to be masculine, and what it is like to be feminine, are distinctively different. Moreover, consciousness is sexed too, and obviously sexed, because the physical realities of what it is like to be male, and what it is like to be female, are distinctively different. And that is why the answer to our two questions is not just 'Yes', but 'Obviously yes'.

3.7: Two objections

At this point I predict that I will face two objections: one (so to speak) from the right, and the other from the left. The right-wing objection will be about what I have just said about masculine/feminine and political oppression. It will be: 'But that was *Homer's* time. You can't argue that gender is oppressive *now* by pointing out that it was oppressive *then*.' The left-wing objection, by contrast, will be about what I said earlier about male/female and physical difference, and it will be: 'Wow, innate differences between males and females on the basis of their bodies? What a sexist you are.'

To the objection from the right, my answer is that gender is an ideology that oppresses people in our society as surely as it did in Homer's

---

[7] I quote in French because of the beauty of Weil's prose. I translate: 'Such a piling-up of acts of violence would fall cold artistically, but for a tone of unhealable bitterness that we continually hear, even though it is sometimes signalled only by a single word – or even by a cutting-off of the verse, by a refusal to say something. It is because of this that the *Iliad* is something unique: because of this bitterness that arises from tenderness, and which is extended to all human beings alike, as equally as the shining of the sun.'

– though, to be sure, the oppression is much less extreme now than it was then. The objection is quite right to draw our attention to the fact of historical change: a fact that is always relevant when thinking about politics, but all too apt to go missing when we are doing philosophy. People don't always manage to notice that ethics is a study that is conditioned by history and politics. Even when they do notice that, they are still (as I said before) very prone to make the mistaken assumption that, in contrast to ethics, philosophy of mind is an apolitical study.

Our enquiries into a question like 'Is consciousness gendered?' can easily be undermined by this mistake. There isn't a timeless fact of the matter that answers this question: gender is ideological and political, and ideologies and politics change. So even if consciousness is in fact always gendered, there are different *ways* for it to be gendered, corresponding to those different political and ideological possibilities. And since ideology is not always equally bad or harmful – since some ideology, indeed, is not harmful at all: cp. my comparison with smell and accent in 1.13 above – it becomes possible for us to ask the question what a *benign* ideology of gender might look like. Are there ways of keeping the, or a, masculine/feminine distinction in our society that are not harmful, that are perhaps even positively beneficial? Yes, I think so. To ask whether *ideology* is always bad is, in a way, to ask whether *politics* is always bad; whether it is even possible to have a more or less harmless politics. Despite some bitter experience, I am not entirely pessimistic about this possibility. But I just note it; I won't here try to explore it any further.

I turn to the objection from the left. This is the objection that it is sexist to say, as I have said, that consciousness is not only gendered but also sexed, because there are physical differences between males and females. My answer is: not at all, *provided* we notice that the male/female distinction is not the only axis of physical difference that we might observe among human bodies. As well as distinguishing human bodies as male/female, we can also distinguish them as old/young, well/ill, fat/thin, strong/weak, able-bodied/disabled, and in many other ways as well. If my question had been 'Is human consciousness modified by health/illness?', my answer to that too would have been 'Yes, obviously'. If it had been 'Is consciousness modified by age?', the same again. Likewise for fat/thin, strong/weak, and all sorts of other bodily distinctions that we might draw as well.

In all of these respects I am simply following out the logic of my own argument. I started by saying that a crucial determinant of human consciousness or subjectivity is our experience of our own bodiliness: what it is like to be a human being is determined, in key part, by what it is like to have a human body. But there are many different *kinds* of human body. For very many of the particular kinds of human being that we distinguish by reference to their bodies, what it is like to be a human being of that kind has a distinctive nature, determined by reference to the kind of body in question. *One* of the distinctions we make about human bodies is, of course, male/female. But *only* one. What prompts the allegation of sexism here is the perception that I have said that the male/female distinction is *the single key distinction* that we make among human bodies. But I haven't said that. I didn't say that at any point; and what I have just said is an explicit denial of it.

Let me say it again: there are lots of ways of distinguishing among human bodies; the male/female distinction is just one of those many distinctions; to take this to be *a* distinction is both natural and reasonable; to take it to be *the only distinction that matters* is neither inevitable nor even correct. It is, in fact, a dangerous piece of ideology, and one that has been absolutely crucial to the process whereby the physical distinction male/female has normally been deployed to rationalise the political distinction masculine/feminine. According to the ideology of gender that still dominates our world today, biology itself vindicates the idea of a world that is and must be *authoritatively and definitively binarily divided* between the masculine and the feminine. But biology itself does no such thing. Biology certainly recognises *a* distinction between the male and the female bodies; but biology also recognises distinctions between rhesus-positive and rhesus-negative bodies, left-handed and right-handed bodies, tall bodies and short bodies, and so on as above. Which of these distinctions between body types we choose to foreground, and which to pass over as less important or not important at all, is not a *biological* decision; it is a political one.

My question has been: 'Is consciousness gendered, differentiated by the masculine/feminine distinction?' My answer is: 'Yes; and consciousness is sexed too, differentiated by the male/female distinction.' But it is also differentiated in lots of other ways by lots of other distinctions. Which of these distinctions we decide to treat as more or less important is not settled solely by the unthinking power of ideology. It can be, and sometimes is, consciously settled by us.

3.8: Is consciousness trans*gendered?*

There is another distinction that you might expect me to make here. This is the cis/trans distinction, the distinction between those who are transgender and those who are not. We have been asking whether consciousness is gendered. What about whether it is *trans*gendered? Is there, in other words, anything that it's specifically and distinctively like to be transgender?

Speaking as a trans woman, my answer is 'Yes, there most certainly is'. To be transgender is to stand in a *very* distinctive relation both to the masculine/feminine divide, and to the male/female divide. As I experience it, it is to find myself at odds with both those classifications. My own story is about finding myself classified both as masculine and as male when what feels right and natural to me, and what I want for myself, is to be classified on the other side of both distinctions – as feminine, and as female. This is certainly a story about finding, among many other things, that my consciousness has a particular and distinctive quality that clearly isn't there in other people's consciousness – except when they too are transgender.

There are other possible transgender stories. (Even for trans women; trans men and gender-non-affirming people are moving in other directions again.) For instance, someone might care only about moving from male to female, and reject the masculine/feminine distinction altogether (i.e. she might regard it as bad ideology that should just be abolished). Or she might care only about moving from masculine to feminine, and reject the male/female distinction more or less altogether (i.e. she might regard it as unimportant biology that should not be foregrounded in the way we organise society or think about ourselves). But at any rate *some* trans women, including me, think that both the male/female and the masculine/feminine distinctions are capable of being given positive and nonharmful political expressions. And we think that we ourselves would do better on the other side of both distinctions from where we started out.

Now, on the whole, people (including transgender people) are demonstrably correct in their judgements about what would be better for them. And we live in a society where everyone is supposed to have a wide latitude of freedom to choose what they think is better for them even when they *aren't* correct. So it is not easy to see why anyone would struggle to allow transgender people the same simple right of self-determination that cisgender people take for granted.

However – welcome to the UK, 2024.

PART IV

The Adoption Analogy

4.1: The analogy

Part II's fourth myth was 'Trans women are men really' (2.10). I have a bit more to say about this myth. I'll say it here.

Maybe we should look at it like this: Trans women/men are to women/men as adoptive parents are to parents. There are disanalogies of course, and the morality of adoption is a large issue in itself which I can't do full justice to here. Still, the analogies are, I think, important and instructive.

An adoptive parent is someone who desperately wants to be a parent but can't be one in the normal biological sense. (At any rate usually – there are families with a mix of biological and adopted children. But here I'll focus on the commoner and simpler case.) So society has found a way for them to live the role of a parent, and to be recognised socially and legally as a parent, which kind of gets round the biological obstacle.

'Kind of': plenty of adoptive parents report an abiding regret that they aren't biological parents, and there can be problems on either side of the adoptive relationship. It is clear that the existence of adoptive relationships creates psychological difficulties, both for the parents and for the children, that would not otherwise exist. But these problems are not big enough to make adoption a net bad thing.

One reason why not is that adoptive parents are, in the nature of the case, deeply committed to parenting. Unlike some biological parents, they aren't parents by accident. (Like trans women, they treasure things that their biological counterparts often don't even notice.) And by and large – though unfortunately adoptive parents do suffer some sorts of discrimination – society recognises and values their commitment, and accepts them for many purposes as parents like any others, though of course there are contexts (blood transfusion, organ donation, testing for inherited illness) where the fact that they are adoptive parents makes a difference.

4.2: Spelling it out: what nobody thinks

Nobody sensible thinks that it's all right, when you find out that someone is an adoptive parent, to get in her face and shout 'Biology! Science! You're running away from the facts! You're delusional! You're not a real parent!'. As well as being incredibly rude and insensitive, that would be importantly false: there is a perfectly good sense in which an adoptive parent most certainly is a real parent. Yet since this aggressive accusation is also, alas, only too intelligible to the parent who is subjected to it, it would also be stamping up and down in the crassest and cruellest way on what anyone can see at once is likely to be a sore point for her. (Here I speak, I'm sorry to say, from personal experience of analogous shoutings.)

Nobody sensible thinks that it's an infraction of Jordan Peterson's or Germaine Greer's human rights, or rights of free speech, to impose on them a social, ethical, and sometimes even legal requirement that they call adoptive parents parents. (Notice how I put that: crossing this line shouldn't *always* be treated as a crime. Sometimes it's a crime, but sometimes it's just gratuitously offensive: just bad manners. And nobody sensible thinks that being rude should or even could always be a crime.)

Nobody sensible thinks that, if you refer to an adoptive parent as a non-parent, then you don't owe it to that parent, as a matter of basic courtesy, to retract, correct, and apologise.

Nobody sensible thinks that the existence of adoptive parents under-mines our understanding of what it is to be a parent. On the contrary, it extends it.

Nobody sensible thinks that adoptive parents are, typically and as such, a threat to other parents. Or that they only went in for adoptive parenting as a way to get their hands on vulnerable children or vulnerable parents. Of course it's not impossible that someone who is an adoptive parent might be bad or dangerous in either or both of these ways, and of course it would then be right to protect ourselves and other potential victims from that person. But if that happened, it wouldn't throw any shade on adoptive parenthood itself, as such. (This is one of those points in discourse where we are reminded how bad humans are at risk assessment. When we just go by instinct and intuition, we consistently overestimate the probability of *sensational* risks, like nuclear disasters, and underestimate the probability of *boring* risks, like getting run over by a car.)

Nobody sensible thinks that there's automatically a problem about having adoptive parents in parents-only spaces. There might be some special spaces that should indeed be reserved for biological parents only – pre- and postnatal groups, for instance, or a group like this that helped my wife and me when we had a still-born child in 1995: https://www.sands.org.uk/. We should be prepared to listen carefully and sympathetically to the case that might be made sometimes for biological-parents-only spaces. But in general, adoptive parents have similar enough concerns and interests to biological parents for it to be, in most cases, both natural and useful to include them in such spaces.

Nobody sensible thinks that adoptive parents are necessarily buying into an oppressive ideological agenda of parenthood, and, by their choice to be parents, imposing that agenda on other parents. There are oppressive ideological agendas about parenthood; of course there are. But to be an adoptive parent is not necessarily to buy into them. It might even be a way of subverting them.

Nobody sensible thinks that there's just one right way to be a good adoptive parent, any more than there is a unique right way to be a good parent in general. Though there are some things that have to be in common between all good parents, there are lots of different ways of being a good parent. The broad schema of what parenthood is, adoptive or not, is set by biology and sociology. But sociology can certainly be challenged, and often should be (fighting back is called *politics*), and even biology is not always just to be accepted (fighting back is called *medicine*). Within the general role of 'a good parent', there is all sorts of room and scope for creativity, self-expression, and imaginative invention and re-invention.

We don't always know, on meeting some parent, whether she is an adoptive parent or a biological parent. Often there are visible clues and give-aways, or at least we can see things that make us strongly suspect an adoptive relationship. But in most contexts it would be rude and intrusive to ask. The implicit social convention is loud and clear: you don't ask, you wait to be told. But when we know all the facts about any parent, we know which they are, biological or adoptive, without any difficulty.

This implicit social convention is, of course, one that ramifies. It's first about adoptive parent–child relations. But secondarily it is about other things too. As Cora Diamond writes to me in a private communication, commenting on an earlier version of this section:

> One thing that I hope you mention some time is (in addition to adoptive parenthood) adoptive brothers/sisters. My two step-grandchildren are adopted. I would be aghast if anyone asked whether they are 'really brothers'. There may indeed be contexts in which someone is concerned with their health, and in which the fact that they are not biologically akin is relevant. The case is somewhat different from the case you discuss, of adoptive parents. The boys never decided to be brothers, in the way adoptive parents have decided to be parents, have taken on being parents. But they may well be subjected to intrusive forms of scepticism on the part of others, in the light (for example) of their lack of resemblance.

In our society, the role of adoptive parent is almost completely uncontested. (Almost, though there can be some resistance, and it can be unreasonably hard to get into the role in the first place.) If you're an adoptive parent, you're a parent – for most purposes – and no one sensible scratches their head or clutches their brow over that, or decrees that you can't sit on school parents' councils, or sees it as somehow dangerous or threatening or undermining of 'real parents' or dishonest or deceptive or delusional or a symptom of mental illness or a piece of embarrassing and pathetic public make-believe. On the contrary, people just accept you as a parent, and value your commitment to parenthood as an important contribution to the well-being of our society that you could not have made if you didn't have the psychological set-up that you do.

4.3: A little terminology

We can imagine adoptive parents, when talking among themselves, needing and finding a phrase for parents who aren't adoptive parents. You can see why the phrase they'd choose might not be 'real parents'; that would be doing themselves down. (And you can see how that phrase might be weaponised against adoptive parents, by unkind other parents.)

Anyway, these adoptive parents might choose, for this purpose, a phrase like 'biological parents'. Then, language use being what it is, maybe they shorten it to 'bio-parents'. Now in this scenario that I'm imagining – for all I know there are subcultures where it is real – two extreme stances strike me as overdone and unreasonable. One is for the adoptive parents to insist that all biological parents always call themselves bio-parents. The other is for bio-parents to take offence at ever being called bio-parents. Yet apparently both these stances are actually taken in discussions of 'cis' and 'trans' (cp. 1.19). Here what I want to say is: Maybe we should all calm down a bit?

Maybe we could follow the philosopher Derek Parfit and say that 'once we know all the facts', the further question 'Are they really women/ men?' is an 'empty question'.[1] Or maybe we can say what I actually want to say, which is related to Parfit's move, but different. I want to say that the question is not *empty* at all, but it has different substantive answers for different substantive purposes. And that, provided we keep the score carefully in our language-game(s), there's no reason at all why anyone should be confused about any of the semantic-logical ins and outs of 'trans woman/man' any more than they are with 'adoptive parent'.

Perhaps this proposal is best seen as a modest piece of conceptual engineering? I consider that possibility in Part V, where my topic is the prospects for conceptual (re-)engineering in the area of our gender concepts. I propose a number of possible analogies, some less and some more serious. My outlook on these possibilities is, broadly, optimistic.

4.4: A disanalogy?

Here is a possible line of objection to the adoption analogy:[2]

The alleged analogy is between the terms '(adoptive) parent' and '(trans) woman'. But the analogy fails, because there is a significant difference between how the two terms behave semantically. 'Parent' can be a noun or

---

[1] Derek Parfit, *Reasons and Persons* (Clarendon Press, 1984), p. 262.
[2] The clearest statement of the objection that I have seen is from Jane Clare Jones, in a Twitter exchange at https://twitter.com/SophieG32294014/status /1508798897778536462; my thanks to her.

a verb: we know what it is *to* parent, and adoptive parents count as parents because parent*ing* is something that they do. But 'woman' is only a noun. There is no verb 'to woman', and if there was, it would mean 'to play the gender role of woman'. But gender roles are pernicious. So the analogy either fails, or gives pernicious results.

Now, first, it is not a problem for the adoption analogy if there is – to date – no English verb 'to woman'. (Or 'to man', though in practice proponents of this line of argument are usually focused exclusively on the case of trans women.) For there very easily can be. It is perfectly easy to invent or stipulate such a verb; as I shall be pointing out at length in Part V, such linguistic and conceptual extension and innovation goes on all the time, in English and in any other natural language.

If we do so, then what are the rules about what this verb 'to woman' must mean? We stipulated its existence; why shouldn't we also stipulate its meaning? 'To woman' does not have to mean 'to adopt a regressive and oppressive social role'. For there is a debate to be had about whether being a woman has to be a regressive social role. As I've said already, I am a gender reformist not a gender abolitionist, so I don't think gender-based social roles are automatically bad or oppressive. I agree they usually have been, but I think we should use our imaginations here: more about such imaginings in Part VII.

Alongside the debate about whether being a woman has to be an oppressive social role, there is another debate about whether being a woman has to be a role at all. The sides don't always line up here quite as one might expect; most trans-exclusionary theorists are perfectly happy to say that there is a distinctive thing called 'the lived experience of womanhood', and in agreement with that I have just argued myself, in Part III, that consciousness is both sexed and gendered. So there can be such a thing as identifying with the lived experience of womanhood, or manhood. And that identifying – as the trans-exclusionaries themselves are keen to emphasise – is something quite distinct from playing any social role, whether regressive or progressive or neither.

'But trans women can't identify with the lived experience of womanhood.' Can't they? Why not? If the answer to that is 'Because they're not women', this is question-begging; it's also false (cp. 1.18, 2.10). Also, remember again that some trans women pass, and some don't.

Those who pass are, by definition, living under the same political and social conditions as cis women. Those who don't pass are living under the political and social conditions of visible trans women. Why isn't this a way of having the lived experience of womanhood? If the answer is, again, 'Because they're not women', then, once more, the question is being begged.

There is a lot of elasticity in quite a few of our concepts; perhaps in all of them. In particular, there is an inevitable – and indeed desirable – elasticity or bendiness in our thick concepts (2.6), including our gender concepts. To explore this elasticity in more detail is the task of Part V.

Gatekeepers, Engineers, and Welcomers

5.1: Some bendy concepts

Apocryphally (though it would be lovely if it were true), the statutes of King's College Cambridge at one time included the following clauses:

> 16b. No dog shall be permitted within the grounds of the College.
>
> 16bi. For the purposes of these Statutes, any pet animal belonging to the Provost shall be deemed to be a cat.

Not apocryphally but truly (alas; I was there), the following has certainly happened. Three people sit and wait in a departmental meeting room, two professors and the department secretary. A third professor enters the room, sits down, looks around, and says 'So, we are only three people in this meeting today, right?'

In my first example, we might say that the fellows of King's consciously decided that, for a certain particular purpose, their concept of a cat had in it a certain particular outward bulge – what we might *see* as a bulge – that admitted the Provost's Jack Russell, allowing it to count as an honorary cat. And we might want to applaud their decision as a superficially flippant, but basically sensible, response to a minor practical-administrative difficulty.

In my second example, we might say that the third professor acted on an *un*conscious decision: that for the purposes of departmental meetings his concept of people had in it a certain particular inward dent – what we might *see* as an indent – that excluded the department secretary, denying her the standing of a person present in the meeting. And this decision we might well want to decry as a piece of rude and obnoxious status-mindedness, and also, given the pronouns I've just used, of rude and obnoxious sexism.

Take a third example, from Richard Hare's well-known paper 'Abortion and the golden rule'. A city park has a sign at its gate that says 'Wheeled vehicles prohibited'.[1] So according to this piece of quite literal gatekeeping, what counts as a 'wheeled vehicle'? Cars, motorbikes, and bicycles definitely count. Skateboards, Nordic skis customised for summer use with little wheels, Segways, and tiny-wheeled fold-up electric executive scooters all probably count, especially if they are furiously conducted. Park-keepers' wheelbarrows and sit-on lawnmowers and wheelie-bins definitely *don't* count. Prams and wheeled suitcases and shopping trundlers and heelies probably don't. (In case you don't know, heelies are a type of trainers much favoured by little girls and often found, accordingly, in sparkly pink varieties, that have small but functional wheels embedded in the heels of the soles. Terrifying to watch at pedestrian crossings.)

What about roller-skates? Does the park sign cover them? Hare asks us to suppose that a case comes to court where an adjudication is sought on the roller-skates issue. As he points out, the judge 'may have very good reasons of public interest or morals for her decision;[2] but she cannot make it by any physical or metaphysical investigation of roller-skates to see whether they are really wheeled vehicles. If she has not led too sheltered a life, she knew all she needed to know about roller-skates before the case ever came into court.'

Hare's point is an analogy with the concept of a 'person' that we might (or might not) want to use in philosophical discussion of abortion. The point is that the world does not *just give* us a single, uniquely authoritative way of deciding whether any beings born or unborn count as persons. To determine this for the first time (whenever *that* was), or to reopen the issue at some later date, is to extend our concept of a person, and/or to argue about how to extend it, and how not. And as with any concept, while there are clearly better and worse ways of extending it, no single extension can be straightforwardly read off 'the nature of things' and declared, by judicious application of that large and painfully studded bludgeon called What Science Tells Us, to be uniquely rational.

---

[1] R.M. Hare, 'Abortion and the Golden Rule', in *Essays on Bioethics* (Clarendon Press, 1993), p. 150. I am indebted to unpublished work by John Hare for reminding me of his father's roller-skates case. Apparently, Hare got the case from H.L.A. Hart's book *The Concept of Law*. Cp. also *McBoyle v. US*, 283 US 25 (1931).
[2] In just one respect, I have subtly altered Hare's original text. See if you can spot where.

5.2: Maybe all concepts are bendy?

'As with any concept'? Yes. Nietzsche famously says in *On the Genealogy of Morals* that 'all concepts in which an entire process is semiotically concentrated elude definition; only that which has no history is definable'.[3] Nietzsche is focusing, as his book title shows, on evaluative concepts; but there is a plain sense in which there are no human concepts at all that 'have no history'. For example, you can go to the library and find histories of our number-concepts.[4] Any of these will tell you how long it took for early-mediaeval European minds, steeped as they were in the Platonic-Aristotelian-Christian tradition, to take seriously a notion already found in Ptolemy's *Almagest* and in Indian-influenced Persian mathematicians like Al-Khwarizmi – the notion of zero (from the Arabic *al-sifr* via the Italian *zefiro*): no solid reality but a mere breeze in the empty air, a Parmenides-defying Is-Not-That-Is, a Euclid-resistant number that is not any number, an amount of which Plato would surely say 'But that "amount" is a *non*-amount – and you can't count a non-amount!'

In this conceptual transformation of European mathematics, the key figure was the great Italian number theorist Leonardo Fibonacci (1170–1250), whose *Book of the Abacus* (Pisa, 1202) was the crucial text that led to the general adoption of Arabic over Roman numerals, and so, because of the decimal nature of the Arabic system, to the general use of zero in European mathematics. To quote Fibonacci's *Liber Abaci*:

> My father ... had me in my boyhood come to him [in Bugia/ Bejaia in Algeria] and ... be instructed in the study of calculation for some days. There [I was introduced] to the nine digits of the Hindus ... I realized that all [calculation's] aspects were studied in Egypt, Syria, Greece, Sicily, and Provence, with their varying methods; and at these places thereafter, while on business, I pursued my study in depth. But all this, and the algorithm, and the art of Pythagoras, I considered as almost a mistake compared to the method of the

---

[3] *On the Genealogy of Morals*, 2.13, in *Basic Writings of Nietzsche*, trans. and ed. Walter Kaufmann (Modern Library, 2000), p. 516.
[4] Or to Wikipedia, which has a fascinating article on zero: https://en.wikipedia.org/wiki/0 – and from where, with some editing down, I have lifted the Fibonacci quotation below.

Hindus [with numerals]. Therefore, embracing more stringently that method, and taking stricter pains in its study, while adding certain things from my own understanding and inserting also certain things from the niceties of Euclid's geometry, I have striven to make this whole book as comprehensible as possible … Almost everything which I have introduced I have displayed with exact proof, in order that those further seeking this knowledge, with its pre-eminent method, might be instructed, and further, in order that the Latin people might not be discovered to be without it, as they have been up to now. If I have perchance omitted anything more or less proper or necessary, I beg indulgence, since there is no one who is blameless and utterly provident in all things. The nine Indian figures are: 9 8 7 6 5 4 3 2 1. With these nine figures, and with the sign zero (0), any number may be written.

What Fibonacci is proposing here is both a notational and a conceptual reform of his readers' ideas of number. Don't fall for calling it a *merely* notational reform: what Fibonacci is saying is not like just telling us to put a bar through the waists of our 7s to distinguish them from our 1s. The switch from Roman to Arabic numerals is a profound change in how we represent and manipulate numbers, with enormous expressive potential both for mathematical theory and for the purposes of practical finance.

In his modest and unpretentious way, and quite without grand philosophical fanfare, Fibonacci is proposing *to change his society's concept of number.* He is also commendably open to the possibility that the conceptual change that he proposes is in some sense an incomplete revolution: he says both that he has made his book on number theory as rigorous as he knows how, and also that it may well be possible for future researchers to improve on the formality and cogency of his work. For Fibonacci, then, our concept of number is quite explicitly a work in progress. Given, moreover, that he himself is proposing a wholesale rethinking of that concept, he must also, at least implicitly, be open to the possibility that someone else might come along with a *further* rethinking of the concept to propose, no less revolutionary than his own. (As indeed has happened since, several times.)

If this can happen even with our concept of number, or again with our concepts of space, time, and causality (the Kant-Einstein-Planck contrast is familiar enough) – then a fortiori it can happen with our value concepts, and especially our political and ethical concepts. In fact, if it doesn't sound too *rive-gauche* to say so, changes in our mathematical and physical concepts can be evaluatively potent too. That was true of Fibonacci's discoveries, which transformed not only the mathematical but also the economic thinking of his time. In the economics of our own time, at at least one cutting edge there has been a veritable explosion in abstruseness that is directly reliant on the discovery (or invention, as you like) of new or relatively new mathematical concepts. (No polynomials, no pseudorandom functions; no pseudorandom functions, no cryptography; no cryptography, no Bitcoin.) But to repeat the basic point, the a fortiori: even our basic mathematical and physical concepts can be and often are engineered or re-engineered to meet or supply new needs or aspirations. If that can legitimately happen with them, then all the more can it happen with our value concepts.

5.3: The very ideas of 'regularity' and 'irregularity'

Whether or not they are 'officially' value concepts, and whether or not we define them with IFFs, none of our concepts is completely fixed in its content.[5] Room for reform and change is built into our concepts,

[5] *None* of our concepts. So I go further than Morris Weitz ('The Role of Theory in Aesthetics', *JAAC* (1956): 27–35), who, arguing for Wittgensteinian anti-theory in the philosophy of art, writes this – note my added italics: 'The basic resemblance between these [aesthetic] concepts is their open texture. In elucidating them, certain (paradigm) cases can be given, about which there can be no question as to their being correctly described as "art" or "game", but no exhaustive set of cases can be given. I can list some cases and some conditions under which I can apply correctly the concept of art but I cannot list all of them, for the all-important reason that unforeseeable or novel conditions are always forthcoming or envisageable. A concept is open if its conditions of application are emendable and corrigible; i.e., if a situation or case can be imagined or secured which would call for some sort of decision on our part to extend the use of the concept to cover this, or to close the concept and invent a new one to deal with the new case and its new property. If necessary and sufficient conditions for the application of a concept can be stated, the concept is a closed one. *But this can happen only in logic or mathematics where concepts are constructed and completely defined.* It cannot occur with empirically descriptive and normative concepts unless we arbitrarily close them by stipulating the ranges of their uses.' Here too notice the distance between saying 'Conceptual extensions are a matter of decision' and saying 'Anything goes'. (Thanks to Dan Cavedon-Taylor.)

both of the open-texture kind that the Wittgenstein of *Philosophical Investigations* is pointing to in his famous remarks about the notions of a game and family resemblance, and of the rule-following kind that he is pointing to when he says that even with highly formalised concepts like 'plus', what counts as 'going on in the same way as before' is determined at least partly by 'agreement in form of life', by a constitutive and at least largely inarticulate social agreement. In both contexts – both open-texture and rule-following – I think the debates have often been run into the sand by a failure to understand that both are constitutively diachronic notions: we are talking not about disengaged games of Spot The Difference or Guess The Next Number, but about socially embedded understandings that develop over time, within a wider diachronic context of the kind that Alasdair MacIntyre (in *After Virtue* and elsewhere) calls a tradition, and also of the kind that everyone calls a society.

It is not necessarily always completely obvious what counts as 'going on in the same way' with our concepts, nor – connectedly – with our rules. Nor is it necessarily a manifestation of eccentricity when 'going on in the same way' looks at least to some eyes like not going on in the same way: when there is, in some identifiable respect, what I started by calling a dent or a bulge in the extension of the concept. There is an identifiable thing that it is for verbs to be regular. Or at least so we think, though in fact I doubt that there is any *uniquely* identifiable thing: the notion of regularity is less determinate than we imagine. Still, by all accounts, not all verbs are regular: the aorist of the English *to go* is not **goed*, and the imperfect of the ancient Greek *lambanw* is not **elambanon* but *elabon*. That is because English borrows the conjugation of a separate verb, *to wend*, to form the aorist of *to go* (though *went* is not regular either); and it is because the Greek *lambanw* is one of those double-nu stems (*lanthanw, lagkhanw, tygkhanw, manthanw, thigganw, kinduneuw, punthanomai* …) that give me at any rate so much distinctively philological pleasure.

Again, chess is not a less reasonable game than draughts simply because the pieces don't all move in the same way. Nor a less interesting one. On the contrary, we might say that the different rules for the different chess pieces *thicken the plot*: they are a principal part of the explanation why chess is a far better game than draughts. To think, as George Bernard Shaw famously thought about English spelling, that 'irregularities' are somehow a sign of irrationality, is to misunderstand what rationality *is*. Rationality is not rationalism. In certain cases, indeed, there are few things less rational than rationalism. And this is one of them.[6]

5.4: Brushing up our ideas

In some circumstances, as with the offside law in football and the tackle law in rugby, we can improve a game (or try to) by changing its rules in ways big or small. In some circumstances, likewise, we can increase our heuristic power and our explanatory scope by re-engineering our concepts more or less ambitiously. As David Chalmers has put it:

> Philosophy has many aims distinct from discovering truths. Philosophy also aims to raise questions, to help us understand, to help us see the world differently, to live better lives, to improve the world, and so on. New and improved concepts certainly can help with those things. For example, once you have the concept of epistemic injustice, you see all sorts of old situations in a new way, and this can help achieve more just outcomes.[7]

Now, obviously, it is not necessarily the case that every widening of a concept is an improvement in that concept. To take a specific example, it was clearly a good thing to narrow down from uselessly broad and inaccurate concepts of disease like 'the bloody flux' to more precise, and

---

[6] 'There is nothing irrational in exercising other powers than our reason. On certain occasions and for certain purposes the real irrationality is with those who will not do so. The [person] who would try to break a horse or write a poem or beget a child by pure syllogising would be an irrational [person]; though at the same time syllogising is in itself a more rational activity than the activities demanded by these achievements. It is rational not to reason, or not to limit oneself to reason, in the wrong place; and the more rational [someone] is the better [they] know this.'
I am quoting C.S. Lewis's 'Priestesses in the Church?', in his posthumous collection *God In The Dock* (Penguin, 1979). With deliberate pointedness, since Lewis was arguing that though it might be 'more rational' for the Church of England to recognise women priests, there were reasons of mystical theology why such an argument from rationality did not apply. (My square-bracketed emendations of Lewis's prose are pointed too.)
[7] David Chalmers, 'What is conceptual engineering and what should it be?', *Inquiry* (2020): 12.

more usefully scientifically networked, concepts like gastroenteritis, food poisoning, and peptic ulcers. More generally, concepts do need edges if they are to be of any use at all; a word that can mean *anything at all* is a useless one.

(Notice, by the way, how limp this 'But then, anything goes!' worry is as an all-too-familiar form of protest against some sorts of proposal for conceptual change. How much bite does an anything-goes protest have against changes in the offside law, or against irregular linguistic inflections? Hardly any at all. True, with J.R.R. Tolkien's invented language Sindarin, I find it awkward that pluralisation often happens through vowel shift: the pluralisation of *orod* 'mountain' may be *ered*, but what if we wanted to have *ered* itself as a word? Still, despite that type of qualm, which is of course equally applicable to English words like 'geese' and 'mice', the rational distance between *not entirely regular* and *anything goes* is in general huge; and important to remember in the face of glib rationalist rhetoric.)

For sure, *more inclusive* is not automatically *better*. All the same, it is very common to find our political and ethical concepts improved by widenings of their scope, and worsened either by narrowing, or by an insistent refusal to countenance any widening. The authors of the American Declaration of Independence wrote that 'all men are created equal'. But since many of them were, notoriously, slaveholders, they clearly didn't mean *black* men: their concept of 'men' had an indentation in it that excluded black people. They didn't mean women either, though they no doubt were in the habit of using what is sometimes called the 'inclusive' sense of 'men'.

('Inclusive' is absurd, by the way. A better name might be the 'gender-unary' sense of 'men', since the point of the usage is not to include women, but on the contrary to treat them as a degenerate or non-focal case of being human – which is to *ex*clude women, by erasing them. A close semantic parallel, attested in writers from William Shakespeare to A.J.P. Taylor,[8] is the wide sense of 'England' in which 'England' is, or

---

[8] For Shakespeare, see *Richard II* (Act 2, sc. 1), John of Gaunt's famous 'scepter'd *isle*' speech – about *England*. For A.J.P. Taylor, see his amusingly testy remarks about 'England' 'Britain', 'Great Britain' and 'the Scotch' in the Preface to his *English History 1914–1945* (Oxford University Press, 1965), p. v.

was, a synonym for 'Britain'.[9] This sense *includes* Scotland, Wales, and Ireland as the python includes the rabbit. But more about Scotland in a moment.)

Nor, to note a third implicit exclusion, did Jefferson and his colleagues really mean, by 'men', to include babies and children, who are no doubt equal with each other, but certainly not of the same status as (male) adults. This third exclusion perhaps makes less comfortable reading than the first two – since where children are concerned we ourselves are very likely to make something like the same exception in our practice, if not in our profession. Perhaps the fact that the exclusion is uncomfortable to us, and that some very astute philosophers are now thinking about it in some detail, is a (hopeful?) sign of (positive?) change in our concept of who counts as a full moral and legal 'person'.

Notice, by the way, what I have just implied in this last paragraph: that 'man' (as Jefferson had it), or 'person' (as we say today), is an ethical and political concept. And not by accident; *of course* 'person' is an ethical and political concept. More exactly, it is one of the thick ethical concepts.

'American' and 'Scot' are thick ethical concepts too; so indeed are 'German' and 'Jew'. In Chapter 2 of my book *Knowing What to Do*, talking about the moral imagination and about how we imaginatively frame other humans when we meet them, I mentioned Hitler's question about the Jews he met in 1910s Vienna.[10] Hitler asked 'Is that a German?', and his own answer was that they were not just Germans of another religion; rather, they were 'a separate nation'. Yet it was possible for people in Hitler's day to take a quite different attitude to the concept of Germanness: one that, just in philosophy, might have counted as Germans such giants of the tradition as Lessing, Heine, Mendelssohn, Husserl, Schlick, Scheler, Cassirer, Waismann, Feigl, Popper, and Wittgenstein, and that, today, is happy to count as Germans the two scientists of Turkish extraction who recently pioneered the

---

[9] Alex Barber, who lives in Wales, tells me of the following gem from the index of the *Encyclopaedia Britannica*, 1888 edition, under W: 'WALES: see ENGLAND'. Likewise a book I am currently reading, William Shirer's *The Rise and Fall of the Third Reich* (Mandarin, 1960), includes both the following index entries: 'England, *see* Britain' and 'Great Britain, *see* Britain' (pp. 1207, 1212).

[10] See *Mein Kampf*, Ch. 1.

COVID vaccine. To put it informally and roughly, Hitler could have said something more like: 'Germans are all those who *want to be* Germans.' And that would have been a way of thinking about Germanness, which would have given his nationalism a quite different shape – and a healthier one.

(Including a *logically* healthier one? If he had said this, wouldn't he have been using a viciously circular account of what it is to be German? Not necessarily, no. 'Germans are all those who *want to be* Germans' can be parsed as: 'There is historically a tradition of what it is to be German – and it is part of that tradition that it is open to anyone who wants to, to become part of it themselves.' This may be recursive; but it isn't viciously circular.)

5.5: No true Scots(wo)man?

A parallel debate to this at-least-possible early twentieth-century debate about Germanness, and a less wearisome and sullying one to think about, is the actual debate in recent decades, within the Scottish independence movement, about the concept of Scottishness.

At times the Scottish independence movement certainly has harboured, at least in some quarters, a hardcore blood-and-soil nationalism, a rhetoric of racial and historic exclusiveness, gatekeeping, and purity tests that is disturbingly reminiscent of some other nationalisms. It has not been at all like that in recent decades. The last generally visible sign of the gatekeeping attitude about Scottishness is a bumper sticker that was commonplace in 1991, but that I'm glad to say you hardly see any more: the bumper sticker that says 'I'm a real Scot from [insert name of town]'.

On this account of what it is to be Scottish, there is no real prospect that anyone might become Scottish. By your birthplace or your parentage or both, you're born it (or not); you don't and can't become it. And any attempt to do so, or to announce, perhaps after marriage or long residence, that you now identify as Scottish is strictly self-defeating. If you really were Scottish, you wouldn't need to claim to be. And apparently, if you are a Scot but not 'a real Scot', then in the eyes of the makers of that bumper sticker you are, with shameful literality, a second-class citizen. When we lived in Edinburgh in 1989–91, a mild but near-universal paranoia about this whole business of 'being a real Scot' palpably filled the air. It always seemed to me that this insecurity about identity was there even in the bumper sticker itself: if someone is a real Scot, why protest about it so loudly and defiantly?

A huge change for the better in the dominant concept of Scottishness came, in particular, from the influence of the SNP's leader from 2014 to 2023, Nicola Sturgeon. The attitude to Scottishness that she stands for is summed up by saying, in her own words in a speech to the SNP conference in (I think) 2018: 'It's not about where you've come from, it's about where you're going.' Never mind about stags and unicorns, glens and bens, tartan and bagpipes, haggis and neeps, buts and bens, Irn Bru and deep-fried Mars Bars, ginger wigs and 'the Doric', Sean Connery, Billy Connolly, Brian Cox – and blood and soil. Instead, on this new account, a Scot is anyone who identifies with Scotland enough to make their home here, and to seek to join in the project of building a new nation together. For Ms Sturgeon and her political allies, the concept of Scottishness is not a tool for racial-cultural gatekeeping; it is an inclusive and welcoming idea.[11] And that means that it is entirely possible for someone like me, born and bred in England and of English parents, with only the most threadbare genealogical entitlement to a clan or a tartan (Macdonald of Clanranald, if anything), and with an accent mostly in between Lancashire and Received Pronunciation and with only the occasional even-hint of Dundee, to decide one day that from now on *I will identify* as Scottish.

The day in question, if you care, was 24 June 2016, on which day I also transitioned from No to Yes about Scottish independence. But things had been building in that direction for a while. In particular, the UK general election campaign of 2015 was disfigured by a great deal of disgracefully cheap and nasty anti-Scottish scaremongering on the part of the Conservative and Unionist Party. I was surprised by how angry that racist scaremongering made me (its electoral effectiveness in England was even more dismaying). And I wasn't just angry in a detached way, on general cosmopolitan principles of justice and racial-cultural respect. I took it personally: the content of my anger was: 'This

---

[11] I am no expert on Wales, but Alex Barber tells me that a parallel move away from ethnic nationalism has happened with Plaid Cymru.

is my people you're talking about.' But then that gave me pause: 'Hang on, *my* people? The Scots are my people now?' Well, at that point I had been living continuously in Scotland for seventeen years, and for another nearly three-year period a decade earlier than that; and I had (and have) every intention of living in Scotland for the rest of my life. So yes, my people: then, now, and always.

So what I now say, post-24/6/2016, is that I identify as Scottish and am proud to do so, despite my stereotypically English origins and demeanour. Does saying this make me a fraud? Am I an impostor? Should we say 'Genealogy matters', and that I am ignoring the genealogical facts? Should we say that 'you can't ground objective nationality in subjective feelings', and that I am basing on mere emotional attachment what can only be based on history and breeding? Am I an implausible failure because I don't look like a Scot or sound like a Scot, or at any rate not like a stereotypical Scot? Am I a cultural entryist, diluting and corrupting historic Scottish culture? Should 'real' Scots feel 'flooded' or 'overwhelmed' or pushed to 'breaking point'[12] by incomers, 'white settlers',[13] like me? Am I merely fetishising a crude cheap stereotype of pantomime Scottishness which is itself part of the historic oppression of true Scots? Must I fail to count as a Scot because I have not, myself, had a lifelong inculturation as a Scot, and so cannot know for myself the full depth and reality of anti-Scottish prejudice? Or again, is the very notion of Scottishness – of any nationality – a historical relic that we should abandon in favour of an austerely global, particularity-erasing cosmopolitanism? Or must we say that I, and those who think like me, define 'Scots' simply as 'those who self-identify as Scots', and therefore that we are trapped in a vicious circularity? Consequences like these might, I suppose, follow if we were sufficiently insistent that the only acceptable concept of Scottishness is a blood-and-soil-nationalist one. But on any more inclusive concept of Scottishness, it seems to me, the

[12] https://www.theguardian.com/p.olitics/2016/jun/16/nigel-farage-defends -ukip-breaking-point-poster-queue-of-migrants.
[13] https://www.independent.co.uk/news/uk/home-news/the-little-england -over-the-water-white-settlers-make-up-15-of-skye-s-population-1450967.html. Cal McCrystal talks here, in 1994, about a Scotland-for-the-Scots organisation called 'Scottish Watch'. I'm happy to say that, as far as I can find out from the internet, this no longer exists.

answer to all the above questions is one and the same: Yir talkin pure glaikit blether.

5.6: Drawing another analogy

Someone who combines an exclusiveness about Scottishness, with a protestation that their view of what Scottishness is depends only on 'the objective facts', does not look like an innocent investigator; actually, their combination of views has a decided air of disingenuousness. Decisions about how to define Scottishness are not determined solely and completely by some set of neutral worldly facts. They are determined also by how inclusive we want to be. We might even say that this willingness to welcome rather than gatekeep is the decisive factor. If that willingness is in place, then all sorts of theoretical options for a greater or lesser degree of conceptual engineering about Scottishness are left open. Yet, in a sense, it barely matters which way the theory goes. The key thing is not the theory but the inclusiveness. I am reminded here a little of the famous debates in the early church about how to provide a theological justification for extending the new covenant to the gentiles: to tell the truth, it wasn't actually crucial how the church's leaders justified this extension – just so long as they did justify it.

It's not exactly difficult to get from where we've just been to analogous conclusions about transgender; and here as in Part IV, an analogy is what I'm aiming at. Analogies of course are never perfect: if they were they would not be analogies, they would be qualitative identities. My adoption analogy in Part IV was neither perfect nor intended to be perfect, and neither is the one that I'm now suggesting, between coming to identify as a Scot and coming to identify as a woman. Still, I do at least hope to have made it reasonably clear why I am happy to say both 'I am an English Scot, and English Scots really are Scots' – and also 'I am a trans woman, and trans women really are women.'

And if this section is to have anything as reductive as takeaways – in Scotland we call them kerry-oots – then here are three conclusions that I'd like to draw.

First: despite a great deal of recent *Sturm und Drang*, there is nothing particularly special about the proposal to submit the notions of 'woman' and 'man' to conceptual re-engineering in order, among other purposes, to make the social world more welcoming for, and less gatekeeping against, transgender and gender-incongruent people. Conceptual changes of this sort happen all the time, all over the place, to all sorts of concepts (if I have any objection to manifestos for the philosophical programme of 'conceptual engineering', the main one is that no manifesto is needed – conceptual engineering is already pervasive in philosophy, and has been at least since Plato's time.) Such conceptual changes can be and sometimes are both socially and conceptually progressive, and when they are, they're unambiguously for the better.

Secondly, therefore, there is no mileage at all in trying to object to conceptual revisionism about 'man' and 'woman' simply because it is revisionism. There is nothing sacred about the concepts we currently have or had, or about the concepts that something called 'the tradition' had. The idea that we are somehow necessarily stuck with those concepts, that they are unalterably 'just there', that accepting them is accepting 'obvious facts' and rejecting them is buying into some sort of 'ideology' (1.13), is often offered to us as if it were itself an obvious truth. But it is neither obvious nor even in fact a truth, and it is often right to see something disingenuous in the offer. The connected idea that there is something automatically enlightening and correct about some past phase of 'ordinary language' well deserves to be called by the rude name that Bertrand Russell gave it: the metaphysics of the stone age.

Thirdly, and finally, what I have said leaves it wide open exactly how revisionary we want to be about gender concepts. Some approaches to these concepts, such as Sally Haslanger's, propose wholesale reforms; such approaches aren't ruled out by anything that I've said here. But other proposals are much less revisionary than that; and they aren't ruled out either.

(Some recent reports in the UK press of revisionism, or alleged revisionism, about our gender concepts have been, to put it mildly, of dubious honesty. One example: in February 2021 Brighton and Sussex University Hospital published employee guidelines about trans-inclusivity which suggested the use of phrases like 'birthing parent' and 'chest-feeding' as suitable for patients who are trans men, *to be used alongside* more traditional phrases like 'mother' and 'breast-feeding' for cis patients. This *suggestion* was immediately reported – by *The Times* no less – as an *order* to *replace* those traditional phrases for *all* patients, *across the board.* It is hard not to see this kind of dishonesty as straightforward anti-transgender propaganda.)[14]

One example of a non-revisionist proposal, one that is conservative about our gender concepts, is my own adoption analogy, as presented in Part IV. As far as I can see, we hardly need to change our concept of parents at all to accommodate adoptive parents. I mean, we might change our concepts in the process of accommodating them. But we might also say: 'Parents are still defined as biological progenitors; and the existence of adoptive parents doesn't change that definition – they just stand as by-your-leave or honorary parents, if you like as "an exception that proves the rule".'

This is close to what apparently happens with the case I started this section with, the case of the Provost of King's' Jack Russell. I intended that case as a warm-up and as a joke. My serious view about it is that it would be overblown to say of this case that the College's statutes really redefine the concept of 'cat'. As I suspect Herman Cappelen would agree,[15] it would be much nearer the mark to say that what they do is establish a *local legal fiction*, and/or the existence of at least one honorary cat; though even if it is only that much that the statutes do, it is surely both striking and interesting how easily they do it.

Pari passu, then, we might say that the existence of trans women and men doesn't change the existing definitions of 'women' or 'men'. There is therefore nothing whatever for a trans-inclusive philosopher to object to if someone wants to define women and men as adult females and males respectively. (Though there are further complexities to address about what 'male' and 'female' mean – as we saw in 1.18.) It's simply that, just as the Provost's Jack Russell is an honorary cat, so trans men are honorary men, and trans women are honorary women.

This last view clearly does not go far enough to satisfy most trans-inclusionary philosophers. Some of them, for instance, may have had their moral-conceptual antennae sensitised by a South African

[14] https://www.thetimes.co.uk/article/breastfeeding-is-now-chestfeeding-brightons-trans-friendly-midwives-are-told-pwlvmcnc7. https://katelynburns.medium.com/no-that-british-hospital-didnt-ban-the-word-breastfeeding-coca19fde8b0.
[15] Herman Cappelen, *Fixing Language: An Essay on Conceptual Engineering* (Oxford University Press, 2018).

background to the apartheid regime's disgracefully condescending use of the notion of an 'honorary white'.[16] But it does go far enough to bring out how there can be a perfectly good sense in which 'trans women are women' is true even if we take the King's College case as our closest analogue, and take that sense to be very much a by-your-leave one, indeed a distinctly nod-and-a-wink one. However, for now, the point is not whether this is the right way to think about our gender concepts. The point is merely that this possibility, along with a whole range of other possibilities, is still on the table. The options for conceptual engineering about our gender concepts are wide open. And that, as I think we should be aware, makes this an exciting moment to live in.[17]

[16] https://en.wikipedia.org/wiki/Honorary_whites. Thanks to Alex Barber for reminding me of this historic injustice. There is also, as Wikipedia points out, the notion of an honorary male, https://en.wikipedia.org/wiki/Honorary_male, which is equally worrying. In philosophy, I suppose most of us are aware that Wittgenstein, who seems to have been something of a misogynist, explicitly regarded Elizabeth Anscombe ('old man') as an honorary male.

[17] Part V was originally an essay written for a panel on gender at the American Philosophical Association, Central Division, February 2021. Thanks for helpful comments to participants there, and other readers since.

PART VI

An Open Letter to J.K. Rowling

Dundee
10 June 2020

Dear Ms Rowling

I am as far as I know the only professor of philosophy in the UK who is also transgender. Because my own research is in ethics, because I have in the past been a Governor of the British Association for Counselling and Psychotherapy (though I'm not their spokeswoman here), and because obviously I am also personally involved, I have said a few things in public on transgender issues. So I hope I won't offend you if I chip in with a few thoughts about the current furore over your recent remarks.

I have long been an avid reader of your books. My wife and I read the Harry Potter series to our four daughters when they were small, between 1998 and 2010, and there was much in them that resonated with me as an emerging trans woman. Perhaps particularly the Mirror of Erised, which, especially before I transitioned (in stages between 2008 and 2014), struck me as a really heartbreaking image for my own condition. If I looked in the magical mirror, and saw myself exactly as I most long to be, what would I see? It was a key moment for me when I first read that passage in *The Philosopher's Stone*, and realised more clearly than I ever had before that my own answer to that question was, unavoidably, 'Myself as a woman, of course'. But your secret werewolf Remus Lupin resonated too: he tries to be a normal member of society, but there is something dark and terrible and hidden in his nature that, from time to time, he can't help transforming into. 'Remus', I would think, in the days when I was still trying to hide my own true nature, 'I know exactly how you feel'.

Once upon a time I thought my own nature as a trans woman was something dark and terrible about me. Your books, Ms Rowling, were one part of what helped me to come to terms with myself. Another and older help was Ursula Le Guin's extraordinary depiction of Ged in *The*

Wizard of Earthsea. The demon that Ged unleashes, the demon that chases him down until he turns and chases it down, the demon that he has to battle and come to terms with: it's Ged's *own nature*. A Jungian would say, his *anima*.

Here, in the depths of the psyche, there be monsters. Yet we cannot truly deal with the demons by, well, *demonising* them or extirpating them, as happens in another fantasy epic that you and I both love. In *The Lord of the Rings* Frodo successfully kills off his own obsessive, addictive, fetishistic lust for the Ring. Yet in the process, he also kills quite a lot of himself; he certainly and avowedly kills most of the ancient elvish world around him. I often wonder what Frodo teaches us about Tolkien … But anyway, the deep psychological truth is that we have to come to terms with our monsters, not just crush or incinerate them. And when we do, it can turn out – as it does for Ged, and as it has, I'm happy to say, for me – that those monsters are not monsters at all. They're just misunderstood and misdirected energies.

Perhaps you, Ms Rowling, think that there's something dark and terrible – and monstrous? – about trans women. You certainly seem to frame us as a threat. You've faced appalling and inexcusable abuse and threats (misdirected energies for sure) from some trans women and other activists, especially online. And you've now had the courage – which I applaud – to speak out about the male violence that you've suffered in earlier parts of your life. So if you do see us as a threat, I can understand your feelings. If it's worth anything to you, I am happy to denounce all such threatening and abusive behaviour: I don't want even to seem to be that sort of monster. But I urge you to look a little more closely, and from a different angle, at some of the issues that you're raising.

First, a quick harrumph of exasperation. You wrote on Twitter: 'I'd march with you if you were discriminated against on the basis of being trans.'[1] To be honest, that tweet took my breath away. *If we were*

[1] On 10 April 2022 at 1pm, there was a march in London precisely about trans people in the UK being 'discriminated against on the basis of being transgender': it was a protest against the UK government's decision to exclude conversion therapy practised on trans people from its proposed ban on conversion therapy in general.

Despite her undertaking of June 2020, J.K. Rowling did not in fact join this march. Instead, she had lunch with a selection of hardcore trans-exclusionary activists, and put photos of her lunch date on Twitter.

discriminated against?? Trans people are one of the most discriminated-against groups in the world! What have you been reading for the past few years, if you haven't noticed that?

But let's let that pass; perhaps it was a Saturday night lapse. Let's move on to some points of simple and straightforward agreement. First, free speech matters, and must not be silenced by threats and intimidation. Yes, absolutely, and I've been in places where I was shouted down or otherwise silenced (e.g. by having speaker invitations withdrawn) both by socially conservative bigots and by trans-unsympathetic feminists. It isn't always easy to speak out for transgender rights either. The climate of hatred does none of us any good. And it is particularly toxic for trans women who, like me, have grown up (at school and elsewhere) in an atmosphere of derision and rejection. I see from what you say that you understand how that kind of hatred can be internalised if you're exposed to it long enough. When trans-unsympathetic feminists deliberately misgender trans women, or deride our appearance, or tell us 'You're men really', or stigmatise us as perverts and predators, just the same thing is going on. It's a raw nerve for us, and angry (and sometimes inexcusably violent) responses are evoked by that kind of hate speech, because *we ourselves* have had to battle our way to self-acceptance, in the teeth of our own internalised transphobia.

Next, you raise some doubts in effect about whether everyone who transitions 'really means it', and whether some of the transitioning, particularly in the female-to-male direction, is perhaps really triggered by society's misogyny, and/or by people misunderstanding their own natures, and wrongly thinking that they're transgender when really they're gay.

You don't – I'm relieved to see – try to claim that *all* transitioning has these causes. I have heard eminent 'gender critical' philosophers make exactly that claim, and frankly it horrifies me. It is patent 'cisplaining' and gaslighting of trans people to say that. The claim is contrary to all the existing evidence, and it's a clear instance of what Daniel Radcliffe, Eddie Redmayne, and Katie Leung (bless them) have all recently spoken out against in public – attempts to erase transgender identities altogether.

Since you only think that *some* gender transitioning is 'not genuine' but has these other causes, we aren't in deep disagreement here. Of course *sometimes* there might be those poor reasons for someone's decision to transition. If so, two things follow. First, we need a society that clearly and unambiguously rejects misogyny and homophobia, to get rid of the false prompts that may have led some people in directions that don't help their own self-understanding. Secondly, it's an empirical matter, and a particular one, how to deal with individual people who are or may be in this plight. I'm sure we agree that they should be treated sensitively and caringly and discerningly; and that no pressure should be put on them to go in *any* particular direction – the counselling and help that they receive should be client- (or patient-) led. The results of any other policy for young people's well-being can be, and often are, devastating. Parental or teacher-led gaslighting and 'dissuasion' strategies can and often do lead vulnerable young people towards depression, self-harm and even suicide. That remains the majority view at the Tavistock Centre, and it is certainly what's suggested by my own biography, by my experience as a sometime BACP Governor and by my own attempts to help other transgender people.

This brings us to safeguarding. I have recently read some outstandingly good online materials about how to safeguard all school students' well-being, including transgender students; I'm thinking of Brighton and Hove City Council's online 'transgender toolkit', which I recommend to your attention. What struck me about those materials was how sensible and tactful they were. And also, how client-led: these are clearly materials that have been developed in response to the lived reality of students in Brighton and Hove schools. That, I think, is the approach we should all be taking. Start where people actually are, not from some pre-existing ideology or from innately hostile assumptions; above all, don't use young people as your mouthpieces for your own theoretical convictions. By and large, schools in the UK have been very good about this, I think – at least until recently.

At this point we come to the different debates about female-only spaces. These are *different* debates, and they have different outcomes (particularly in the case of women's refuges), and I can't discuss all of them here. So I'll focus on the one that affects more people than any other, the toilets debate. A debate that is already deeply bogged-down (sorry), is full of utter crap (sorry again), and doesn't, alas, seem likely to get unblocked any time soon (OK, I'll stop now).

You write – with evident passion – that 'When you throw open the doors of bathrooms and changing rooms to any man who believes or feels he's a woman … then you open the door to any and all men who wish to come inside. That is the simple truth.' But with the greatest of respect: that isn't true at all. Let me try and explain why not.

The first thing to say is that – like many others – you're making a connection here between this debate about toilets and changing rooms and another bogged-down debate, the one about legal self-identification. But the two are completely unconnected. For one thing, it's not currently an offence in UK law for a man to enter the Ladies'. (And there is some justification for this: the Ladies' can be the best place for a father to take a 4-year-old daughter; it can also be the only place with nappy-changing facilities.) So no legal protection on ladies' toilets is being *removed* by gender self-identification.

For another thing, have we really lost sight of the fact that, when anyone goes to the loo, they are not asked to present their papers first? So it is *already* possible, both in law and in practice, for 'male sexual predators' to access women's toilets for nefarious purposes. It always has been. And here's a newsflash: they don't have to disguise themselves as women to do so, either. A much simpler tactic, surely, would be for such a predator to disguise himself as a male toilet attendant. So where is the outrage and orchestrated suspicion about *that* category of natal males in women's toilets?

It is extraordinary that people think that a change in the law about gender identity recognition is what matters here, when what matters is patently not that law, but the policing of public safety in public spaces. Trans women, including me, have been routinely using the Ladies' for decades now. The law on how officially to declare yourself a woman has simply nothing to do with this social fact. We're here, have been for ages, and all we want to do is – well, use the loo. What else would we want, for heaven's sake?

Women of every kind should be and feel safe in the public toilets. Of course they should; *everybody* should. But trans women are simply not a threat to women's safety – not as such. As you say yourself, 'the majority of trans-identified people not only pose zero threat to others, but are vulnerable for all the reasons I've outlined. Trans people need and deserve protection.' If we google hard enough, we can find bad anecdotes about trans women attacking other women in the toilets; the tabloids go to town on such anecdotes whenever possible, and so do some trans-unsympathetic feminists. But anecdotes aren't data. And you can find bad anecdotes about *natal* women attacking other women in the toilets, too. All of that should stop; of course it should. But trans women are not the problem here. Violence is.

Those of us trans women who 'pass' as natal females aren't even a perceived problem. Those of us who don't pass, like me I suppose, aren't a problem even if we're perceived as one. And we find it deeply offensive to be profiled as we are now sometimes being profiled, as threatening, creepy, deceptive, predatory – and as *men*. Violence against women (including trans women) is a blot on our society. But treating trans women, as such, as somehow uniquely culpable for that violence is a ridiculous slur, and a deeply discriminatory one – in just the same way as it would be a discriminatory slur to blame black people, as such, for it.

About the law, incidentally. The Scottish government is, as you say, proceeding with a gender-recognition bill. I welcome this, myself. Currently, a formal change of gender is a humiliating, protracted, and medicalising process; you can be knocked back in the process and if you are you have no right of appeal, ever; what counts in the process is not who *I* know myself to be, but what a panel of doctors make of me. That does need changing, and I think the Scottish government is right to seek to replicate in our law a change that has already happened in some countries – for example Ireland in 2015 – with no bad or even dramatic effects at all. (Up to 2017, this is how many Irish transgender people had availed themselves of their new right to change their gender by self-identification: *230*. Does that sound to you like a tidal wave of opportunistic predators?)

You describe the proposal as 'a law that will in effect mean that all a man needs to "become a woman" is to say he's one'. But surely that's not a fair description. To quote Shirley Anne Somerville, the minister responsible: 'The term "self-identification" is routinely used but in my view this does not adequately reflect the seriousness, or the permanency, of the process envisaged … applicants will be required to make a solemn statutory declaration that they intend to live in their acquired gender permanently and that they have already been living in their acquired gender.' What the Scottish government is talking about is a serious, legal, and irreversible step. To take it insincerely would be both to commit perjury, and also to leave yourself in a legal limbo, since you can't change back. To think that this matter of law has anything at all to do with the danger of men impersonating women in order to access spaces where they can harm women – that just doesn't seem like clear thinking at all.

Ms Rowling, it's certainly not my intention, or the intention of any trans activists whom I personally know, to erode or erase the biological reality of (cis) women's experience. Certainly not. Natal females start in a different place from trans women, and have a different journey and a different story, and undergo different things both good and bad. *All* these stories are worthwhile and valuable, and no one should be trying to prevent any of them from being told. Like the rest of the world, I look forward eagerly to seeing which of all these stories, in the future, you yourself choose to tell.

With all best wishes,
Professor Sophie Grace Chappell
Department of Philosophy, The Open University

PART VII

Lissounes

Prefatory remarks

As the epigraph below from Le Guin suggests, this little sci-fi or fantasy fable is an exercise of the philosophical imagination about what gender and sex are, and what they might be under other conditions. As the epigraph from Paglia suggests, it is tongue in cheek (which is not inconsistent with being serious).

Sometimes two different words in classical Greek have the same Latinisation. When Sir Thomas More named his most famous book *Utopia*, he was exploiting an ambiguity of this sort to make a pun: Ou-topia is no place, Eu-topia is the good place. To be perfectly clear from the outset, I am not offering Lissounes as a picture of how I think things should be. It is more like an allo-topia, an other place, a way that things could be different that is, I hope, instructive. Maybe it's even attractive, to others – it certainly is to me, up to a point.

Lissounes is clearly not a place where the categories or scripts or cages of gender are abolished. But it is a place where (as we might say) the cages are much bigger, at least for most, and differently shaped too.

The View From Lissounes:
A Thought Experiment

It doesn't take a thousand men to open a door, my lord.
It might to keep it open.

Ursula Le Guin, *The Left Hand of Darkness*

If civilisation had been left in female hands, we would still be living in grass huts.

Camille Paglia, *Sexual Personae*

It may be we shall touch the Happy Isles.

Alfred Lord Tennyson, *Ulysses*

In recent years Lissounian society has liberalised greatly: men even have the vote now. In fact, they have had the vote for more than twenty years, and, before that, they had already been legally permitted for nearly a century to hold property within the family as well as privately, at least if they lived *in* families. For more than forty years now, too, the law has allowed men to attend the Great Council of Peynelpoli as witnesses (*martîs*), though of course they cannot be Councillors. They now have the right to speak in debates in our Assembly, the *fismoforiya*, and what bawdy jokes *that* has evoked at the prospect of male assembly-goers. Naturally their right to vote (*ostrayyín*) does not apply until they have reached the age of discretion and maturity, but we have lowered this twice in reforming legislation, and it is now only twenty-seven – a mere nine years after women reach that age.

Of course many sage voices have spoken out against these innovations, and I think they definitely have a point. Wise counsellors have urged the preciousness and the enduring power for peace and well-being of Lissounes's own ancestral ways and traditions, contrasting them sharply, and surely altogether justly, with the disastrous and unnatural alternatives seen in other lands. They have descanted unrelentingly on the fecklessness, the impulsiveness, the permanent and apparently irremediable immaturity, the acquisitiveness and greed and pushiness and attention-seeking and thoughtless, aimless, destructive combativeness of men; men who do not understand how much better it is to accumulate learning than coins; men whose only thoughts, for the most part, are to roam and hoard and feed and breed. Making lavish use of historical and topical illustrations – big things like the wars that men start and the pointless dog-in-the-manger 'properties' that men accumulate; little things like the way a man who is cycling in the town seems unable for even half an hour to avoid angry finger-jabbing conflict with a man who is driving in the town – they have reminded their peers of men's hopeless subjugation, as the classic poets, philosophers, and theologians of Lissounes have always insisted, to the *fumos* in them, 'the cloudy smoke hovering over the fires of anger'.

The *fumos*, say our Lissounian poets and storytellers and psychologists, is the principle of aggression, and it is a dark principle in us all whatever our sex or gender. It is the blind dark force in us that only knows how to fight and push, and so pushes and fights constantly against whatever comes in its way, including and in particular the other two principles in us. One of these is the *loios*, the pure white overarching principle of Reason, of law and moderation and compassionate justice. The other is the multifarious *eivfumii*, the scarlet-and-blue principle of Rhyme.

Rhyme: it is the skill of the scansion or interweaving (*synvloki*) of our so-various desires for all that is most enjoyable in life. It is the delicacy of food and wine or the intriguing mazes of close and careful thought, and the creative concentration of the literal weaver, at her loom. It is the health-ache of a leg muscle well-stretched by wanderings in the snow-peaks of the Mezhorye or by the flickering green light of the Aurora on the great northern ice-sheet of the Mellyepaiyi. And it is the gentle, laughter-filled, delirious mutual yieldings and surrenders of the all-night warmth of the bedchamber in midwinter, when the snow is up to the lintels, the sun won't come up for a fortnight, and there is no point in being anywhere else but in bed, nor in doing anything else but offices of tenderness. (Every Lissounian hospital knows that it needs to budget for the late September birth-rate spike.)

Push of course is always useful – to good ends, such as those set by the things and the poems and pictures and the songs that we all make. (It is the hallmark of Lissounes that we have always prized not *money-making*, but *making*.) Push is useful in a fight, and fight of course we sometimes must – occasionally even literally, with our fists or weapons; as when pirates or imperialists raid or invade. (We have defeated the pirates and the imperialists so embarrassingly often that we are now a blank space on their maps, somewhere up there in the Mercator-distorted latitudes between Iceland and Spitsbergen.) But one of the key passages in Lissounes's history is the century-long struggle in the time when the Vikings pressed us, a millennium ago: our struggle to end the need for our defence militias so as to win, and to keep enduringly, the constitutionally guaranteed right that all Lissounians of every gender so prize today, the right not to bear arms. We never forget our struggle for that right, and the blessed freedom that it brings with it from men's nonsense about the 'drunk delight of battle'; freedom too to relax, to be off-guard, and to trust each other even when we are strangers.

We say accordingly that the wise one's life is not controlled by pushing and fighting. A wise one knows how to attune a harmony in her being of *loiyos, eivfumii, fumos*, Reason, Rhyme, and Push. She understands how so to yoke her Push that it pushes to some purpose, and helps not hinders the good work of Reason and Rhyme. She sees how black, pure white, and scarlet-and-blue together can make one tapestry, or the flag of Lissounes. And that, the sage voices repeat, is exactly what men do not know, and never have known; that is why, in *our* gender unary, women are the norm, and men a variety of degenerate cases of failure to meet that norm, of fallings-away from that focal case. Most men (they say) have no idea how to rhyme their desires. Reason in them, poor clumsy oafs, is a tenuous flame, not to be exposed to the winds that will extinguish it. Better for men to be at all times good students of life's harmony than at any time its bad masters.

Just that is what men traditionally were in Lissounes, in deference to our island's two great foundation myths. Both myths say first that the island's *yeiyyeinis* are all feminine – that it was originally peopled only by women (men only allowed in briefly for purposes of fertilisation, and then *out they go again*); and that it is and always has been a *yinartsiya*, a land where women rule. The one myth continues that when Thetis very sensibly hid the young boy Achilles from Odysseus and the other recruiting sergeants for the warmongering Greek armada against Troy, it was not, as Ovid claims in the thirteenth book of his *Metamorphoses,* at Lycomedes' court on the Aegean island Skyros that she hid him, nor yet, as the Irish might claim, on Achill Island, but among the pretty girls of Lissounes in the far north of the Outer Ocean. And a joyous and contented and extremely comely girl Achilles made too, with his slender agile figure and his pale round smooth cheeks and his bright lilac-blue eyes and his shimmering bright-red hair. For a while he was at peace in his flowing scarlet silks and his shimmering frills, with his lyre and his loom, in the summer orchards of Mellyevorn. There for a while he was permitted to learn the happy ways of Lissounes, until the miserable ways of other lands, and above all the stupidity of war, overmastered him and de-learned him back into the paths of death.

The other myth says that Lissounes was found by the wandering ships of Odysseus on his last voyage: found again as if by a homing instinct, maybe the same instinct that had taken Odysseus there in the first place, so many years before, when he and his press-gang were hunting down the harem-hidden Achilles. One bright morning in some long-ago May, his stubble-jawed, sabre-scarred, pot-bellied sailors and he waded again ashore, the melting pack-ice knocking in the seaweedy shallows against their numbed fat hairy scab-pocked shins, swords out, all combat-ready and anxiously blinking in on-guard watchfulness, and impertinently renamed their new home after their own warlord: Oulisseou Neysos, Odysseus' Isle. The aboriginal inhabitants were amusedly tolerant, and smilingly allowed them their new name, which in time was worn down to Lissounes, a name with three liquid es-es in it, and the same shape of pitch and stress to it as 'wilderness'. The indigenous women of the island even took up, for the most part and with changes, the newcomers' Greek language (before that they had spoken something like the languages of the older parts of Britain). We still read the incomers' ancient poets too; we take the *Iliad* as a tragic case-study in masculine pride, bloodlust, rapine, and folly, and the *Odyssey* as a massive relief from the *Iliad*. (Your scholar Richard Bentley says that the *Iliad* is for men, the *Odyssey* for women. Well, yes: the *Iliad* ends where two mortal men, both shortly to die, agree to end a truce and resume a war; the *Odyssey* ends where one ever-living goddess commands an end to a war and the beginning of peace.) Though of course our favourite of the old Greek poets is Sappho, whose complete works, and not just her fragments, we have right here in our libraries. How tantalising for you.

And so Penelope – Peynelwvi, who as our tales tell came *with* Odysseus on their last voyage, no doubt to keep him out of trouble for once – became our first Queen In Council, while Odysseus we allowed as her consort, uncrowned of course. But once the old sea-dogs made Lissounes their home and put war-roving and war-striving aside, a lotus-eater's happiness overcame them all, healing the self-inflicted wounds of masculine anger and battle. They became like Penelope (or Sappho); they became weavers not swordsmen, creators not killers. And in the end very many of them went quite native, and chose to live at peace as women too. Under the gentle but powerful magic of our hyperboreal lotuses, they, as you would say in your language, *unmanned* or *emasculated* themselves; though our word for that transformation, *enyinaikwsis*, has a quite different tone to it from yours.

And so, to this day in Lissounes, most who have suffered the misfortune of male birth still live (at least in appearance and mien, and sometimes physiologically too) as aspirant or adoptive women (*fetiyinis*), even once they are adults. As such they are permitted at least some of the full rights and honorifics of a born woman in our *yinartsiya*. They have the same rights to marry (each other, or born women) as born women do; their unions with born women are, of course, one of the main places in Lissounes that babies come from. And from birth on, all babies in Lissounes are always dressed and treated and grow up as girls until they insist otherwise, or fail for too long to celebrate (even in boastful show only, as often happens) their *prwtomeynaia*.

Most of our children are very happy like this. A child only takes on a boy's role if they absolutely demand it, and there is much social pressure against the demand. Children in school, despite the gender-equality-ideology-based reproaches that it is nowadays the fashion for their teachers to make, still sometimes follow the understandable old habit of using *boy* (*meyraki*) as a taunt for one who is clumsy, rude, uncouth or aggressive. And they still sometimes call someone who decides to transition to boyhood a *vwfetiyini*, 'someone who will never make it even as an adoptive woman', or even more cruelly *leipsiyini*, a 'failed woman'. The taunt is unkind, but it has some biological justification – after all, as our scientists will tell you, the embryological processes *do* tend naturally towards producing a female, and only produce a male when they glitch in some way. Biology matters, and reality matters; still, we mustn't mix up the norms of science with the norms of the school playground.

It is a shameful thing, too, when a male is first seen in boy's clothing. (Or a female for that matter; adoptive men do happen, but they are rare and *very* countercultural, and I must admit that they *are* rather stigmatised by our customs.[2]) In Lissounes when someone 'comes out' as a boy, and eccentrically ditches the exhilarating freedom and grace of his floaty satins and the intricate lace of his petticoats for dull, coarse, lumpen, constricting trousers, he can get laughed at and teased. As our tradition sees it, such beings are confessing that they do not have, don't know how to have, the admittedly greater beauty of a girl, or the virtue that it takes to live as a girl – the sunny, contented blend of graceful wisdom, peaceful good humour and measured, confident self-control that we Lissounians call *sao-frosini,* health and well-being of mind, and see as the crowning virtue of a supremely good and ideally admirable female, a queen of a woman, whether born or merely adoptive.

Anyhow, it is not as if males who live as men were really all *that* ill-treated under the old traditions. Of course their status was always lower – and really still is – than the status either of born women or of adoptive women. But how else can it be, if society is to be protected from the restless anger and violence, from the blind intransigence and ugly conflict-seeking Push of the *fumos,* that – as the history of all other nations so tragically shows – lurks so close to the surface in the psyche of so many men?

Don't forget that those who *insist* on living as men have always had more rights and freedoms in Lissounes than even our most venerated animals, the she-eagle and the white bear-dam and the mother wolf. They are never forced, once they have made that choice, to stick to it irrevocably; they can always desist if they like; there are potions and herbs, and there are bindings and tricks of clothing, that can rescue

---

[2] Our speaker rather skates over this point. But it should be very obvious that, whatever else might be right in Lissounes, the position of trans men there is not good at all. Like I said at the outset, this is (designedly) not a *eutopia* but an *allotopia.*

from stubble and masculine shape even the most inveterately male. And Lissounian men have always been permitted (as no animal is, or at least no tame animal) to wander and roam and explore as they love to, to wonder at the eagles of the white mountains of Perevorn, or herd sheep and goats in the green hill country of Prihorye and the shadowy pine forests of Helyevorn, or sail fishing boats on the wide cold ocean, sometimes discovering things that benefit all society. True, their permission to roam traditionally, and until recently, always came at the price of their owning no property except for personal use, and having no status within any family, even the one they were born in. But to roam is to opt out of family responsibilities; so it *should* come at a price. And after all, to pay that price is what men often choose anyway.

Yet so many voices in Lissounes, it seems to me, are now under modish influence from modern cultures, elsewhere in this cruel and confused world, that are truly alien to us because they are precisely that *andrartsia*, that dominion of males, that we got free from and left behind forever when we began here. Those are cultures that pollute their own culture with such gender ideologies as sadly as they pollute their airs and their waters – and these days, even more sadly, ours too; cultures that are full of gratuitous violence and pointless, environment-ravaging acquisitiveness and wasted, self-indulgent, self-advertising energy; cultures that are choking to death on the bitter black smokes of *fumos* run amok. This vocal minority now clamours that we should *be like them*? They say our ways are unfair on men; that men too can be all that women are; that the essential differences between men and women that are so obvious to us are nothing but the result of so many centuries of our *yinartsiya*; that, if we only chose to, we could inculturate men too to be all that women are; that our *subjugation* of men, as they call it, is almost as bad as other societies' subjugation of women. A moment's glance at those other societies shows that this last charge at least has got to be nonsense. Even if they could show that our *yinartsiya* is not as good as equality, whatever equality might mean, surely no one can sanely hold that *yinartsiya* is anywhere near as bad as the *andrartsii*, the places where the *men* are in charge. I mean, just look at them.

Nonetheless, nowadays men can even be priests in the Orthodox Church of Lissounes. There has been much difficulty on this painful issue of conscience. The theological controversy (in which men, I fear, have often been marked in their debating style by a grievous excess of Push) has centred on the question whether it can possibly be a good idea to put the clock back, as the advocates of so-called 'men's rights' seem to be advocating, to the primitive and undeveloped condition of the church that the New Testament holds up to us as a dire and instructive warning lesson – a condition in which so many of the leaders of the early church actually were, embarrassingly enough yet undeniably, men. (Well, most of them were sandal-wearing fishers too; does that mean any of our priests have to be sandal-wearing fishers?) As if the Christian life were not all about putting away the 'man of sin', the *andrartsiya* of the old Adam of cruelty and violence and rashness, and being transformed, in Christ, into the *kenye shtisi*, the new Eve, the new creation. As if that angry male German philosopher with the epic moustache (I'm sorry, in Lissounes we all find facial hair of any kind pretty comical) had not been absolutely right, albeit not in the way he meant, to call our faith a feminine one. No wonder the early Christians made so many mistakes, and fell, on the whole, so badly away from the standards of Mary, Christ's Mother, and Mary Magdalen who herself came to Lissounes at the last and founded our church, and Joanna and Salome, and the other leading disciples. (And what humility it incidentally was in God, I've always thought, to be incarnated as a man, at least at first and before Christ was resurrected as the *Sofiya*, the Eve who is the true morning, the divine and grace-filled wisdom of God.)

All these calls for 'equality' are all very well, if you ask me, but they overlook some basic facts of simple physiology. In the context of the family in particular, equality for men goes obviously against the grain of nature. How can a man take turns with the breastfeeding, or agree to alternate pregnancies with his spouse, as *meytres* who want large families usually do? Is a man likely to be better than a woman at understanding what it means to suffer a breech birth, or a torn perineum, or mastitis, or postnatal depression? Is a man as likely as a woman even to stick around, given that a man is by his very nature so prone to wander off, to roam, neglecting his children and his spouse alike? Or if he does stick around, will his spouse and children be safe from his simmering *fumos*?

Despite these obvious ethical barriers, some, especially in recent times, make the rather countercultural choice to marry and live with someone who is openly a man. Some say they do so out of natural inclination;

maybe, though I myself tend to agree with those who think that they've just never met the right girl. In Lissounian law living with an overt and self-declared man has never been actually illegal, and it can nowadays be done with very little prejudice against it.

So when a woman marries in Lissounes these days, she may marry as she likes among our overlapping two genders and two sexes – a born woman or an adoptive woman, whichever she chooses; or, if she really insists, a man. And if their biology interfits, that spouse of hers will be the parent, usually *meytir* but occasionally *patir*, of whatever children she may choose to conceive. In Lissounes it is this relation, the relation of parenthood (*meytria*), of nurturing and instruction and love over decades and longer, that matters legally for inheritance and for the protection of each other and of children; the family, whether *meytres ki pajes* or *meytir ki patir ki pajes*, is defined as the unit where the children's upbringing happens, and where whoever is pregnant or breastfeeding is helped through that. And no one is stronger than we are on family values.

The question of who biologically seeds the child is a different matter, a private one, and one of no legal significance at all. A man does not get to be a *patir*, a nurturer and upbringer of children, just by being their *sporitis*, their seeder. Well, of course he doesn't. What after all is it to seed a child but a sweet warm five-minute spasm that leads to a life that the seeder need know nothing about, a life that he may contribute absolutely nothing to after that tiny gluey blob of DNA? It is not even necessarily a five-minute spasm of enjoyable or skilful sex, or of anything anywhere near as good as another woman could offer the mother – as we all know from Sappho and Teiresias, and as men themselves seem to admit in the poor dog-eared random jottings that pass among them for erotica. What is it to seed a child, compared with what it is to be pregnant for nine months or give suckle for eighteen, or again to help your spouse through these things, or through a day and a night of the piercing agony of childbirth?

The mother, therefore, is sovereign: she is free to choose whoever she wishes to seed her. It might be her spouse, but it might be some friend on the quiet, or it might be a professional backstreet *sporitis*. Unless she chooses to say – and saying is generally regarded as laughable and embarrassing immodesty – who seeds her is nobody's business but her own.

Every Lissounian understands that not even a born woman spouse has the right to be told that, lest jealousy be given something to work on.

One corollary is our distinctive Lissounian notion of marital faithfulness, which has relatively little to do with who a woman (yes, all right, or a man) has sex with. For sure it is not seen as ideal if she (*sigh* ... or he) even occasionally has sex with someone she is not married to, unless she is looking for a *sporitis* (or he is acting as one). But because of our custom of the *sporitis*, for us one-night stands are not really a central definer or even necessarily a symptom at all of unfaithfulness, as I understand they are in other societies. Faithfulness for us is all about what is habitual, including who is one's habitual sexual partner, and even more than that it is about staying with the family that you have committed to. Correspondingly, unfaithfulness is all about deserting your family, or even setting up with another family. (This happens. But happily, not very often. When it happens, it meets with immediate and strong social condemnation; which means, in practice, that lots and lots of friends ring up to ask if there is anything they can do to help.)

A life as a professional *sporitis* is always an option for a male who lives openly as a man; and those who know about it say that such a life, strangely enough, can on the whole be an enjoyable one. But of course being an open and habitual *sporitis* has – given its rather sad rootlessness – never been thought a very reputable life, even though, by an odd asymmetry, no opprobrium at all has ever attached to a woman who *uses* a working *sporitis*. Even today, when a Lissounian man is jokingly called a *sporitis*, the joke is on him, and it is usually considered a harsh one, almost as harsh as calling him a *leipseyini*.

This is just how we go on in Lissounes. This is simply what we do. And to me the question whether we Lissounians need to change so as to treat men better is the question whether any likely alternative arrangement of our whole society is at all likely to be better, not just for men, but for everyone. Well, maybe we could do more about a few outliers and minorities, like adoptive men for instance. But overall, I just can't see any other way in which things could easily be better. The gender egalitarians say that we 'put men down' in our society, and maybe they have a point; but do men really do better in other societies, societies where their dangerous, violent, inegalitarian, plundering, and sociopathic tendencies are not only allowed but positively encouraged to cause havoc? Of course they don't. And neither do any of their victims.

I see myself as quite liberal on these questions – it's not like I am one of those hard-line traditionalists who thinks that the only good sex is necessarily Lesbian sex, or that everyone should at least try to live as a woman, or that men are 'only there for one thing'. (To serve as *sporiteis*. There is a rude old Lissounian saying that corresponds exactly to a very idiomatic phrase of English: *andris havlws fallui eyse*, 'men are just dicks'. However tempting at times, I am liberal enough to think that it is an unkind and unfair saying.) But I have always thought, and I go on thinking, that it is best for all of us if we continue to do things the good old Lissounian way that long experience and tradition – and nature itself – have all taught us is the truly human way. That means accepting and enjoying the clearly different and complementary roles that the good Lord has assigned by nature to men on the one hand and to women, whether born or adoptive, on the other. And that means, if you'll forgive my bluntness, that in the end, it's simply best for everyone, including them, if Lissounian men just know their place.

Alles Vergängliche
Ist nur ein Gleichnis;
Das Unzulängliche,
Hier wird's Ereignis;
Das Unbeschreibliche,
Hier ist's getan;
Das Ewig-Weibliche
Zieht uns hinan.

Goethe, Faust Part II

Extended Contents